The MIT Press Essential Knowledge Series

THE BOOK

AMARANTH BORSUK

The MIT Press | Cambridge, Massachusetts | London, England

This book was set in Chaparral Pro by Toppan Best-set Premedia Limited. Printed and bound in the United States of America.

Library of Congress Cataloging-in-Publication Data is available.

ISBN: 978-0-262-53541-0

10 9 8 7 6 5 4 3 2 1

CONTENTS

SERIES FOREWORD

The MIT Press Essential Knowledge series offers accessible, concise, beautifully produced pocket-size books on topics of current interest. Written by leading thinkers, the books in this series deliver expert overviews of subjects that range from the cultural and the historical to the scientific and the technical.

In today's era of instant information gratification, we have ready access to opinions, rationalizations, and superficial descriptions. Much harder to come by is the foundational knowledge that informs a principled understanding of the world. Essential Knowledge books fill that need. Synthesizing specialized subject matter for nonspecialists and engaging critical topics through fundamentals, each of these compact volumes offers readers a point of access to complex ideas.

Bruce Tidor
Professor of Biological Engineering and Computer Science
Massachusetts Institute of Technology

PREFACE AND ACKNOWLEDGMENTS

The book would, at first glance, seem to be an object about which we all possess essential knowledge. It is, for many children, among the first playthings we encounter, whether in the soft cloth books of contrasting colors and bold patterns often kept in the crib to stimulate vision, or a little later in board books like Dorothy Kunhardt's *Pat the Bunny* (1940), with contrasting textures to activate our sense of touch and simple words and phrases to help us imagine a world arranged neatly into narratives. The book would seem like a solid object, yet it is presently poised to melt into air, or, if we are honest, has been threatening to do so in popular consciousness for at least a decade, thanks to the advent in 2006 of the Sony Reader and in 2007 of the Amazon Kindle, digital reading devices many seem to think will render books obsolete. We might trace fears over the book's decline even earlier, to the first part of the twentieth century, a period of rapid technological change in which the phonograph, film, and television reinvented storytelling on a grand scale. Book history and Victorian studies scholar Leah Price, in a 2012 *New York Times* essay, chronicles such admonitions, following them back to the Romantic period, when Théophile Gautier professed that burgeoning newspapers would kill the book.[1] Such reports of the book's death are abundant and, perhaps, overstated.

Digital reading devices existed prior to e-readers, but none has challenged our definition of the book in quite the same way or raised as much of an outpouring of print nostalgia on one hand and digital futurist rhetoric on the other. These devices—flat, lightweight screens that can show us any volume in a whole library of texts—look much different from the one most of us picture when we hear the word *book*: a stack of paper sheets printed on both sides, bound on one end, and encased between covers. We seem comfortable assuming the term refers to a single object: the *codex*, whose name comes from the Latin for "tree trunk,"[2] and whose image is likewise firmly rooted in the Western psyche.

This form, which emerged around 150 CE, has enjoyed a long history. It was predated, however, by the long-standing use of clay tablets and papyrus scrolls, both of which emerged over two thousand years earlier. It seems fitting, then, that e-readers have come to prominence in the twenty-first century, nicely bookending the codex as a hinge in the middle of a four-thousand-year span of textual proliferation. Codex-like forms, in fact, precede the book of bound leaves: accordion-folded scrolls and *polyptychs* of wax tablets facilitated the combination of sequential reading and random access the codex made possible.

And though they lend themselves to infinite scrolling text, our digital reading environments maintain codex-like features, from bookmarking and page turning on-screen to iPad cases that simulate hardback books. So how do we define *the book* when the tablet and scroll have come back to us in full force? And why does the proliferation of new reading devices cause so much speculation about the death of the book in popular media?

The codex has endured over two millennia thanks to its utility as a device for the dissemination of ideas. It's no wonder many readers, even those who have embraced the e-reader, have a soft spot for its predecessor and will claim to read both kinds of book (digital and print) in different contexts: e-reader on the train or bus, paperback at the beach; e-reader when traveling, hardcover books at home; or e-reader for schoolbooks and print for graphic novels, to name just a few variations. If you don't use one of these devices, chances are you have read books (or parts of them) on a computer or phone, or on one of many precursor digital devices. But the fact that an e-reader is not tethered to a specific text serves as a handy reminder that the term *book* commonly refers interchangeably to both medium and content, regardless of our acculturation to the codex.

At a moment when the dual subjects of the death of the book and the future of books (two halves of the same debate) have taken hold of popular interest, where paeans to print fetishizing the sensory pleasures of books are published alongside encomiums on the storytelling capabilities of virtual reality, many of us want a better sense of what a book is and has been—and what it may become. As a poet, scholar, and book artist working at the intersection of print and digital technology, I have long been fascinated by the book as a malleable medium for artistic inquiry and by writing technologies as spurs to authorship. My goal in this short work is to bring together several perspectives on the book that illuminate its long history of transformation. While this volume will communicate essential aspects of book history as they pertain to the idea of the book, it is outside my scope to cover the full breadth of this robust discipline. For those interested in pursuing a more rigorous study of print history, I have provided a list of "further reading" at the back of this book that includes seminal texts in the field. I also believe that a thorough understanding of what a book is and can do requires a certain amount of hands-on engagement, and have likewise appended a list of "further writing" that includes opportunities to study book arts.

While I take the history of the book as a starting point for understanding an object that is by its nature slippery, the goal of this Essential Knowledge volume is to give readers purchase on the "essential" contours of debates, issues, and ideas around how we define the technology we know as the book in order to address a historical moment in which many of us are fascinated by it and concerned about its future. Rather than presenting the book's development as a linear path from cuneiform impression to touchscreen interface, I have punctuated this timeline with digressions and hypertextual connections on book structure, fabrication, and culture to allow us to explore the many apparatuses that keep the book in circulation—both in our cultural landscape and imaginations. Bridging history, the book arts, and contemporary electronic literature, this volume reminds us that the book is a fluid artifact whose form and usage have shifted over time under numerous influences: social, financial, and technological.

As the quotations scattered throughout this volume suggest, defining the book is no easy feat. Tracking the book as "material text" helps us see the ways its physical form, readership, and artistic content have inspired one another's evolution, suggesting they will continue to do so in the years to come. To see where books might be going, we must think of them as objects that have experienced a long history of experimentation and play. Rather than bemoaning the death of books or creating a dichotomy between print and digital media, this guide points to continuities, positioning the book as a changing technology and highlighting the way artists in the twentieth and twenty-first centuries have pushed us to rethink and re-define the term.

Providing a focused exploration of the manifold arti-facts we think of as "books" alongside short forays into the interdisciplinary arenas that have influenced the study of book history, I take the artist's book, which uses its con-tent to interrogate book form, as an instructive paradigm for thinking about the way forward for digital books. Rather than inscribing a teleological story of ever-improv-ing legibility, distribution, and engagement, the book's mutations tell us about our highly contingent cultural ide-als of authorship and art. In mapping these shifts, I hope to offer a path forward for those interested in shaping the book's future. Perhaps our hand-wringing over the death of the book is as misplaced as fears regarding the decline of reading a decade ago, when the National Endowment for the Arts published its study *Reading at Risk,* documenting a "decline of ten percentage points in literary readers from 1982 to 2002."[3] The losses that report bemoaned have since been debunked—we are not reading less, but simply differently. Humans' interaction with language and litera-ture necessitates certain kinds of portable reading experi-ences. It seems only natural that the book should grow and change with us.

My own growth as an artist and thinker on these is-sues has benefited greatly from a community of collabora-tors with whom I have had the opportunity to explore the book's boundaries. I am grateful to Brad Bouse, my partner in all things, who first encouraged me to make my study of electronic literature material. I am also indebted to Nick Montfort, a rigorous thinker and generous friend who introduced me to regular expressions and who was this work's first reader. Sandra Kroupa, special collections librarian and living index to the University of Washington's artists' books collection provided invaluable guidance. A number of interlocutors have influenced and inspired my creative and critical thinking about the juncture of print and digital media, especially Jessica Pressman, Dene Grigar, Kathi Inman Berens, Stephanie Strickland, Élika Ortega, and Alex Saum-Pascual. I am grateful, as well, for invitations to the Reva and David Logan Symposium on the Artist's Book in San Francisco, Máquinas de inminencia: estéticas de la literatura electrónica in Mexico City, the Digital Technologies and the Future of the Humanities at City University Hong Kong, and Sprint Beyond the Book at ASU's Center for Science and the Imagination. Some of the ideas between these covers began gestating during my time as a Mellon Postdoctoral Fellow at MIT, where I had the honor of co-hosting the symposium UNBOUND: Speculations on the Future of the Book with Gretchen Frances Bennett. My completion of this volume was made possible through the generous support of the School of Interdisciplinary Arts and Sciences at the University of Washington, Bothell, as well as a Worthington Innovation Fellowship, which provided much-needed time to focus on writing. Part of this manuscript was completed at the University of Washington's Whitely Center, which served as both refuge and scriptorium, for which I am deeply thankful. Finally, my own love of books in all their forms started with my family: thanks, Practive Associates.

THE BOOK AS OBJECT

The story of the book's changing form is bound up with that of its changing content. The book, after all, is a portable data storage and distribution method, and it arises as a by-product of the shift from oral to literate culture, a process that takes centuries and is informed through cultural exchange, both peaceful and forcible. In the development of the book from clay tablet to codex, each medium's affordances—the possibilities for use presented by its form—facilitate certain kinds of expression. As certain modes of expression—whether they be iconographic Egyptian alphabets or interactive video clips—gain prominence, the medium that best supports them develops and, in some cases, supersedes the one that preceded it.

We know this intuitively, but it would be incorrect to think of this series of shifts as determined solely by the expressive needs of scribes or authors (whether they

This work treats a "book" as a storehouse of human knowledge intended for dissemination in the form of an artifact that is portable—or at least transportable—and that contains arrangements of signs that convey information.

—FREDERICK KILGOUR,
THE EVOLUTION OF THE BOOK

are tracking the sale and exchange of goods, recording administrative regulations, codifying religious tenets, or transcribing myths and epic tales) or the desires of a hypothetical readership (needing receipts, consolidating regulatory power, seeking spiritual guidance, or hungry for romance). Content does not simply necessitate its form, but rather writing develops alongside, influences, and is influenced by the technological supports that facilitate its distribution. We would also be wrong to presume that these storage mechanisms supplant one another in a tidy timeline of forward progress. Book historian Frederick Kilgour refers to the book's development as a series of "punctuated equilibria" driven by "the ever-increasing informational needs of society"[1]—a useful way of thinking about the book's transformations. Different technologies of the book exist side by side throughout its history: tablet and scroll, scroll and codex, manuscript and print, paperback and e-book. Looking at the changing object of the book gives us a deeper sense of the history of relations between form and content that help define it.

The Original Tablet

The transition from clay tablets to papyrus as a writing support, modes that coexisted for two thousand years, reveals the extent to which the book's form and content influence one another's development. The use of clay to record information arose in Sumer (modern Iraq), which shifted from a nomadic to an urban culture between 8500 and 3000 BCE. As people settled in villages and a system of kingships formed, Sumerians needed a way to track trade and record information about their governance. Cuneiform writing developed in Southern Mesopotamia around 2800 BCE thanks to a confluence of material availability, linguistic development, and utility.[2] Sumerians had long relied on clay, an abundant and renewable material supplied by the Tigris and Euphrates, the two rivers that give Mesopotamia (which means "between two rivers" in Greek) its name, in their architecture and crafts. While their region did not provide stone or wood in any great quantities, they had highly developed techniques for sifting and working with clay to create durable and lasting artifacts, making it a natural fit as a support for writing.

Initially, Sumerians used clay tokens in various shapes for their accounting, in some cases tying together groupings with string. Around 3500 BCE, they began containing these tokens in spherical clay envelopes, or *bullae*, impressed with each token's shape to demonstrate the sealed pod's hidden contents (see figure 1).[3] Rather than associating three conical tokens with three sheep in the world, for instance, this system associated three impressions of tokens with the tokens themselves, a level of abstraction

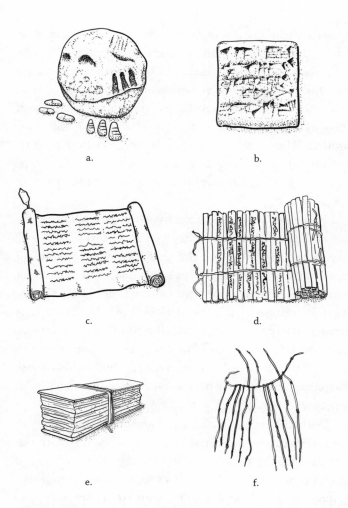

Figure 1 (a) Clay bulla, based on Louvre Museum SB1940 (ca. 3300 BCE); (b) cuneiform tablet, based on Metropolitan Museum of Art 11.217.19 (ca. 2041 BCE); (c) scroll (ca. 2500 BCE); (d) *jiance,* based on The Museum of the Institute of History and Philology, Academia Sinica 128.1 (ca. 95 CE); (e) palm leaf manuscript/*pothī* (ca. 200 BCE); (f) *khipu/quipu* (ca. 1500 CE). Illustration by Mike Force for Lightboard.

necessary to make the representational leap from spoken language to writing. With impressions standing in for objects, they no longer needed the receipt to serve as a container, so around 3200 bullae became solid, a shape that gradually flattened to create the clay tablet that would serve as a portable recording device for several millennia. Around 3100, scribes began to add designs inscribed with a *stylus* depicting the goods these token impressions represented, and a pictographic writing system in clay was born.[4]

While impression in clay worked well, the medium was not really suited to drawing, given the resistance of wet clay to the stylus tip and the challenge of standardizing drawn forms—your sheep and my sheep will likely look quite different unless we have a shared approach to drawing it. Working with the affordances of the clay, Sumerians developed a special wedge-shaped stylus (hence *cuneiform*, from the Latin *cuneus*, or "wedge"), also drawn from the material they had in abundance: reeds, which could be easily split and peeled to generate one of these beveled implements ready-made.

With the stylus in one hand and the damp tablet in the other, a scribe impressed a corner of the reed into the clay at an oblique angle, using combinations of wedge shapes to make characters, thus transitioning from pictographic to syllabic writing. This shift from shapes depicting words to signs representing sounds had the additional benefit of reducing the number of characters required to convey information. Rather than a one-to-one correspondence of drawing to object or idea, language could be abstracted from the things it represented, and this reduced phonetic character set could be adapted to represent other spoken languages in the region during the second millennium BCE, facilitating the spread of writing across the Near East.

This early medium, the tablet, takes on epic proportions in popular imagination. The term conjures up images of Charlton Heston as Moses, bearing the Ten Commandments on two stone slabs the size and shape of small headstones. While the Mesopotamians did carve texts into stone, because it was rare in the region it is thought to have been reserved for recording important events.[5] The reality of the clay tablet was far more modest—most were small enough to fit comfortably in the palm of the scribe's hand, and their shape, generally rectangular with a slightly convex bulge, suggests the cupped palm that formed them (see figure 1). Ranging from the size of a matchbook to that of a large cell phone, cuneiform tablets were highly portable, could be inscribed on multiple sides, and could rest stably on a flat surface for storage or consultation. Some were cured in ovens, but most were simply allowed to dry in the sun.

As the need for written documentation of law, commerce, religion, and cultural history increased, so too did

Although the history of writing might have to include anything from the cave walls of Lascaux to ancient stellae, to a computer disk or sky-writing, our definition of the book must be narrowed to records in portable form, going back at least as far as the Sumerian clay tablets, and following the availability of materials and techniques of material manipulation.

—THOMAS VOGLER,
"WHEN A BOOK IS NOT A BOOK"

the need for specialists who could both read and write. Thus scribes were born, though in this early period they were seen more as transcriptionists than authors. One notable exception, the Sumerian princess and high priestess Enheduanna composed poems to the moon goddess Inanna in which she addresses her, not on behalf of a king, but as herself:

> my Lady
> what day will you have mercy
> how long will I cry a moaning prayer
> I am yours
> why do you slay me[6]

Her name appears both in these poems and on tablets of temple hymns she composed, making Enheduanna the first named author.[7] Drawn from upper-class families, the young men who predominantly served as scribes were accorded important status for their skill and received an education befitting their task.[8] Scribal schools provide many of our surviving tablets: copies made by students on clay discs whose rounded form kept them distinct from official documents.

The increase in writing also led to the development of archives to store these texts. The most impressive such collection, that of seventh-century Assyrian King Ashurbanipal of Nineveh, included more than 30,000 tablets and used a topic-based indexing system, laying the foundation for contemporary libraries. Thanks to their clay form, these tablets survived the great fire that destroyed the city in 612 BCE, though countless scrolls and wax tablets were likely lost.[9] Among the collection were letters and government documents, but also astrological, mathematical, medical, and scientific texts, as well as proverbs, songs, epics, and myths. These were dispersed among a series of rooms, each with a tablet by the door describing the subject matter within. Unlike today's libraries, the collection was developed not as a public good, but as a symbol of King Ashurbanipal's stature and scholarly achievement. Evidence suggests the library was also consulted by priests, professionals, and members of the learned class—some tablets are inscribed with threats to would-be thieves demanding borrowed tablets be returned the same day.[10]

Perhaps the best-known cuneiform tablet in King Ashurbanipal's collection is a fragment of an Assyrian translation of the epic of *Gilgamesh*. Known as the "flood tablet," it made waves when it was translated in the 1860s because of the similarity of its narrative to the biblical flood story in the book of Genesis.[11] *Gilgamesh* originated as a series of Sumerian praise poems about the king of Uruk (ca. 2700 BCE), raising him to myth-like status. These were combined to create a long epic poem detailing the adventures of King Gilgamesh and his bellicose sidekick Enkidu. Their escapades include war, rivalry, romance, and brotherhood—all the makings of a great road movie.

The version of *Gilgamesh* found in Nineveh, spanning twelve tablets, forms the basis for most contemporary translations and reveals much about the ways cuneiform literature was shaped by the tablet structure. To facilitate reading, scribes sometimes marked off sections with horizontal lines (easily made by impressing the side of the stylus into the clay) and indented the opening line of the subsequent section. They used special marks to separate words and to indicate a word was a name, and they developed determinative marks that categorized the words to which they were appended (as, for instance, related to people, place names, divinities, or specific materials). These latter are a particularly fascinating case in that they would not be voiced, but rather served as a kind of readerly metadata for disambiguation of words with multiple possible meanings.

Scribes developed finding aids for works spanning multiple tablets like this one, using the tablet's reverse to provide, in some cases, summaries, a *colophon* with the scribe and/or owner's name, the work's title (generally its first line), and the opening line of the subsequent tablet (known as an *incipit*) if the text continued. Incidentally, these terms, colophon and incipit, come from manuscript studies, and while they are useful to us in mapping the shifting conventions of the book, they would not have been applied to such texts by their creators. *Colophon*, Greek for "finishing stroke," suggests the use of pen and ink to close a text with information about its production on the final page. *Incipit*, Latin for "here begins," comes from the scribal tradition of beginning a text with this term to name what follows.

The Papyrus Scroll

While the Sumerians were developing a book from the materials at hand, the Egyptians reached to their own river for a support to writing: papyrus, which only grows in the Nile Valley. Egyptians used the plant widely: for building materials, clothing, and even food. The earliest Egyptian writing appears on stone faces inscribed with *hieroglyphics* that date from the fourth millennium BCE.[12] Hieroglyphics are sure to be familiar to many readers as a system in which drawings of figures and objects are combined to represent things (*pictogram*), ideas (*ideogram*), and sounds (*phonogram*).[13] Hieroglyphs were inscribed on temple walls and obelisks, providing religious and historical records, but they also appear on potsherds as more ephemeral notes. As the need for documentation increased and Egyptians sought a more portable surface for writing, they developed an ideal material from *papyrus*: a paper both smooth and flexible that could be sized to the needs of a given document.

To write on this surface, they developed a water-soluble, charcoal-based black ink and a red ink from oxidized iron, as well as a brush-like rush pen that allowed for smooth and rapid transcription, which gradually transformed hieroglyphics into a simplified script known as *hieratic*. One of the many ways the material form influenced its content was the indistinguishability of up-and-down strokes in hieratic, which some scholars associate with concern for piercing the papyrus.[14] The uniform thickness of the line suggests even pressure, unlike the thick downstrokes and hairline upstrokes associated with calligraphy on paper and parchment. It might also be attributed to the reed pen itself, a soft brush with a fine tip. Whatever the case, in the fifteen hundred years in which papyrus prevailed, scribes took great advantage of their chosen medium.

Pliny the Elder (23–79 CE) provides a useful, if limited, explanation of Egyptian papermaking (a description he copped directly from Theophrastus) as part of his *Natural History*.[15] The *cyperus papyrus* plant, which was used so extensively in ancient Egypt that it was nearly eradicated by the first millennium CE, consists of clusters of long, triangular stems (up to eighteen feet tall) with tasseled heads. Papyrus was made by cutting the stalks into uniform lengths, removing the outer green rind, and making strips from the plant's pith using one of two methods. According to Pliny, papermakers sliced the pith into strips that gradually decreased in size (given the triangular shape of the stalk), discarding the smallest section. Contemporary research, however, suggests that in some cases the triangular stems were carefully peeled, working inward in a spiral fashion.[16] This would have resulted in a wider continuous sheet and less waste. In both methods, these strips were laid out in two layers—one vertical, the other horizontal—and beaten until the fibers fused, using the plant's natural sap as an adhesive. The resulting sheets averaged between eight to thirteen inches high and eight to ten inches wide, much like contemporary office paper. These were dried and bleached by the sun, then burnished with a piece of stone or shell, leaving behind a smooth white surface with natural flecks.

Egyptians glued these sheets end to end using starch paste to make rolls of twenty, which could be trimmed into shorter widths as needed and for easier handling.[17] Such rolls were generally inscribed on only one side and in columns so they could be held open to reveal a narrow portion of text, much like a newspaper. The two layers of pith created a natural paper *grain* that dictated how papyrus could be inscribed and rolled: with the horizontal grain on the inside and the vertical on the outside to prevent cracking as the sheet curled.[18] Once a scroll dried, its curvature would set, making curling it the other way difficult, so in

A book might be best understood as the material support for inscribed language, a category that includes rolls and codices and even monumental inscription, both written by hand and printed by many different mechanisms, and also a wide variety of digital media.

—JESSICA BRANTLEY,
"THE PREHISTORY OF THE BOOK"

those rare instances in which scrolls have been found with writing on both sides, the reverse generally contains a second text, suggesting reuse rather than continuation (see figure 1).

Among its affordances, papyrus was durable, could be extended by adhering additional sheets, and allowed texts written on it to be amended, unlike hardened clay. The smooth surface made possible the development of curvy hieratic script, and the use of the brush facilitated the development of colorful illustration, of which Egyptian papyri offer some beautiful examples. Among the best known is a collection of texts to facilitate passage into the afterlife, referred to by ancient Egyptians as the "book of coming forth by day." Known colloquially as the Egyptian Book of the Dead, this collection of two hundred spells, originally written on burial chamber walls and sarcophagi, was codified around 1700 BCE, when it began to be composed on scrolls for interment with the deceased.[19] The order and number of spells varied from roll to roll, and its design reflected the status of its owner: from elaborately illustrated custom versions for the wealthy, who both selected their preferred spells and were depicted within them, to more anonymous prefabricated templates with gaps for the name of the deceased.[20]

The papyrus scroll contains precursors to both the codex book and contemporary digital reading devices. The *scroll*, after all, which allowed continuous writing in columns on a surface that could be thirty to forty feet long, provides the verb we use for horizontal or vertical movement in a text that extends beyond the screen's bounds. Many finding aids developed for the scroll persisted into codex form. The work's contents or first words and the name of its creator were written on the outside edge of the scroll, providing an early title page, though the unfortunate placement at the scroll's vulnerable edge meant that most of these fragile bits were lost over time.[21] Egyptian scribes took advantage of ink's variety and incorporated *rubrication* into their work, using red ink to highlight important words and ideas, as well as to indicate the start of new paragraphs. Such contrast was not possible with cuneiform impression. Rubrication would be adapted by Greek and Roman scribes in their manuscripts, and the tactic persisted into early printed books. Headings, glosses, and titles might be written in red, as would dots and dashes used to separate sections and sentences. In every case, scribes developed techniques to facilitate the reading of written work, one of the hallmarks of the book as not only a storage, but also a retrieval, device.

While papyrus facilitated the development of writing and illustration, it was not an ideal archival material because it becomes fragile as it dries and is susceptible to moisture and insects, particularly in European climates. We have very few intact papyrus scrolls as a result. Another drawback to the scroll form, its tendency to snap shut due to its curled shape, required readers to use both hands to hold it open or lay it on a flat surface and place objects on it, tactics that sounds cumbersome to us today, but that scholars point out would have become second nature among Egyptian readers.[22] This normalization of reading practices bears remembering, since from the vantage point of the twenty-first century, our own codex book has been normalized to such a degree that we question the "book-ness" of anything that challenges our expected reading experience, with little regard for the fact that reading in one direction rather than another, scanning text silently, and putting a title and author's name on a book's cover are all learned behaviors.

Mineral, Vegetable, Animal

Despite their drawbacks, scrolls persisted for more than two millennia as the dominant book form in Egyptian and Greek culture, to which it was exported. Parchment, developed around 1600 BCE, provided a durable alternative to papyrus and ensured a long life for the scroll in Greece and Rome, where the Latin name for such a roll, *volumen*, gives us an important foundational term for the book.[23] The term *parchment* itself comes to us from the Latin *pergamum*, for Pergamon (in modern Turkey), a key center of its production in the fourth century BCE.[24] Made from animal hide rather than plant fibers, parchment was flexible, strong, could be cut in larger sizes than papyrus, provided an exceptionally smooth writing surface, and was opaque enough to allow clear writing on both sides. These features helped it eventually replace papyrus, but its greatest asset was mobility: parchment could be made wherever there was land to raise cattle, goats, and sheep—unlike papyrus, whose manufacture and export Egypt had cornered.

Like Egyptian papyri, Greek and Roman scrolls were inscribed in columns, which the Greeks called *paginae*, providing both the foundational term and the concept of the page, establishing what scholar Bonnie Mak calls its "cognitive architecture."[25] While we associate the word *page* with trimmed sheets sold by the ream or bound in volumes, we might, instead, think of it as ancient scribes did, as a means of guiding the reader's eye and containing information for easy access. These *paginae*, after all, were similar in size to the content of an 8.5×11 in. page, though scroll dimensions varied with content and quality. Works of Greek poetry, for instance, were trimmed to around five inches in height, and epigrams appeared on short, two-inch scrolls suited to their pithy texts.[26] With the development of *concertina* scrolls, discussed in this chapter, the shape of the page as we know it emerges. Folding the parchment between each *pagina* emphasizes its discrete edges while still allowing continuous reading.

Some scrolls were wound around rods that extended beyond the top and bottom of the roll to facilitate opening and closing. This *umbilicus*[27] (a term that points to the rollers' centrality but also suggests a Cronenbergian connection between the hand at one end of this cord and the text at the other) could act as a weight if allowed to drape over a table's edge, holding the scroll open.[28] Generally, readers would unroll a scroll with the right hand while rolling it with the left, an active process revealing only a column or two at a time, which meant that to read it again one had to rewind it, much like a reel-to-reel, cassette, or VHS tape. This process takes a ceremonial form in Judaism, where the Torah scroll is publicly rewound on a holiday known as *Simchat Torah*, or "rejoicing of the Torah." After the final portion is read, the scroll is paraded around the congregation before being returned to the start so the opening portion can be read as well, symbolizing the cyclical nature of both the year and the text.

While one might expect parchment to have quickly superseded its more fragile counterpart, scrolls of both kinds existed side by side for centuries, much as tablets and scrolls did. Some scholars attribute this parity to the difficulty of systematizing and scaling its production. Parchment and *vellum*, its highest-quality exemplar (typically of calfskin), were made by skinning an animal, removing the hair from its pelt, bathing the skin in lime, stretching and drying it slowly, then treating the surface to make it hard and smooth. In addition to requiring utmost care, the process necessitated the slaughter of great quantities of livestock, a costly prospect. Much as in our own technological moment, where print books and e-readers continue to be used despite staunch proclamations in favor of the portability, durability, and cost-effectiveness of one or the other, established systems of production and use take time and resources to change.

The Alphabet

The material text, as we have seen, arose largely for administrative purposes: it helped burgeoning cities keep records and accounts, established the power of rulers, and codified ceremonial practice. The movement from orality to literacy plays a central role in the further development of writing to produce literature and its necessary audience: readers. It is through the Greek development of the alphabet that writing gained enough of a foothold to foster the book in the West, so we'll take a short diversion here to establish how Greeks revolutionized the written word.

Much like Egyptians, early Greeks initially relied on pictographic writing (ca. 2200 BCE), from which a syllabic system (peppered with a few *logograms*: symbols representing a word, phrase, or concept) developed in the seventeenth century BCE. Syllabics, in which characters

The term "book," then, is a kind of shorthand that stands for many forms of written textual communication adopted in past societies, using a wide variety of materials.

—MARTYN LYONS,
BOOKS: A LIVING HISTORY

represent sounds rather than objects or ideas, both simplify writing and enable a vast increase in vocabulary. Their reliance on consonant-vowel combinations, however, means such alphabets require large character sets to express that vocabulary: upward of ninety in the Minoan script scholars call Linear A and seventy-five in its fourteenth-century Cretan successor, Linear B. This made writing so ponderous only a select group could master it. Such linear written forms, suitable for inscription in clay, were thus used primarily for administrative records.

The alphabet as we know it arose not from a syllabic source, but a consonantal one that developed in the Sinai Peninsula around 1700 BCE through the mutual influence of Egyptian and Semitic languages. The Phoenicians developed this system of consonants into a twenty-two-character alphabet during the tenth century BCE.[29] The Greeks, in turn, adapted these letters to their own spoken language, swapping consonants they didn't have for vowels and adding new letters for missing Greek sounds. Establishing a writing system of consonants and vowels with one symbol for each sound, the Greeks exploded the capacity of language, magnifying the number of words and ideas it could represent. Not only could these letterforms transcribe spoken Greek, they could adapt to any number of regional dialects and languages, ensuring their spread and development in the West. The Romans adapted Latin from an Etruscan variant of Greek around the seventh century BCE, and as their writing developed over the next two centuries, they established the familiar letterforms that would become the most widespread in the world.

The Greek invention of the consonant-vowel alphabet assured the development of literacy and the shift from tablet to scroll. This alphabet proved easier to learn and write than its predecessors, since it involved far fewer signs. And, like Egyptian hieratic script, it was better suited to papyrus than clay, leading to widespread adoption of scrolls. This reliance upon papyrus led to another important Greek invention: the pen. Cut from a reed and possessing a sharp split tip, the ink pen ensured clarity and speed—it was a vast improvement over the Egyptian reed brush and was eventually adopted, along with the Greek alphabet, by the Egyptians themselves in the fourth century.[30] The enhanced speed of writing in turn influenced the alphabet. Initially written in straight-sided majuscule only, Latin grew curves in the fourth century CE, and minuscule letterforms arose in the fifth century, perhaps because of the increased production of Christian codices at that point. We'll return to upper- and lowercase letters when we look at the invention of movable type, but it bears noting that writing's form and materials developed in dialogue with one another, even in this early stage, shaping the form of the book to both writers and readers.

Scrolls and the Advent of Paper

Like Mesopotamians with clay and Egyptians with papyrus, the Chinese developed their earliest book form, *jiance*, from the plant fiber they had in abundance: bamboo. A versatile material, it supported architecture, agriculture, and the arts before its adoption as a writing substrate. At around the same time King Ashurbanipal was amassing his library, Chinese artisans were cutting bamboo stalks at their natural joints, splitting them into strips about half an inch wide, cutting these into slips of equal length, and curing them over a fire. They polished these slips smooth on one side (known as the yellow side), and tied them together with cords of silk, hemp, or leather so they could be rolled up like a mat for storage and transport (see figure 1).[31] Though in most cases their cords have disintegrated, some *jiance* include gaps in the text or notches in the bamboo that indicate where such bindings would have been placed. The very name for these Chinese scrolls, scholar Liu Guozhong points out, "*ce*," which translates loosely to "volumes [of strips]" (as in *jian*/bamboo strip + *ce*/volume), is a pictogram representing uneven strips of bamboo encircled with string: 冊.[32] Incidentally, this form provides an excellent model for the idea of *grain*: the direction in which a sheet of paper's fibers lay. One folds paper parallel to this grain to get the smoothest crease and ensure pages will turn easily. As book artist Scott McCarney demonstrates to his students with a sushi mat, folding a jiance against the grain will snap it like a bundle of twigs and likewise crack the paper's surface.[33]

This preliminary form influenced the very shape of Chinese writing. *Jiance* were inscribed in ink using a fine, stiff-bristled brush. As with Egyptian and Greek scrolls, a knife was used to scrape away mistakes, though saliva and water also did the trick. The traditional Chinese style of writing from top to bottom arises directly from the book's materiality—a bamboo slip was too thin to permit more than one character per line. They were thus inscribed from top to bottom in a column of single characters, and the text continued to the left. One would expect scribes could just as easily have developed a top-to-bottom, left-to-right orientation, but here the form again impacts the content. Because scribes wrote with their right hands, blank slips were held in the left. Moving the painted strip to the right to dry and adding a blank slip to the left was the most expedient approach, and thus they were bound in this fashion.[34] In addition to this columnar orientation, scribes established other characteristics that would continue into manuscript and printed books at this point, numbering their slips either at the bottom of the yellow side or on the back, including chapter numbers and titles on the outermost slips of a roll, and inscribing titles or colophons on the reverse (much as we saw with clay tablets).

The narrowness of the strips contributed not only to the way texts were laid out but also to the evolution of the characters themselves. Because the strips were so thin, scribes developed vertical ideograms that could be written more easily on them. Guozhong gives the example of the characters for horse and pig, both of which appear to be standing on their hind legs, rather than on the ground, as we might expect.[35] In addition to fitting comfortably on their supports, figures for humans and animals also face to the left, indicating the direction in which writing and reading will proceed.[36]

While writing on other surfaces, including tortoise shells, pottery, bronze artifacts, and seals, appears as early as 1400 BCE, *jiance* provide the first portable method for distributing information in China, including funeral lists, divinations, and civic records early on, before expanding to include medical books, philosophical and scientific treatises, and literature (a pattern that repeats in nearly every culture to develop writing). The best-known example of a book composed of slips might be the *Yijing* or *I-Ching* (*Book of Changes*, ca. 1000 BCE), a divinatory text consulted by casting lots to generate hexagrams whose meaning must be interpreted. The oldest complete *jiance*, whose seventy-seven intact strips are threaded together with hemp cord, dates from between 93 and 95 CE and consists of a monthly weapons inventory for the platoon to which it belonged.[37] While bamboo slip scrolls were durable and portable, in lengths over two feet the rolls would have been cumbersome to transport and read. Light, durable silk, another fiber whose production the Chinese perfected, was also used for writing and illustration, particularly between the third and fifth centuries, but it was far more expensive to produce, and those silk scrolls that have been found are thus thought to have been luxury goods.[38]

For the book to take hold, a cheaper, lightweight alternative to bamboo and silk had to be developed: paper, attributed to Cai Lun, a eunuch of the Han imperial court, though examples precede him by two centuries. Cai Lun reportedly presented a method to the emperor in 105 CE whereby a mash of hemp, mulberry bark, fishing nets, and rags was suspended in water (known in papermaking as a slurry) and then sifted through a fine screen to lift out the matted fibers, which were then dried and bleached.[39] The random orientation and interlocking of the fibers made paper durable and flexible. These sheets were adhered into scrolls much like those in use in Egypt and would be inscribed in the same method as *jiance*. Once again, while we might expect this new technology to have quickly superseded its predecessor, scrolls of paper and bamboo continued to be used alongside one another through the fifth century, when Emperor Huan Xuan felt the need to issue an imperial decree commanding bookmakers to use paper and stop relying on what he believed were antiquated techniques.[40]

We should keep in mind that no text exists outside of the physical support that offers it for reading (or hearing) or outside of the circumstance in which it was read (or heard). Authors do not write books: they write texts that become written objects—manuscripts, inscriptions, print matter or, today, material in a computer file.

—GUGLIELMO CAVALLO AND ROGER CHARTIER, *A HISTORY OF READING IN THE WEST*

Paper and Islam's Golden Age

Despite its superiority as a material, paper did not reach the West until 751. Its arrival was fortuitous, circuitous, and linked to the spread of the Islamic Empire. When Muslim soldiers captured a group of Chinese sailors in battle, they immediately recognized the utility of the paper found aboard their vessel.[41] These Chinese prisoners of war built the first paper mill in Samarkand, and the papermaking techniques they taught their captors spread rapidly throughout the Arab world, replacing papyrus entirely by the tenth century.

As the Islamic Empire expanded, bookmaking flourished, fed, in part, by the availability of paper. Islamic artisans developed the process they inherited, and the essentials of their paper milling system continue to this day: the replacement of mulberry fibers, unavailable in the region, with linen rags; employing trip hammers to mechanize the slurrying process, rather than beating the fibers by hand; and the use of laid-wire screens that leave faint lines on the finished sheet. The high value placed on writing and intellectual pursuits in Muslim culture, coupled with the expansion of the empire, led to a boom in bookmaking between the eighth and thirteenth centuries. Some calculations suggest Islamic book production during this period of expansion was greater than that of Greece, Rome, Byzantium, and Christian Europe combined.[42]

This "golden age" of Islamic culture, marked by significant advances in philosophy, mathematics, science, and medicine, also saw extensive translation and annotation of ancient Greek texts inherited through the conquest of Egypt and Syria. Caliphs collected millions of books in libraries in Baghdad, Cairo, Lebanon, Córdoba, and elsewhere, furthering scholarship and book production throughout the empire. It was ultimately through Islamic Spain that Europe would receive paper in the twelfth century, at which point the codex had become the dominant book structure. The founding book of Islam, the *Qur'an*, had embraced this form from the outset. The text was initially transmitted orally by the prophet Muhammad and his followers in the first decades of the seventh century, but because they were soldiers actively engaged in conquest, the narrative was threatened by their own bodily precarity. To prevent its loss, Caliph Abu Bakr had the text committed to the page soon after its appearance.[43] After Muhammad's death, Caliph Uthman compiled an authoritative version, and the *Qur'an* took shape as a parchment codex.

A Networked Text

While we are considering the deep history of the book's material forms, we should look briefly at an example that arises elsewhere, outside of the lineage of the codex. The South American *khipu* (or *quipu* in the Spanish spelling) provides an entirely different method of recording—knots (*khipu* in the Quechua language) in string. While our earliest samples come from the first millennium, most archeological specimens represent the Inka Empire (roughly 1400–1532).[44] At least one proto-*khipu*, which includes twigs knotted into the strings, likely dates to the third millennium BCE, making it concurrent with cuneiform tablets.[45] These devices consist of a main cord of cotton or wool with pendant strings affixed to it, most descending, while a few are attached in the other direction (see figure 1). Some of these pendants include further, subsidiary strings dyed in a range of colors and spun in multiple plies. When displayed in museums, *khipu* are often mounted linearly, like a timeline on the wall, or radially, like a clock face or dramatic rope necklace. While some are relatively simple, a handful include over fifteen hundred pendants, making them intricate and beautiful objects of study.

Scholars are still deciphering these dense systems of knots, based on around 750 specimens found in burial chambers in the Peruvian Andes and on descriptions of their use by the Spanish colonists who first encountered them. The opacity of the *khipu* is a legacy of colonization: Spanish authorities outlawed their use in the sixteenth century, destroying many of them in the process. The only *khipu* to have remained within their community are those of Rapaz, Peru, where they were kept until the 1930s.[46] While they are still maintained and used in ritual, they are no longer updated. In 2012, Chilean artist Cecilia Vicuña published a contemporary, conceptual artist's *khipu*. Produced in an edition of thirty-two, her *Chanccani Quipu* (2012) takes the knot-book as metaphor, in her words, for "the clash of two cultures and worldviews: the Andean oral universe and the Western world of print."[47] Knotted to a bamboo spine, four-foot cords of unspun wool cascade like soft white hair to the ground when the piece is hung. Stenciled in rust-colored ink onto their surface, fragmented Quechua phonemes extend across and down each strand, inviting eye and ear to sound the chords of language.

Khipu were maintained by a specialized bureaucratic class of knot-makers, *khipukamayuq*, who understood the conventionalized signs represented by different configurations of knots, colors, and types of string. Their role was to breathe life into the threads, conducting the census, documenting taxation and labor, and maintaining calendars of ritual practice. The chief question, whether their knots served as mnemonics or as a written system that could be read, remains unanswered. These devices were certainly portable, like a book, and they could contain both accounting records and narratives. Scholar Gary Urton, founder of Harvard's Khipu Database Project, contends that the system represents a form of binary coding that helped keepers recount narratives based on relational pairs.[48] On some quantitative *khipu*, knots are arranged in a decimal hierarchy based on distance from the primary string, with the 1s being furthest, then 10s, then 100s, and so on. Other *khipu* have a more complex arrangement, which suggests they were used to record some other kind of information, like images, ideas, or sounds.

While the *khipu* represents a distinct departure from the kinds of record keeping we have so far traced, it is knitted to the history of the book's changing forms by its materiality. Like the clay tablet, papyrus sheet, and bamboo scroll, it was made from a material both abundant and highly refined within the culture in which it arose: cloth. The cultivation of alpacas, llamas, and other camelids in the Andes provided raw material for the perfection of weaving. Incan cloth was pliable, three-dimensional, visual, and already embedded in the culture as a marker of status.[49] Colored embroidery and geometric designs had clear symbolic significance, and knotted tapestry patterns in royal clothing were used to establish authority. As in each of the other early book forms we have looked at, the chosen material formed part of the fabric of existence for its users and likely shaped not only how information was transmitted but also the very nature of thought itself. Our challenge, as students of the book, is to think about the way its materiality is both a product and constituent of its historic moment.

In China, an entire mountain can be a book, a calligraphic catalogue of historical events. For example, in Quanzhou, there is a mountain whose cliffs are inscribed with maritime stories, such as historical accounts of Zheng He's travels to the Western Ocean. In this way, even nature can be considered a medium for writing books.

—CAI GUO-QIANG, STATEMENT IN *SHU: REINVENTING BOOKS IN CONTEMPORARY CHINESE ART*

From Roll to Accordion to Codex

Given this range of antecedents, where does the codex, that ubiquitous structure we all recognize, come from? How do bookmakers transition from continuous scrolls to bound volumes, and why? There are a few different ways to answer this question, depending on which material you used to make your scrolls. In China, paper's strength and malleability led to the development in the eighth century of sutra-folded books, named for their use in producing copies of the Buddhist sutras. Scrolls were folded back and forth in even widths to create an accordion (see figure 2). Such folded books facilitated reading by allowing access to any part of text and would play a key role in both spreading Buddhism throughout Asia and establishing the codex in China. Incidentally, the term "role" itself is a legacy of the scroll, a reference to the rolls on which actors' parts were written during the Renaissance.[50]

The folded book, also known as an *accordion* or *concertina*, was a flat, rectangular volume, and its height came directly from the scrolls that preceded it, since the paper sheets used were generally the length of the papermaker's arm. The format may also have developed from the *palm leaf manuscript*, or *pothī*, carried by monks between India and China starting at the beginning of the Common Era. Produced in many scripts and languages, such collections of Hindu and Buddhist teachings were copied and

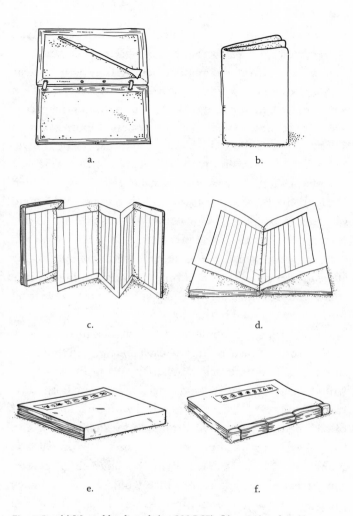

Figure 2 (a) Wax tablet diptych (ca. 800 BCE); (b) quire/parchment notebook (ca. 55 BCE); (c) accordion/concertina (ca. 700 CE); (d) butterfly binding (ca. 800 CE); (e) wrapped back binding (ca. 1200 CE); (f) stab binding (ca. 1300 CE). Illustration by Mike Force for Lightboard.

memorized as a form of devotion by scribes across Asia. Using dried palm leaves that had been flattened, polished, and trimmed into rectangular strips, they wrote these sutras with an early *intaglio* technique: text was inscribed with a stylus, ink or soot was applied to it, and the excess was wiped away, leaving behind darkened impressions.[51] The leaves were bound in a style reminiscent of the venetian blind: encased in wooden boards of the same size and shape as the leaves, one or several holes were drilled through the lot and a cord passed through to hold them together (see figure 1). The name *sutra* itself relates to this form: it derives from the proto Indo-European root *syū*, "to bind, sew," which yields the Sanskrit *sūtram*, meaning "thread [or] string."[52] The Chinese accordion book turns this volume on its side, adapting it to the vertical writing method established in the *jiance*.

The earliest example of a woodblock-printed book comes from China as well. The *Diamond Sutra*, a fourteen-foot scroll commissioned in 868 CE by Wang Jie, was made from a series of carved wood blocks containing both illustration and text.[53] These were rolled with ink, and a sheet of paper placed on top was rubbed to transfer the ink to the page. This type of printing, known as *xylography*, was highly portable and could be completed by a single person (unlike early movable type, which would require a heavy press and several artisans to operate). It had the added benefit of enabling the reproduction of multiple sequential pages simultaneously.

The rubbing technique, coupled with the thinness of mulberry paper, meant that only one side of a page could be printed—rubbing the inked side to print on the reverse would have smudged it. This restriction likely led to the development of glued bindings from the concertina.[54] For the butterfly binding (ninth to thirteenth century), individual sheets were printed with two facing pages, then folded in half, stacked, and glued along their crease. This results in a codex whose open, printed folio perches like a spread-winged butterfly on the closed folios on either side (see figure 2). Unfortunately, it also leaves two blank pages between each printed pair, a trait that both breaks readers' concentration and encourages skimming.[55] To create an uninterrupted reading experience, printers developed the wrapped back binding (thirteenth to seventeenth century).[56] Sheets were folded outward, so text appeared on both sides, and piled, and holes were drilled through the open edges of the stack (see figure 2). Bookmakers threaded these holes with thick paper pegs to keep the pages together, then glued the spine and wrapped a stout paper cover around it, creating a stronger *book block* and hiding the blank sides of the page while also producing the first glue-based or *perfect binding*.

Because glued bindings attracted insects, they eventually gave way to a thread-based system: the stab binding most associated with Chinese and Japanese books. This sewn binding used the same folded-folio technique as the wrapped back binding, but rather than gluing covers on, a single thread was passed through a series of holes along the spine to create a decorative geometric pattern. In addition to being less appealing to bugs than glue, the sewn binding was easier to repair, since it could be taken apart without damage to the pages (see figure 2).[57] The stab binding remained popular until the early twentieth century, when the Chinese book began to more closely resemble the codex.

The Greeks and Romans had an accordion-like structure of their own before the introduction of papyrus or paper: wax writing tablets. Employed as early as the eighth century BCE in ancient Greece (and borrowed from the Assyrians, who used them from the fourteenth century BCE on),[58] they were made by carving a rectangular depression in a wood slate and filling it with wax. Known as *pugillares*, their name derives from *pugnus*, or fist, suggesting these "handbooks" offered sturdy and portable writing surfaces that could be held with one hand, much like a contemporary e-reader.[59] They also clearly demarcated the boundaries of the *pagina*. A similar device can still be found in novelty shops—the magic writing pad that so intrigued Sigmund Freud, a gummed surface protected by a layer of cellophane. Using a plastic stylus or the tip of a retracted ballpoint pen, one can write secret messages on the surface of the plastic that are easily "erased" upon reading by lifting the cover away. Early wax tablets were used for secret messages as well. According to Herodotus, when the exiled king Demaratus wanted to warn Sparta of an impending Persian attack (ca. 480 BCE), he carved his message in the wood of a tablet and covered it with wax to avoid interception. The warning reached its readers who were, at first, perplexed by the blank slate. Herodotus credits Queen Gorgo with the idea to scrape the wax away, revealing the secret message in time to warn the people.[60]

Wax tablets were inscribed with a stylus that was sharp on one end and flat on the other, allowing one to erase one's mistakes. Writers might warm the stylus with their lips for easier inscription, as some ancient artworks suggest. Tablets could be used singly but were often threaded together with leather cord into pairs or *polyptychs*, gatherings of as many as ten tablets. When more than two tablets were threaded together, either end to end or along one edge, those in the middle could be inscribed on both sides.[61] The bound group of tablets, known to Romans as a *codex*, is suggestive of the form's wooden supports, though the term was also used for tablets carved from other materials, including ivory and bone.[62] Representations of such bound tablets on Greek vases suggest they were held not

A book is never simply a remarkable *object*. Like every other technology, it is invariably the product of human agency in complex and highly volatile contexts.

—D. F. MCKENZIE,
BIBLIOGRAPHY AND THE SOCIOLOGY OF TEXTS

like our codex, with the hinge running up the middle, but more like a laptop, with a horizontal hinge between two writing surfaces (see figure 2).

The Greeks initially used wax tablets for important documents like wills and birth announcements,[63] but with the introduction of papyrus and parchment rolls, they began to use them in education and for more ephemeral documents like notes and household accounts. Romans used *pugillares* and *codices* extensively, particularly for legal documents (giving us the term *codicil*). They are credited by most scholars with shifting the material of the codex from wood to skin in the first century CE—a process that likely began with the use of small parchment notebooks, or *membranae*.[64] Horace (ca. 65–8 BCE) mentions their use for drafting in both his *Satires* and *Ars Poetica*, suggesting groups of folded pages provided a lightweight alternative to the wax tablet for composing longer texts before committing them to papyrus rolls.[65]

These bundles of folded pages provide the essential concept from which the codex developed in the Common Era, though the inventor of the form remains unknown. Folded papyrus and parchment sheets from the first to the fourth century CE, wrapped with leather and sewn with a loop of thread along the fold—a sewing now known as the *saddle stitch*—provide some of our earliest codices, each using a slightly different method to produce a *quire*, or gathering of folded pages (see figure 2).[66] A single sheet can be folded into a variety of gatherings named for the number of smaller sheets (known in bookmaking as *leaves*) they generate: *folio* (two), *quarto* (four), *octavo* (eight), *sextodecimo* (sixteen), etc. (see figure 3), and book historians use these names to describe a work's size. Papyrus gatherings consisted of nested *folios*, sheets folded in half with the grain, and are thus the same height as papyrus rolls. Parchment gatherings, however, were made from a range of pelt sizes and, given the malleability of the material, could be folded and cut several times before binding. The most common such folding, in octavo, yields the gathering of four nested folios that give the quire its name.[67]

When a large sheet is folded down, the resulting pages are called *conjugates* because they are still attached. When the conjugates have been sliced along their folds, the pages become *leaves*, each with two sides: *recto* (front) and *verso* (back). These terms come from the names Romans gave the sides of a papyrus scroll: *recto* for the horizontally ruled interior that was the right place to write, and *verso folium*, for the "turned leaf" of the scroll's back.[68] When looking at a two-page spread or *opening* in a codex, the left-hand page is always a verso and the right always a recto.

This easy-to-assemble format, in which a single sheet is folded down into a quire, played an important role in European publishing from the sixteenth to the nineteenth

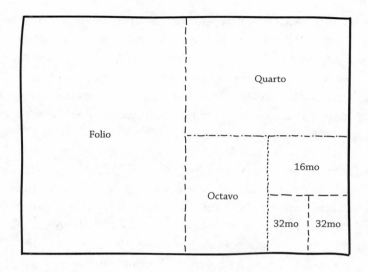

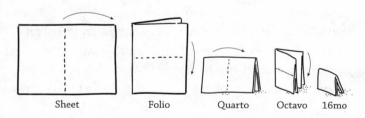

Figure 3 Single sheet folding and resulting book sizes. Illustration by Mike Force for Lightboard based on A. W. Lewis, *Basic Bookbinding* (New York: Dover, 1957), 9.

century, with itinerant peddlers known as chapmen hawking such cheap pamphlets to the masses at a time when books were luxury goods.[69] These *chapbooks*, ranging in length from four to twenty-four pages, continue to play an important role in small press publishing today, where they are used for compact, inexpensive collections of poetry.

It bears repeating that the advent of the codex doesn't mean scrolls disappeared—scrolls and codex books made of both parchment and papyrus existed side by side within Roman culture for centuries. Archaeological evidence shows a gradual decline in the number of rolls from the third century onward, with codex books increasing, until the two reach parity between the third and fourth centuries.[70] The extant codex books from this time include works by Homer and Plato as well as treatises on medicine and grammar, which suggests they were used in education. Each tends to be only as long one or two scrolls, evidence that the predominant format had established in readers' minds some concept of a book's duration. To make the leap from the pamphlet-like notebook to the codex as we know it required more complex bindings that could link several quires tightly together. Our earliest complete example, the Mudil Codex, a fourth-century psalter discovered in an Egyptian Graveyard in 1984, reveals the bound book's Roman roots: its thirty-two quires are enclosed in wooden covers and stitched with leather.[71]

The Manuscript Tradition

The side-bound book as we know it is well suited to the needs we have seen so far. It is portable and durable, it is easy to reference, and its economical pages allow writing on both sides. Unlike the scroll, it does not require both hands to pry apart, and like the tablet, it can rest open on a surface for consultation. But perhaps its spread is most attributable not to what it is, but to what it isn't: a scroll like that used for the Hebrew Scriptures—the Torah— and pagan religious texts. Early Christians, the essayist and book historian Alberto Manguel suggests, embraced the codex as a means of clandestinely transporting texts banned by the Romans.[72] This differentiation would serve an important purpose with the rise of Christianity in the Common Era, as Christians and Jews selected bindings for their religious tracts to reinforce their distinction—monks even bound the Septaguint into codex form for inclusion in monastic libraries, suggesting the extent to which such differentiation was internalized.[73]

It is through the rise of Christendom that codex book production developed in the West—in the form of monastic manuscripts. In the sixth century, as the first monasteries were establishing Catholicism in Italy, St. Benedict of Nursia issued a rule requiring Benedictine monks to read daily, complete a book during Lent, and carry books when traveling to peruse each time they stopped.[74] The emphasis placed on literacy led to a boom in book production within monasteries, each of which had its own library and a *scriptorium* for copying texts by hand. Staffed by scribes, correctors, calligraphers, and rubricators, it produced codex books for trade or sale to other monasteries predominantly for the consultation of other monks. Monasteries monopolized book production until the thirteenth century, and when you picture early books, it is likely monastic *illuminated manuscripts* that come to mind. These ornate productions included both Christian texts and ancient Greek and Roman works, copied and recopied by scribes who hadn't exactly signed up for the task of preserving and disseminating literature.

The monks who served as scribes did not, in fact, relish the task. While their brothers worked in the fields or traveled, they spent six hours a day hunched before the page in a cold scriptorium, incurring back-aches, headaches, eye strain, and cramps, all while wasting away the daylight hours, since candles were costly and fire was a great risk to their highly flammable materials.[75] They labored in silence, communicating by hand signal when they needed materials or simply wanted to commiserate about their lot. This they sometimes did in the margins of their pages, leaving complaints in ink among the text's glosses like this one, reminiscent of a schoolchild's plea: "St. Patrick of Armagh, deliver me from writing."[76] Scribes need not have understood the Latin, Greek, and Hebrew texts they copied, since literate correctors and proofreaders ensured the quality of their work.[77] Some roles in the scriptorium could be filled by laity, including calligraphy, rubrication, and illumination. Manuscript production thus employed a great number of people in the manufacture of a single book through a time-consuming process. Bound in wood and leather covers, sometimes encrusted with jewels and filigree, and decorated with bright colors and gold leaf, the labor and expense that went into each codex manuscript shows tangibly on every page.

Scribes worked on gatherings of four parchment folios, known among book historians as *quaternions* (the source of our term *quire*), whose sixteen pages were arranged with "hair" sides facing "hair" sides and "flesh" to "flesh," an effect of the octavo fold described above.[78] The two sides of a sheet of parchment, though treated, scraped, and stretched, bear the history of the animal from whom it was made: the "hair" side is visibly darker and freckled with tiny follicle holes.[79] Dividing manuscripts into these smaller sections enabled several scribes to work on the same volume simultaneously, speeding up the process, but multiplying the potential for error, since each quaternion had to align in appearance and content with its neighbors in the finished book. To keep their writing clear and uniform, scribes pierced or marked lines and margins on their pages. Their layout was drawn from a familiar source—Roman scrolls and codices: a series of justified columns, two to a page, both efficient and pleasing to the eye.

Scribes copied the text before them with a goose quill in one hand and a knife in the other, the latter allowing them to hold pages flat, sharpen their pens, and scrape away mistakes. They wrote in a majuscule style, or *hand*, known as *uncial*, developed from Roman letterforms, but with curved edges.[80] This hand persisted for religious texts through the eighth century, when Charlemagne commissioned a more legible, lowercase hand to standardize manuscript writing. Known as *Carolingian* for its association with his reign, it was much faster to write, so scribes could produce more quickly with this small affordance and keep up with an increasing demand for books.[81] By the fourteenth century, Gothic scripts in a variety of regional styles had developed across Europe, and these would provide the basis for our earliest typefaces, a subject we will return to in chapter 2.

When a quaternion was completed and proofread by a corrector, the rubricator took over, continuing the Egyptian tradition of embellishing important passages in red ink. At this point, titles, chapter initials, and headings were added. If the manuscript was important, or if a wealthy patron commissioned it, the rubricated text was next turned over to the illuminator, whose marginal paintings illustrated and beautified it. Working primarily in red and blue pigment and gold leaf, the illuminator added flourishes to the initial letters of passages (sometimes painting little scenes around the capital to create decorative letters known as *historiated initials*), decorated the page's borders, and introduced illustrations depicting the text's themes (see figure 4). This method persisted through the fifteenth century, when it reached its height with about 10 percent of all manuscripts receiving illumination.[82]

One of the most well-known illuminated manuscripts, the Irish *Book of Kells* (ca. 800 CE), demonstrates both virtuosic technique and the innovations introduced by scribes of the British Isles: an elegant uncial script, richly decorated initial letters, and, most importantly, word spacing.[83] The four gospels and prefatory texts in Latin are written in several colored inks (in addition to the standard black), and are more densely illuminated than any surviving Gospel book of the period. Likely the work of at least three scribes, the *Book of Kells* reflects the intricate and laborious process that made manuscripts such costly and tightly controlled products.[84] Lavishly illuminated throughout its 340 vellum folios, with ten full-page illustrations, it includes interlaced motifs that mimic Celtic metalwork, red dots evoking Roman tradition, and illustrations influenced by Byzantine, Armenian, and Mediterranean iconography.[85]

With its large scale (unfortunately cut down to around 13 × 9 in. for rebinding in the nineteenth century) and

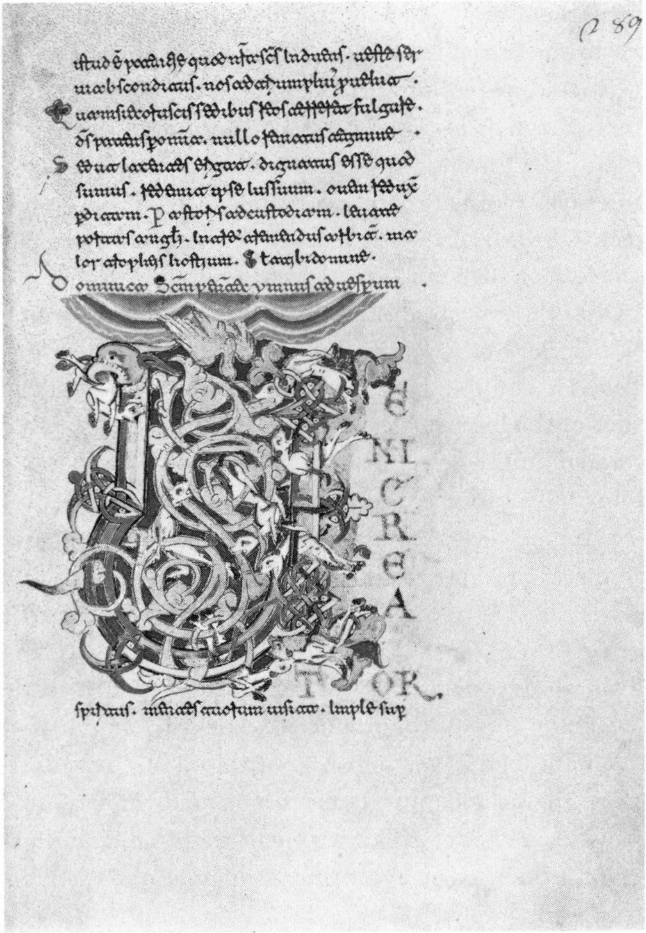

Figure 4 Page from an Italian breviary by an unknown artist. The freckles in the upper left corner are hair follicles. Initial V: The Descent of the Holy Spirit, 1153. Tempera colors, gold leaf, gold paint, and ink on parchment. Leaf: 19.2 × 13.2 cm ($7\frac{9}{16}$" × $5\frac{3}{16}$"). Image courtesy The J. Paul Getty Museum, Los Angeles, via the Open Content Program.

sumptuous appearance, *The Book of Kells* would have been an altar-book reserved for use during special services by a reader who had memorized the text. It was meant more to be seen and heard than studied, as evinced by a number of errors in the text including missing words, repeated passages, and illustrations added to cover up mistakes.[86] Such large volumes required an important seventh-century development in codex binding: the use of stout cords or leather thongs, threaded through the cover and run across the book's spine, to which each quire was sewn. These supported bindings, perfected in the seventeenth century, continue to be standard in both the repair and production of fine books.

Reading and Writing's Shifts

The shape and style of these early manuscripts reflect the reading practices of their day and the needs they were designed to meet. Reading was, in the manuscript era, a practice fundamentally different from the kind of private, meditative engagement we now experience. A monk did not sit silently at a desk or reclining in bed or while in transit from one place to another. He might be read to in assembly by a fluent reader among his brothers, or he might mumble to himself as he learned the Latin text. When he traveled to other monasteries to consult their volumes, he found codices chained to lecterns at pews, ensuring these valuable documents did not walk off. Copying the book would require the significant effort of sliding the neighboring volumes off the metal rod to which they were affixed before he could take his own to a desk that would accommodate his labor. Such chained bindings persisted through the eighteenth century and are emblematic of the different place the codex held in cultural and religious life. Each book was a unique and hard-wrought object to be enjoyed by a limited audience.

Reading had been, since the Hellenic era, an oral practice—one reflected in writing itself. Greek bookrolls were written in a continuous script, or *scriptio continua*, withoutspacesbetweenwords or changes of case and minimal punctuation. They both required and rewarded sounding aloud. As Paul Saenger, curator of rare books at the Newberry Library in Chicago and a scholar of medieval reading practices, explains, continuous script could not have developed without the Greek introduction of vowels, which allowed readers to parse syllables and hold them in memory as the eye traversed the text.[87] While Greek was composed from right to left, like Phoenician, the Romans developed a method of speeding up reading by reversing direction from line to line, allowing continuous reading as one scanned from right to left, then left to right, and back again. This *boustrophedon* form, named for the method of plowing, allowed farmer, writer, and reader to crisscross the field without lifting their instruments, suggesting that it was far less cumbersome than we might assume.

Though it seems awkward to us now, continuous script was not a naïve construction, but a choice, as evinced by the fact that the Romans discarded their own punctuation in the first century in favor of the Greek model. It established literacy as the purview of a cultured elite, who either studied from a young age to master the identification and inflection proper to each text or employed a professional reader, or *lector*, for the task. It also facilitated a culture of shared inquiry, in which challenging texts were read aloud in groups as a springboard for debate.[88] In ancient Greece, literature was primarily a social activity, with audiences gathering for performances of epic poetry and drama. The epic bears the hallmarks of this orality: it relies on repetition, formulaic images, meter, and rhyme as mnemonic aids to the performer.[89] The term used to describe performances of such works, *rhapsody*, means "to stitch together"—suggesting the extent to which oral composition relies on weaving familiar lines.

The great thinkers of ancient Greece, in fact, mistrusted writing as a technology that would destroy the oral arts of debate and storytelling on which they based their sense of the world, of philosophy, of time and space. In Plato's *Phaedrus*, Socrates disdains the written word for separating ideas from their source, citing Egyptian king Thamus as the first to voice this concern when he received the gift of writing from the god Thoth.[90] Transcription, Socrates fears, is a crutch that will both hamper memory and mire philosophical thought in ambiguity, leaving interpretation in the hands of the reader. Texts, after all, can circulate without their author, thus preventing one from explaining or defending them. Despite these fears, the very writing Plato used to record his dialogues proved instrumental in the development of ancient Greek oratory. As scholar Walter Ong points out in *Orality and Literacy*, his study of the ways writing technologies restructure consciousness, the written word enabled Greek scholars to transcribe and codify effective rhetorical strategies.[91] It also vastly increased human vocabulary, since we no longer had to rely on memory to hold all of language at the ready. Writing, in fact, allowed rhetoric to flourish.

For the kind of silent reading we now experience to take hold, reading would have to change its context and text its form. It would have to become a more private experience, which means literacy would have to extend beyond the elite and monastic communities. Texts, too, would need to become more legible, with standardized punctuation and word spaces so that the mumbling of readers sounding out text, common through the sixth century, could dissipate. And libraries designed for quiet, contemplative reading could then develop to serve this new readership.

Insular scribes, like those who crafted *The Book of Kells*, played a key role in making text more accessible. Because

What is a book? A book is an experience. ... A book starts with an idea. And ends with a reader.

—JULIE CHEN AND CLIFTON MEADOR, *HOW BOOKS WORK*

Latin was a second language, and one more challenging to sound out in *scriptio continua*, they introduced several changes to improve its legibility, including word separation (around 675 CE), additional punctuation, and simplified letterforms. Still, it took nearly four hundred years for these small innovations to spread.[92] The translation of Arabic scientific writing in tenth-century Europe likely played a vital role in solidifying word separation, since it was inherent in the language (because unlike Greek and Latin, it is written in consonants). Translators kept Arabic word separation when rendering these texts in Latin, in part because it made the complex technical prose significantly more comprehensible—an important case where content had a direct influence on form.[93]

Ultimately changes in who read and what they accessed were essential in reshaping writing and the look of the page. The population boom in Europe during the late Middle Ages meant a middle- and upper-class laity needed to be educated, and therefore needed access to books. Universities developed in the thirteenth century to provide education for both clerics and the aristocracy beyond rudimentary language and rhetoric. These institutions drove a new market for the exchange of ideas: academia, an almost entirely male province.[94] To meet the rising demand for and production of texts, guilds of stationers, acting as copy services, binders, booksellers, and book lenders cropped up to serve both faculty and students. Using *exemplars* approved by the faculty, the stationers sent quires out to copyists and illustrators who completed the work piecemeal and sent it back, then arranged and bound the finished book in-house.[95] The piecemeal system meant that many more copies could be made, with identical sections interchangeable between them. For a small fee, students could make their own copies from these exemplars, section by section—a highly manual reading process. They then brought these books to class with them, reading along silently with the professor's lecture,[96] thus learning multimodally, with hand, eye, and ear.

Here again we have the Arab world to thank for the spread of ideas and shifts in reading. Scholars translated ancient works preserved in Arabic into Latin, and works of science and mathematics began to spread as well. As a scholastic audience for books developed, so too did the structure of the page and of the codex designed for individual, silent consultation and annotation.[97] This moment swiftly ushered in that period of artistic and intellectual activity we know as the Renaissance, which changed everything for books. Indispensable in the exchange of ideas by thinkers far removed from one another, the easily transported written codex allowed exactly that asynchronous development of thought Socrates and Plato feared.

Their concerns echo contemporary anxieties about the ways digitally mediated reading and writing shortens our attention spans and ability to engage deeply with texts.

The thing we fear is precisely what worried the ancients: mediation. At the root of Socrates's accusation lies a vision of writing as a technology that interposes between thinker and thought, severing the two and allowing them to travel independently of one another. While Socrates believed this would make it impossible to defend oneself against others or clarify one's ideas, this separation proved essential to the development and dissemination of knowledge in a rapidly growing world. It bears emphasizing that writing itself fundamentally changed human consciousness, much as our reliance on networked digital devices has altered us at the core.

THE BOOK AS CONTENT

The Renaissance inaugurated the age of books, at least among the aristocracy, and many of the features we now associate with the codex arose in response to the boom in silent readership. Books of hours, small illuminated manuscripts commissioned by members of the laity, made worship a private act and the codex itself an object of value and status. The period saw some interesting experiments with book structure to draw attention to these precious artifacts. *Girdle books*, a popular form among pilgrims in the Middle Ages, continued to be made: with an oversized soft leather cover whose flaps could be looped under one's belt for easy consultation on the go. *Dos-à-dos* books (sixteenth century) joined two volumes back to back, the spine of one meeting the fore-edge of the other—a useful, though rare, structure for keeping multivolume works together. And a handful of heart-shaped or *cordiform books* (fourteenth and fifteenth centuries)—a book of hours, a collection of ballads, and a volume of love songs—took advantage of the symmetrical opening of the codex to make the work's form suit its content: devotion.[1]

Most important of all, this period gave rise to that feature we most associate with the book: print. When the codex moved beyond the monastery, notions of authorship gradually changed as well, since monastic scribes were not seen as originators of the ideas they put on the page, but workmen transcribing cultural knowledge. With the rise of universities and humanist inquiry into Latin and Greek literature and rhetoric, a picture of the author as an originator began to take shape. This shift, coupled with mechanization, would prove instrumental to reframing the book as content rather than object—its form a mere vessel for the information it contained.

Starting the Presses

As codex books became private items, rather than shared objects experienced publicly, copyists simply couldn't keep up with demand. Woodblock printing, which appears to have developed in the West to produce playing cards, initially met some of the needs of readers. *Blockbooks*, composed of religious images with captions, served a devotional audience through the fifteenth century.[2] Much as in China, whose xylographic printing techniques predate these and are discussed in chapter 1, a folio could be printed from a relief, with both image and text carved into wood. The woodcut technique used to produce block-books played an important role in both influencing and illustrating books produced with the print technology that would set the standard and remain largely unchanged through the twentieth century: movable type.

When you think of early books, chances are the name Johannes Gutenberg comes to mind. One of the few celebrities in the history of the book, his name has become synonymous with the invention of the printing press and with the production of a 42-line Bible that has been widely exhibited and praised as the first Western book printed with movable type. Despite the ubiquity of squares and statues dedicated to him across Germany, a 1952 U.S. postage stamp celebrating his achievements, numerous engravings of him (none of them verifiable portraits), and an initiative to digitize the world's public domain books that bears his name, Gutenberg almost didn't get the credit for the innovations that made that feat possible.

Much of what we know about Gutenberg's work comes from accounts of a 1455 trial with Johann Fust, the press's financier whose 2,026 gulden investment (including interest) Gutenberg failed to repay.[3] As a result of the suit, Gutenberg was forced to forfeit his print shop,

We have already moved
far enough beyond
the book that we find
ourselves, for the first
time in centuries,
able to see the book as
unnatural, as a near-
miraculous technological
innovation and not as
something intrinsically
and inevitably human.

—GEORGE P. LANDOW,
"TWENTY MINUTES INTO THE FUTURE"

retaining only the work and equipment he had completed before 1448 (when the loan was made). Fust and his son-in-law, Peter Schöffer—who had served as Gutenberg's assistant—took control of his shop, half of the completed bibles, and much of the credit for the printing press itself, and Gutenberg died twelve years later, never having profited from his invention or his clean, standardized Bible. Gutenberg's celebrity is all the more improbable, given that he did not write a word of the text, design it, or print his name in the completed codex.[4] To make printing possible, Gutenberg had to develop a wooden screw press based on those used for olive oil and wine, movable type created from molds, and an oil-based ink that could adhere to metal. Though popularly considered the "inventor" of printing, many of the technologies Gutenberg used were already in existence by the time he set up shop. His great achievement lay in bringing these technologies together, perfecting them, and persuading others to fund his vision.

What little we know of Gutenberg's life establishes him as an enterprising young man from early on. Born around 1400 into a wealthy family in Mainz, Germany, he lived for a time in Strasburg, where his ventures included gem-polishing, producing and selling mirrors to pilgrims, and perhaps beginning work on type and the press.[5] In 1448, Gutenberg returned to Mainz and soon thereafter convinced Fust to invest in his newest scheme:

printing. For the next seven years he worked to develop typecasting and printing techniques that would endure for centuries.

Type's Founding

To begin with, printers needed type. In later years, this could be purchased, but Gutenberg and his contemporaries each had to design and cast their own *fonts*, or collections of interchangeable type, from molten metal. Brass stamps had been used to decorate pewter ware and deboss leather, but these were too soft to withstand the pressure of the press.[6] Gutenberg had to formulate his own alloy of tin and lead that was strong but could melt at a low temperatures so as not to destroy the molds, known as *matrices* (from *mater*/mother), into which it was poured. These matrices produced backward characters (or *patrices*, from *pater*/father) that, when printed, produced small, even letters of exceptional clarity.

Though Gutenberg cut his own types, as printing became more specialized these matrices were created by *punchcutters* who carved entire alphabets of uniform letters and matching punctuation, always in mirror image, on the tips of steel bars. Each *punch* was then pressed into a small bar of copper to create a right-reading indented mold. The type founder fitted this mold into one end of a small rectangular chamber, poured in molten alloy, and spun it rapidly (using a pair of tongs, since it would be quite hot) to distribute the liquid evenly. When the form cooled, he unlatched and opened it, releasing a single piece of type: a short metal bar with a raised, backward character on the end. Its rectangular metal shaft enabled this piece of type to fit snugly next to its neighbors generating tight, legible printed text (see figure 5).

Scholars analyzing the letterforms in Gutenberg's Bible have discovered minor differences in recurring letters on a single page (say two *M*'s or two *G*'s), suggesting that he used a less precise approach, sand-casting, rather than punching in copper, and that he composed each matrix from partial letters he combined.[7] His molds were likely made from an amalgam of sand and clay, which meant he had to break them to remove the finished type. This would have made for a far more laborious process, since every matrix had to be recreated each time a piece of type was cast. Given that a single page of the Gutenberg Bible uses roughly 2,600 pieces of type, and two pages were printed at a time, with several others waiting in the wings for their turn on the press, the process of making Gutenberg's font would have been a significant undertaking.

Finished type was sorted into tall storage cases with a cubby for each letter, mark, and space, lending the pieces the name *sorts*. Such cases had to be kept tidy, or a printer might find himself "out of sorts" and unable to complete

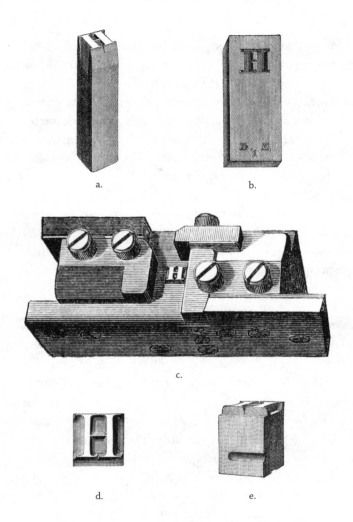

Figure 5 1878 depiction of contemporary typecasting: (a) punch; (b) matrix; (c) type mold with matrix removed; (d) finished type in side and top view. Though a later iteration, the fundamentals of typecasting in the nineteenth century were the same as in Gutenberg's day. These engravings appear in Theodore Low De Vinne's *The Invention of Printing* (New York: F. Hart, 1878).

a given job—an irritating situation. Typesetters, also known as compositors, worked from a manuscript, setting sorts line by line in a *composing stick*, a frame whose width could be adjusted depending on the desired line length. They arranged letters upside down and from right to left, with spacers between words and lines to hold them tightly in columns, creating a mirror image of the text. A completed column, known as a *forme* or *form*, was then tied with string and transferred to a *galley*—a metal tray—for temporary storage and proofing to ensure no words were misspelled or missing. Unlike block-books, in which the design of the page was fixed once the wood had been carved, with movable type the same set of letters could be rearranged to produce an infinite variety of texts. They could also be combined with woodblocks to print word and image simultaneously. Yet while wood carving allowed for all sorts of arrangements of words on the page, including curves and diagonal lines, hand-set type adheres to a rigid grid, making such shapes difficult to replicate.

The Press Itself

Gutenberg's large wooden press required several pressmen to operate. It consisted of a bed in which the type forms were tightly secured, or "locked up," in a frame known as a *chase*. The chase held two forms at a time, which would be printed on a single sheet, creating a folio once both sides had been printed. A pressman called a *beater* applied ink evenly to the surface of the type using handled leather ink balls, and another secured a moistened sheet of paper in a hinged frame, consisting of a *tympan* to hold the paper in back and a protective frame called a *frisket* in front to keep its margins clean.[8] The tympan was then lowered onto the type, and the whole bed slid under the press's platen, a large flat surface at the end of a wooden screw. A *puller* turned the long bar that lowered this platen onto the tympan (much as winemakers used the force of a screw to crush grapes), applying even pressure to the page and the type below (see figure 6). This made the type bite into the moistened surface of the paper, leaving behind an inked impression.

Once enough copies of the forms had been printed, the type was cleaned and the compositor distributed the sorts into the type case again. By the Renaissance, type cases had developed from an upright series of cubbyholes into a system of drawers divided into small compartments for each letter. These were arranged to provide more of the most common letters, like *e*, and fewer of those used less frequently, like *z*.[9] Our terms *uppercase* and *lowercase* come from this system, in which majuscules were kept in the upper drawer and minuscules below. Typographic history also gives us the term *stereotype*. Because typesetters had a limited supply of sorts and had to distribute them for

Figure 6   An etching of an eighteenth-century print shop: a compositor at left sets type from a manuscript page while a beater inks the forms and a pressman removes a quarto from the tympan. Daniel Chodowiecki, "Die Arbeit in der Buchdruckerei," in *J. B. Basedows Elementarwerk* (Liepzig: Ernst Wiegand, 1909). *Source:* Wikimedia Commons, scanned by A. Wagner.

reuse after a page was finished, reprinting texts was a laborious prospect. In the eighteenth century, printers developed a technique for keeping and reusing typeset pages by creating papier-mâché impressions of the finished formes. They used these molds to cast whole pages of type at a single go, enabling them to more easily reprint books whose popularity called for it. The problem with a stereotype, of course, is that it is fixed. Any errors in spelling, spacing, punctuation, or language remain in place, making it difficult to revise both our text and our biases.

It is likely that 180 copies of Gutenberg's Latin Bible were produced, 135 of them on paper and the rest on vellum.[10] Intended primarily for sale to churches and monasteries, each two-volume set included both the Old and New Testament and was printed in two columns with wide margins to allow later illumination. Each volume weighed about fourteen pounds and measured around 17 × 24.5 in. when opened, making these most appropriate for altar use, where the illuminations and rubrication would have helped readers find the requisite texts within them.[11] Of the copies produced, around fifty are currently held in library and museum collections—almost half of them incomplete. And while Gutenberg's Bible is tethered to the advent of the printing press, it was not, in fact, the first text he printed with movable type. Evidence suggests that Gutenberg printed Latin schoolbooks and papal indulgences (receipts forgiving a Catholic person's sins, acquired through prayer or charitable donation) before completing his Bible as a means of supporting his press and currying favor with the Church.[12]

Much as we laud Gutenberg, he was not, in fact, the first person to print with movable type. We can trace it as early as 1041 to the Chinese engineer Bí Sheng who developed a technique for printing from clay type he carved by hand. Chinese printers developed clay, tin, copper, and wood type from the eleventh to the thirteenth century, and the technology spread to Korea, where printers cast copper type to produce *Jikji*, a two-volume anthology of Zen Buddhist teachings, in 1377. Even after the advent of movable type, most printing in China was done from woodblock carvings through the nineteenth century, partly because of its cost-effectiveness and partly because of the fine quality of Chinese paper, which did not require pressure to transfer ink.[13] Not only was he not type's inventor, Gutenberg may not have been the first European to print with movable type, but without an explicit firsthand account he stands at the forefront of printers in Holland, Avignon, and likely elsewhere who were experimenting with type around the same time.[14]

The printing press vastly accelerated the speed of book production by allowing hundreds of identical copies of a single text to be printed. Thanks to its immediately recognized value as a tool of both commerce and communication, the printing press quickly spread throughout

Germany and into Europe, ushering in the first era of printing. Book historians refer to books printed in Europe before 1501 as *incunabula* (or incunables), a term from the Latin that refers to the infancy of the printed codex—its "cradle" period. During this time, printers largely emulated the look of illuminated manuscripts, falling back on the aesthetic with which their audience was already familiar. As they developed the codex for a nonliturgical, literate reader (and customer), punctuation and spacing were gradually standardized, subject indexes were added at the back of books, and "registers" at the front of the book, listing the first word of each section, helped the binder assemble the printed quires in order, providing a precursor to our table of contents.

The Body of the Book

Incunabula inaugurate the form of the book with which we are most familiar: the printed codex. But that object was not at all uniform in the way today's mass-produced volumes are. Scholars of early modern books make a distinction between a "book" and a "book copy," since each codex produced from a given print run will be unique in its circulation, history, and materiality.[15]

For instance, when we look at a volume printed before the nineteenth century, the cover is certainly part

Because what we call a book is a nexus of various histories and fields, it is impractical to insist on a strict hierarchy of such levels, for example, from material to abstract. How we finally organize the elements we see or define in a book will depend always on what questions we wish to ask of that book.

—JOSEPH DANE,
WHAT IS A BOOK?: THE STUDY OF EARLY PRINTED BOOKS

of the codex, but it is not, in fact, part of the book, since early modern book copies were bound to order. Those few books sold already bound at the time were still handmade, and therefore not completely identical to one another either. In addition to minute differences in the binding, each book copy will contain *marginalia* and other residues of reading that adhere to them thanks to their individual history of ownership and circulation. These are part of the copy without being part of "the book." The printing press thus changed the book by both facilitating its proliferation and separating the *idea* of the book from the *object*.

In our own era of proliferating book copies, we have become so accustomed to the codex that we often fail to see it unless it fails us: an unwieldy textbook, a misprinted cover, a missing page. Philosopher and theorist Walter Benjamin's seminal essay "The Work of Art in the Age of Its Mechanical Reproducibility" (1935) suggests that the photography, miniaturization, and distribution of images in the late nineteenth century destroyed the "aura" of art by abstracting it from the hand of the person who created it.[16] Similarly, we no longer sense the hand of the scribe or craftsman when we pick up a mass market paperback, though old books continue to possess an aura for nostalgic readers who hold such volumes like the calfskin-gloved fingertips of a distant ancestor. The codex, like us, has a body, and to know it, we must understand its anatomy.

The language we use for the codex suggests its corpus (see figure 7). The *book block*, those paper pages we read, consists of *signatures*, not unlike Roman parchment notebooks and medieval quires. Stacked and bound in covers, the codex becomes a rectangular volume with a *spine* running down its back, a *foot* or *tail* on which it stands on the shelf, and a *head* where we might insert a ribbon, not to tie up its hair, but to keep our place. A decorative *headband* also reinforces the binding of the book block, allowing it to curve away from the rigid spine when opened. The hardbound codex puts the book block to bed in *covers*, to which the binder attaches it with *endsheets*, often decorative, that adhere to the board on one side and the spine-edge of the book's first or last page on the other. Because of the tension of its *joint* or hinge, this *flyleaf* pulls the pages open ever so slightly, revealing the title page and inviting one into the book.

The endsheets provide an excellent spot to write one's name or paste in a *bookplate*, an identifying label that arose in fifteenth-century libraries and became widespread among bibliophiles in the seventeenth century.[17] Those early modern readers not disposed to altering their books' interiors could identify them during the binding process, both by having all their volumes bound in the same materials and by having a decorative crest or coat of arms stamped into the book's cover or spine. These modes of claiming a book point to a moment when ownership

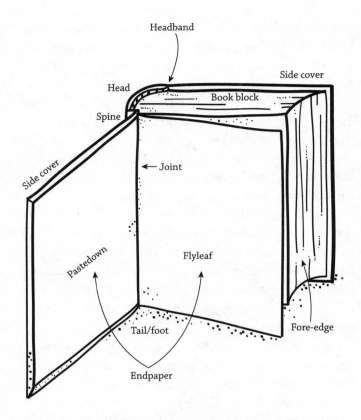

Figure 7 The body of the book. Illustration by Mike Force for Lightboard.

determined aesthetics, before books became uniform, mass-produced commodities whose bodies bear the marks of manufacturing standards, marketing, and bookselling.

Opening the Book

The title page, the entry point into the book we've come to expect each time we open one, developed during the codex's incunable phase, around 1480.[18] The term itself comes from the Latin *titulus*, or label, referring to a tag attached to a scroll to identify its contents, which would have been hard to determine otherwise. Scrolls were stored either in cubbyholes with these tags hanging down, or in upright baskets with these tags at the top for ready access.[19] Illuminated manuscripts did not need a title page either. They began with a rubricated *incipit*, followed by the work at hand, which then flowed onward, providing more than enough information for the work's potential reader: a monk or a wealthy patron who had commissioned it in advance and who likely owned a very small number of books.[20] Any information on the place or manner of the book's production, which we now find at the bottom of the title page, appeared at the end of the manuscript, in its *colophon*.

Early printers continued the manuscript tradition, opening their books with an *incipit*, either hand-rubricated or printed, that gave a work's title and author, relegating publication details to the back of the text.[21] The first incunable to foreground those details was a 1476 printing of astronomer Regiomontanus's *Kalendarium*, which lays out the lunar phases and solar movements for each day along with a calendar of religious festivals. Printed in red and black ink, the volume's title page includes a promotional blurb in verse, the date 1476 in Arabic numerals, and an ornamental woodcut frame of flowers, urns, and flourishes that includes the names of its three printers: Ratdolt, Löslein, and Pictor.[22] This frame evokes the illuminated manuscript through mechanical reproduction, a technique many subsequent printers would follow, creating ever more elaborate entryways to the book over the course of the sixteenth century to entice readers to buy them.[23] Some, designed to look like a portico or a building's facade, symbolized the vast intellectual space within.[24] The term we associate with these opening pages, *frontispiece*, actually originates in sixteenth-century architecture, where it refers historically to a building's face.[25] By the seventeenth century, printers had fully embraced the opportunity for both entry and advertisement, moving colophons to the frontispiece and even printing extra copies of this page to distribute as handbills and drum up sales.[26]

These ornate title pages were not, as we might expect, the first page of the books in which they appeared. That page was generally left blank to protect the contents prior to binding.[27] In the 1600s, as codices were produced in larger quantities, printers began to include an abbreviated title on this blank sheet, inaugurating the "half title" with which we are familiar. This device arose to facilitate distribution: bookshops kept unbound books stacked in bins, so the printed title helped buyers identify the text they wanted while also preventing damage to its interior. In some cases, a volume's owner would cut out this label and glue it inside the cover after binding, folding it over the fore-edge to help identify it on the shelf.[28] Books were, at the time, shelved with spines facing inward, and a book's fore-edge might be embellished with designs, gold leaf, or intricate paintings to help a reader identify it.[29] It wasn't until the mid-sixteenth century, as readers became collectors whose ever-expanding libraries served as displays of both intellect and wealth, that books were shelved with their spines outward to showcase their bindings, leading to the addition of authors' names and titles to facilitate access—a feature of the codex we now take for granted.

The Intimate Book

While contemporary books seem to come in all sorts of proportions, our associations with size reflect its role in the codex's early days: a large book, whether in dimensions or heft, suggests value. We presume such a volume is costly to produce and therefore special. If your home, like mine, contains books in a wide range of sizes, then you have likely experienced firsthand some of the affordances of those dimensions. Exceedingly large codex manuscripts and incunables like the antiphonal and missal were designed to be stable and hefty and to stand open on a podium for prayer. Such large books are nearly always taller than they are wide to reduce stress on the binding and make them easier to handle.[30] Our own large-size books are given the moniker "coffee-table book" because they are best suited to leaving around on unused surfaces for others to admire, on those rare occasions we even open them after our initial purchase. Such books wear their aura outwardly, much as oversize manuscript books with gem-inlaid bindings and gilt-edged pages did. Owned by monasteries or a select and wealthy few, they were objects inspiring devotion in both form and content.

Some incunables were quite large, but the period also saw the development of "quarto," "octavo," and even smaller-size books, enabled by refinements in typecasting. These smaller books were far more portable than their precursors and allowed a more intimate relationship to the book than the large showpiece on the altar. Books of hours, for instance, were designed to be portable both so that one might immerse oneself in prayer at any time of day and so that one might show off one's literacy and wealth by drawing the little volume from one's sleeve or pocket.[31]

We might generalize the historic moment at which the printed text arises as one of increasing intimacy between individuals and texts, which accounts, in part, for the form of the book as we know it today. Although Latin was the language of the church and education across Europe, fifteenth-century printers began to issue vernacular books to serve a wider audience, a move spurred on by the Protestant Reformation, which advocated for a more direct relationship between the individual and God.[32] Martin Luther's best-selling Wittenberg Bible (1522), for example, provided a German translation intended for a broad audience of lay readers. Although it was too expensive for most Lutherans, it was acquired by churches, schools, and priests, and thereby played a vital role in the dissemination of the text across a number of regional German dialects. With Henry VIII's dissolution of the monasteries, and the consolidation of power in the monarchy, there was even more support for the spread of vernacular books, leading to the 1611 production of the authorized King James Bible in English.

Incunables reflect the market of their time. Among these early printed books, more than half are religious: missals for church use, books of hours for private use, and lives of the saints and religious guides for parish priests. Not only did incunabula facilitate a religious Reformation, they aided in the spread of humanism and scientific knowledge. The period saw a rise in interest in ancient

Greek and Roman philosophy, as well as in medicine, in part due to the plagues that were decimating Europe.[33] Aristotle's fear of texts circulating without their authors proved one of print's chief assets. The publication of scientific treatises allowed scholars to engage in dialogue and debate with thinkers far removed, directly facilitating the spread of ideas that would flourish with the Renaissance.

The early years of the printed codex thus mark both an important technological shift (the mechanical reproduction of text) and a philosophical one in terms of how we relate to books. At this point they became the intimate spaces we now expect them to be, whether guiding one through the stations of daily devotion or conveying ancient thought on the structure of tragedy. While we currently enjoy many different kinds of reading experiences, in Western culture "the book" is almost universally seen through this intimate lens. Codices can be owned and shelved in a private library as a sign of one's intellect. They can be wrapped in covers to protect (or hide) them. They can be handed from one person to the next as a love token or symbol of great kinship: *Here, I loved this, and I think you'll love this too.* Whether the volume in question is a travel guide or a romance novel, the perception that books are little worlds enclosed in covers remains the same. We think of ourselves as disappearing into them, only to emerge hours later, changed by what we have read.

A book is a machine to think with.

—I. A. RICHARDS,
PRINCIPLES OF LITERARY CRITICISM

Pundits frequently draw on this romance of disembodiment as a contrast to the passivity of watching television, characterized as a kind of vegetative state. Even in this vanguard moment of complex televised dramas, the stigma remains: *We would be better people if we disappeared into books instead.*

By the seventeenth century, the structure of the book had developed to facilitate this sense of intimacy and cultural value. As the codex became a commodity, printers developed appurtenances to help frame it as one. To differentiate themselves from one another, they developed "printer's devices," emblems incorporating their initials and an icon, which they included on the frontispiece—metonyms that prefigure today's familiar logos, such as the penguin in an orange oval that most contemporary readers will recognize. Long titles helped advertise the book as well by giving readers a taste of what was to come,[34] much as jacket copy and subject area designations today give us a sense of a book's relevance to our field of interest.

The navigational aids we now associate with books—tables of contents, page numbers, running heads, and indexes—arose during this period through a shift from devices that helped printers and binders in manufacturing a book, to devices that helped readers navigate that same text. Scholar Peter Stallybrass has argued such features define the history of the codex, suggesting that "the invention of printing [was] the culmination of the invention of the navigable book—the book that allowed you to get your finger into the place you wanted to find in the least possible time."[35] Most incunabula, for instance, did not include page numbers—readers were expected to number them by hand. Because books were bound by specialists outside the print shop, they had to be clearly marked to prevent the pages from getting out of order in transit. To ensure the binder correctly *collated* the work's sections, printers included folio numbers, signature marks, and *catchwords* (marginal words printed at the end of one page and the start of the next, inherited from the manuscript tradition) to keep the text in order. The efficiency of page numbering in facilitating book use became clear to early modern printers, and, along with running heads, was incorporated by the seventeenth century.

Tables of contents and indexes, an outgrowth of the "registers" of first words that helped binders collate a book's sections, were introduced not only to help readers navigate a text, but also to assure them of its comprehensiveness (despite the erratic and highly interpretive nature of such catalogs).[36] Another type of index, known as a *manicule*, fist, or pointer, was adopted by printers within the body of the book. Originating in medieval manuscripts as early as the twelfth century, these emblems in the margin and body of the text literally "put one's finger into the book" in the form of a closed fist with an extended pointer that draws attention to a specific passage. Such elaborate illustrated hands were used by Renaissance humanist scholars to annotate their books, both as navigational aids and mementos that leave their personal stamp on the text (a hand, scholar William Sherman points out, is a far more individual marker than an underline or arrow).[37] Even after the advent of the printing press, readers used such marginalia to engage more deeply with their books and turn them into private spaces for dialogue with the author.

Authors and publishers actively courted this kind of dialectical relationship. Prefaces as we know them developed to invite readers into the book and instruct them in its goals, setting up a conversation between author and reader. Such intimacy was most explicit in the "treatises" that proliferated during the sixteenth century, providing step-by-step guides to tasks great and small, from how to design buildings to how to mix paints.[38] Illustrations, foldouts, volvelles, and other movable book features invited the reader to engage in a tactile way with the book, treating the page as a space for exploration.

These reader-focused elements were just as important to marketing as to book use. They mark the codex as commodity—an important shift in our thinking about how texts circulate. The value placed on reading during the Renaissance was not simply in absorbing a text, but in actively engaging, consuming, and reframing it. Readers of the period made books their own through the practice of keeping a *commonplace book* in which they copied selections of texts and organized them thematically for easy reference.[39] This practice is emblematic of the highly individual and personal relationship between reader and text prized at the time. Open margins left space for active annotation—a visible and tactile engagement of mind with page. Students could also use such spaces to take down lecture notes, creating a multilayered dialogue with their professor and textbook. Of course, these usages were facilitated by the book design of the day, but they also helped structure the book, which developed in response to the needs and values of readers.

We should remember that the ability to mark up a text to this degree is an effect of codex form—such detailed annotation would have required a paperweight or partner to hold a scroll open on one's behalf, or to take notes on a separate tablet. Likewise, navigating a scroll required an intimate sense of volume if one wanted to return to a familiar passage—one reason ancient readers practiced and memorized their texts.[40] Our conception of the book and access are intimately shaped by the shape it takes. However, lest we imagine that the printing press swiftly ushered in the end of manuscript production, it bears noting that manuscripts continued to enjoy wide use during the Renaissance, for four hundred years after Gutenberg. As book historian Roger Chartier points out, manuscripts had several key benefits—they escaped censorship, were

Books are simultaneously sequential and random access ...; books are volumetric objects ...; books are finite ...; books offer a fundamentally comparative visual space; the two-page opening of a standard codex ...; and last, books are writable as well as readable.

—MATTHEW KIRSCHENBAUM, "BOOKSCAPES: MODELING BOOKS IN ELECTRONIC SPACE" cheaper to produce, and permitted emendation, for example—all of which kept them in circulation.[41]

Type and Face

It is worth a short note on the changing nature of type at this historic juncture in the book's development. Early printers' types were modeled on the manuscript tradition and thus used heavy, formal scripts. Gutenberg's type was modeled on Textura, a German calligraphic style standard among fifteenth-century scribes. Its narrow letterforms and angular pointy ends, or finials, are characteristic of such blackletter scripts. We often think of such heavy lettering as *Gothic*, a legacy that continues in contemporary digital type.

While it has been conventionalized by now, the term "Gothic" is emblematic of the divisive role lettering can play in demarcating national identity. The name was actually imposed on German lettering by Renaissance humanist scholars, who considered the thorny blackletter hand barbarous. For their Latin manuscripts, they revived eighth-century lowercase letterforms associated with Charlemagne's Holy Roman Empire, which they believed had come from classical Rome. Because they were easier to decipher, Renaissance scholars also felt they made texts more accessible, bringing them closer to the forbears they

Figure 8 A sample of Gutenberg's 42-line Bible (1454), set in a Gothic Textura face he designed (at left), and of the Aldine Press's *Hypnerotomachia Poliphili* (1499), set in a roman type designed by Francesco Griffo (at right). "Leaf of the Gutenberg Bible" image courtesy *Digital Commonwealth*, Boston Public Library. Page from *Hypnerotomachia Poliphili* courtesy Henry Walters, The Walters Art Museum.

wished to study. The first Italian printers based their types on this humanist hand, producing "roman" letterforms named for their purported connection to ancient Rome (see figure 8).[42]

As an aside, the Germans developed their own vexed relationship with blackletter type, which was standard in German publishing since the advent of print. In 1933, the National Socialist Party declared Fraktur its official typeface as a sign of German pride. However, the Nazis did an about-face in 1941, claiming Fraktur had been foisted upon them by Jewish printers with the advent of the press, and banning it in favor of the humanist Antiqua letterforms that had arisen precisely to differentiate Gothic and Roman text.[43] This tangled history of type tells us much about the legacy of othering embedded in language's form.

We tend not to refer to the fonts we currently use as *roman type* unless we are contrasting them with *italic type*, the right-slanting face used for emphasis in contemporary typesetting. The styles' names suggest their geography: while roman was drawn from both the Ancient Roman and Holy Roman Empires, italic was developed in Venice in 1500 by engraver Francesco Griffo for printer Aldus Manutius (ca. 1450–1515), who wanted to differentiate his publications from those of his fellow printers. Based on the cursive handwriting of humanist scholars, these letterforms appealed to Aldus as a compact and eye-catching script that would link his books to the intellectual currents of his age.[44] Both roman and italic type are considered "humanist" faces because they emulate writing with a broadnibbed pen, which produces strokes of varying thickness. While such faces continue to be used in both print and digital contexts, we have lost the association with the hand that made them that was so appealing to the Italian scholars.

The Aldine Revolution and Portable Libraries

Aldus himself reflects the Renaissance humanist spirit. Born Teobaldo Manuzio, he adopted a Latinized name because of his love and scholarship of Greco-Roman literature and language. As the personal tutor to a wealthy Italian family, over the years he amassed a network of well-connected patrons who helped finance his Aldine Press in Venice around 1490.[45] Initially publishing textbooks and dictionaries to facilitate the study of classical languages, Aldus built ties to a number of Greek scholars who had fled to the city after the 1453 Turkish invasion of Constantinople, as well as to humanist scholars in Venice and Padua who, like him, were dedicated to the dissemination of Greco-Roman art and thought. So close-knit was this scholarly community that Aldus began including the phrase "in Aldi Neacademia" in his colophons in 1502, turning this society of scholars into an "Aldine New Academy."[46] While they may never have actually founded a physical institution, Aldus and his cohort disseminated their love of Greek and Roman thought through a more intimate, one-to-one method: publication.

Aldus initiated the use of his italic type with a series of octavo editions of the Latin classics and Italian vernacular poetry in 1501 that would change printing and reading forever. These compact volumes, published with prefaces but no notes or commentary, were intended for an intelligent lay reader but were most popular and beloved among scholars, politicians, and courtiers. Machiavelli famously wrote in a 1513 letter to a friend that he took such books with him on hikes through the woods to read of Dante and Petrarch's romances as he savored the scenery or checked his bird traps.[47] Their portable size was made possible, in part, by Griffo's compact type, which was narrow and condensed enough to allow for the reduced page size and count that kept the book affordable. There is some debate as to whether the typeface truly saved any material cost, but it was certainly popular, as evinced by Aldus's attempts to patent it.[48] Though he was granted a privilege protecting his sole right to use the typeface, he could not stop printers in Italy and beyond from copying—and improving—his letterforms.

Aldus's printing is emblematic of an important moment in book history—one in which the aesthetics of the page began to be considered both in terms of artistry and legibility. Competition among printers and stationers, as well as humanist inquiry, led to a careful consideration of the interior of the book as an expressive space. Aldus's first vernacular book, Francesco Colonna's *Hypnerotomachia Poliphili* (1499), the story of Poliphilo's dreamlike erotic quest to find his love Polia, has been praised for the craft of its pages, which include text in Latin, Italian, Hebrew, and Arabic, feature beautiful woodcut illustrations, and use shaped paragraphs to integrate word and image (see figure 8).[49] Renaissance printers sought to differentiate their publications from medieval manuscripts, and in doing so, they merged classical elements with contemporary ones. They removed glosses and critical commentary that cluttered the page to allow scholars unfettered access to the text. Certainly, folio and quarto printings with such additions continued to be produced for a scholarly audience interested in the book as a space of deep conversation among generations of authors. But it was the Aldine octavo that sought a broader audience for classical texts— one with no need for such extras.

While these reprints didn't find the wide readership Aldus expected, due in part to expense and in part to competition from other printers, his practice of reprinting "edifying" and "important" works prefigures the proliferation of "classic" reprints in the nineteenth century. Increased literacy during the period led to greater demand for books, especially since most people didn't have access to formal education. In the words of Victorian scholar Richard Altick, books were considered "fireside universities" and promoted in the press as a means of both cultural and intellectual enrichment.[50] No longer solely the purview of the aristocracy, excerpts from great works were included in the cheap weeklies and newspapers for broad enjoyment, and publishers saw the value in making classics available to this hungry audience at a price they could afford.

But demand alone could not have facilitated the spread of Sir Walter Scott's Ballantyne's Novelists Library (one of many higher-priced series), Constable's Miscellany, or the more than ninety cheap reprint series published between 1830 and 1906 that Altick has cataloged.[51] By the 1880s, publishers were in an all-out price war to drop their reprints to as low as one shilling a volume or less. Printing itself had become cheaper by that point thanks to industrialization: the steam-driven press (invented in 1814), steam-powered papermaking machines that produced continuous rolls (patented in 1807), the development of stereotyping and mechanical typecasting and setting (discussed in this chapter), and machine-made *case bindings* allowed publishers to produce books rapidly, in greater quantities, and at reduced prices.

Intellectual Property

The spread of the book in the nineteenth century was also affected by changing notions of copyright, which influenced both the availability of works for reprinting and the number of new authors making original work. Copyright did not exist during the manuscript era, but ideas about ownership had developed with the rise of print as publishers sought to protect themselves against competition. In the sixteenth century, the exclusive right to a work was tied to the book object and belonged to the printer once he had purchased it from its author or compiler.[52] Possession of the book gave one the right to copy it but didn't prevent others from producing their own pirated versions. Across Europe, a printer might petition the crown or church for a book privilege to protect their right to a certain work. Such privileges, when granted by emperors, dukes, and popes, gave them a certain amount of control over the press, which meant that those agreeable to the government were favored, and newer presses had trouble finding a foothold.[53] In the United Kingdom, publication was carefully controlled by the Stationers' Company in London, a select group of printers that granted and registered licenses for approved books. They gave the rights to the most popular (and lucrative) of these, including the Bible and schoolbooks, to a select few, extending the monopolistic control of printers over British publishing.[54]

With the surge of competition among publishers in England during the eighteenth century, concerns over intellectual property mounted. Debates around copyright mark an important shift in thinking about "the book," transferring rights from the object itself to the text it contained at a moment when it could be not only printed but also translated and adapted for another medium—all of which needed protections.[55] The world's first copyright act, the Statute of Anne (1709), finally gave ownership of a work to its author, enforcing the primacy of content over form, for a term of fourteen years, with the possibility of a fourteen-year extension if the author outlived the first term. Books already in print were granted a twenty-one-year term. This shift improved both the status and solvency of authors, who could earn a living from their work by arranging a profit-sharing agreement with their publisher, selling their copyright outright, or leasing it for a predetermined period.[56] Their copyrights, however, were not enforceable abroad, so international piracy still presented a significant problem, particularly between Britain and the United States. International respect for copyright was established by the 1886 Berne International Copyright Convention and the American International Copyright Treaty of 1891, defining important protections for reprints and works in translation.[57] As authors began to receive a living wage for their work, writing became a profession, and a burgeoning class of novelists and poets provided publishers with still more material to print.

Copyright itself may have had the greatest impact on the resurgence of classic reprints in the nineteenth century. While the Statute of Anne had restricted copyright to a maximum of twenty-eight years, British booksellers fought to maintain perpetual copyright during a sixty-year period known as the "battle of the booksellers." The landmark case *Donaldson v. Beckett* (1774) struck down perpetual copyright and confirmed the copyright term established by the Statute, bringing a wealth of material into the public domain and setting a precedent that would be adopted and adapted around the world in the ensuing decades. The United States would pass its own Copyright Act, An Act for the Encouragement of Learning, in 1790, revising it periodically over the next two centuries.[58] As its name suggests, it aimed to protect the rights of authors while also ensuring works would enter the public domain within a reasonable time frame.

Copyright continues to evolve in response to changes in publishing, legal battles with the estates of artists and authors, and debate over mass digitization projects, which will be discussed in chapter 4. A quick aside, though, on the current status of copyright illuminates the extent to which it privileges a work's idea—what I have been referring to as content. In the United States, publication is not actually required to secure copyright, which applies to original works "that are fixed in a tangible form of expression."[59] An author holds the copyright to their works throughout their lifetime and seventy years beyond their death, at which point it enters the public domain. If a work has been made "for hire," then copyright belongs to the employer or corporation that commissioned it and extends ninety-five years from publication or one hundred twenty years from creation (for unpublished works). Long periods of protection indeed.

The legal shift to conceiving of the book as content, rather than object, is virtually inseparable from its commodification. While new books were expensive during the eighteenth and nineteenth centuries partly because of the cost of copyright, reprints made public domain works affordable to a less affluent readership. Some publishers relied on subscriptions, testing the market for a given work or series by sending out a descriptive prospectus and soliciting advance purchases before deciding to go to press—a bit like today's crowdfunding efforts. While this process raised the necessary capital up front, it also had pitfalls. If subscriptions waned or a publisher encountered costly problems during printing, it would have to abandon the initiative or fold altogether, leaving customers with a partial series they could never complete.[60] The market for new books had a direct impact on their physical form. As readers turned more and more to private circulating libraries and public lending libraries, publishers saw an opportunity: publishing longer books that could be bound in sections, allowing them to sell several volumes instead of one. The "triple-decker" novels of the period were too expensive for all but the wealthiest readers, and thus ensured a robust membership (and income) for lending libraries, who profited from the ability to loan the book's separately bound sections to three readers at once.[61] Publishers seeking to maximize profits experimented with publishing the same work in several forms: first serialized in journals or as pamphlets; then bound for libraries as a triple-decker; and, finally, as a cheap reprint for a mass audience.

The Crystal Goblet

The reprint publishing initiatives of the nineteenth century owe a debt to Aldus's vision—one acknowledged by bookseller William Pickering and publisher Charles Wittingham, who printed the popular *Aldine Edition of the British Poets* in 1830, trading on the Aldine brand. While the myriad reissued classics of the period shared the Aldine impulse, they lacked his dedication to beautiful design and production. Placing their emphasis on content over form, they cut every corner to reduce costs: they used cheap thin paper, filled the page with tiny type, and in some cases included advertisements within the text.[62] To fit as much content into as small a space as possible, such volumes were printed in sizes from the Aldine octavo to the wallet-like 32mo, a tiny format that saved publishers money and buyers valuable space in their already cramped living quarters.

Given this lack of attention to the book object on the part of most reprint publishers, many consider the 1906 Everyman's Library Aldus's true inheritor: it made quality design once again central. As editor Ernest Rhys put it, he and publisher J. M. Dent intended "to produce a book which would be pleasant to see and handle, with a cheerful outside, and print easy to read and good for the eyes within, tempting to look at on the shelf, and of a size convenient for the pocket, one that could be taken for a

country ramble or for a railway journey or on shipboard"—
a goal Machiavelli would have approved.[63] They achieved
these ends with ornate Arts and Crafts–style endpapers
and frontispieces, cloth bindings in thirteen colors to indicate a volume's genre, and gilt-stamped spines, all protected by a paper dust jacket advertising the series and the
volume's low one-shilling price (about the cost of a dozen
eggs at the time). The popular series continued until 1982,
evolving to include bindings in a range of materials to
suit readers' budgets, and paperback editions began appearing in 1960 in deference to public taste and aesthetic
shifts.

The twentieth century saw a number of publication
series that, like Aldus's, sought to help a lay public amass
personal libraries of affordable editions. Unlike those
early printing endeavors, these were truly accessible to a
mass market—printed on cheap paper and perfect bound
with glue in paperback covers, they were designed with the
urban commuter in mind. They were sold at newsstands,
lunch counters, and anywhere a wire rack could be set up
to catch a reader's eye.[64] While many of these were works
of pulp fiction, British publisher Allen Lane (1902–1970)
had a different vision. He founded Penguin Books in 1935
to offer cheap, unabridged works by established authors
designed for educated readers on the go.[65] All books shared
the same cover design featuring the penguin logo and a
typographic treatment of title and author. Colored stripes

The format of the book is determined by its purpose. It relates to the average size and the hands of an adult.

—JAN TSCHICHOLD,
THE FORM OF THE BOOK: ESSAYS ON THE MORALITY OF GOOD DESIGN,
TRANS. HAJO HADELER

at the head and tail of the codex indicated its series: orange for modern fiction, green for crime, blue for biography, burgundy for travel, gray for current events, and yellow for miscellany. At sixpence (less than the cost of a pint of milk), they not only sold well but paved the way for a paperback revolution in Britain, the United States, and France.

The affordability and accessibility of the series certainly contributed to its popularity, but the quality of its design, implemented by German typographer Jan Tschichold (1902–1974), was pivotal to its long-term success. Trained as a calligrapher and self-taught as a type designer, Tschichold embraced modern design in 1923 after seeing the Weimar Bauhaus exhibition. He codified the rules of good design in a seminal manifesto, *Die Neue Typographie* (*The New Typography*, 1927), calling for sans-serif type, wide margins, and asymmetrical page design based on the proportions of the medieval manuscript: a ratio of text block to page known as The Golden Section (1:1.618).[66] Renaissance printers like Aldus had borrowed these proportions, which correspond to the Fibonacci series, from the scribal tradition, determining them most pleasing to the eye.

Tschichold eventually returned to using humanist typefaces and eased up on his earlier ideals. In 1947, Lane appointed him to redesign Penguin Paperbacks, and Tschichold established The Penguin Composition Rules to unify the series' asethetic.[67] This system combined effective branding principles with good design, ensuring the popularity of Penguin for years to come. Like Aldus before him, Tschichold believed good design was not a luxury but an integral part of the book. In his words, "We do not need pretentious books for the wealthy, we need more really well-made ordinary books."[68]

Prizing legibility and accessibility, Tschichold's ideals meant the page and typography had to be put in service of the text, used to deliver content as cleanly as possible from author to reader. This philosophy is reflected in another important typographic manifesto of the period—Beatrice Warde's "The Crystal Goblet, or Printing Should be Invisible" (1932). Aiming to discourage excessive ornamentation and ostentatious typography, her central metaphor of the page as a "flagon of wine" treats the text as an intoxicant, "capable of stirring and altering men's minds," and the page as its crystalline container.[69] This vision reflects the popular conception of the book in the twentieth century: "It conveys thought, ideas, images, from one mind to other minds," and the typographer, designer, printer, and publisher all work in the service of these ideas, trying to transmit them as transparently as possible.[70] With the perception that books are ideas bestowed on readers by an authorial genius whose activity is purely intellectual, the book's object status vanished for much of the reading public as we raised a glass to happily consume its contents.

If the book's handiness has been fundamental to the way we have taken stock of the world, its ability to serve as a *container* has been another way through which we have found order in our lives. Books are things that hold things.

—ANDREW PIPER,
BOOK WAS THERE: READING IN ELECTRONIC TIMES

The twentieth century did indeed see a preponderance of well-made ordinary books, as Tschichold and Warde hoped, alongside some less well made but equally popular ones. To reach a state in which the publishing world could support hardbound books, trade editions, and mass market paperbacks, the book required widespread literacy, an easily reproducible material form, and a means of distribution. All of these had developed by this point. No longer did a chapman travel from town to town selling broadsides and pamphlets to the poor while the affluent enjoyed sumptuous volumes—bookshops either stocked your book or could order the one you wanted. And no longer did the printer serve as both publisher and bookseller, a distinction solidified in the nineteenth century. Distributors arose to traffic between publishers and the libraries and bookstores, warehousing their stock and marketing it to retailers.

Brick-and-mortar bookstores experienced a boom in the 1980s, with major American players Borders and Barnes and Noble muscling out many smaller, independent shops by offering huge variety, best sellers, and cafés where buyers could enjoy a cappuccino while thumbing through their purchases. The infrastructure of such stores is built around the codex and in turn has shaped the book: from eye-catching cover designs, to clearly labeled spines with author and title, to the introduction of ISBN barcodes for managing stock, to genre labeling on the back of books telling the seller where to shelve them and the buyer how to perceive them (for instance, as nonfiction, poetry, science fiction, or fantasy). By Tschichold's time, books were for everyone and were available everywhere, even in grocery store checkout lines. Only fifty years later, the major American chains, including Waldenbooks, B. Dalton, and Crown Books, have all but disappeared, with Borders filing for bankruptcy in 2011. Barnes and Noble has reduced its physical presence and now does much of its business through its Nook e-reader and branded college bookstores. In their heyday, though, such shops played a key role in the commodification of the book and in our changing perception of it as content rather than object. Even though innumerable material elements come together to make the book, these features have been naturalized to such a degree that we now hardly notice them, since we have come to see content as the copyrightable, consumable, marketable aspect of the work.

THE BOOK AS IDEA

The thing we picture when someone says "book" is an *idea* as much as an *object*. As the history of the book's changing form and its mechanical reproduction reveal, it has transformed significantly over time and region. The clay tablet, papyrus scroll, and codex book each were shaped by the materials at hand and the needs of writers and readers. Those materials in turn shaped the content with which such books were filled. The mechanical reproduction of both texts and book objects in the industrial age and the start of the twentieth century helped solidify the codex as an efficient, portable, marketable object, available in hardbound or paperback covers, and distributed through networks of bookshops, libraries, and book fairs worldwide. While we now have Kindles, digital book apps, and a number of web services for accessing books in PDF form, the system remains relatively unchanged: the book is a commodity.

As contemporary publishers seek to embrace digital technology, we find ourselves at a moment in which the form and content of a work often bear little relation to one another. Amazon offers us the same "book" in paperback or Kindle edition, at slightly differing prices, with the digital edition often costing as much as the print now that publishers can control their own e-book prices. When books become content to be marketed and sold this way, the historic relationship between materiality and text is severed.

The twentieth century saw a turn to experimentation with books in response to the very mechanization and mass production that had turned them into an enterprise by the late Victorian period. This experimentation was done in part by printers, whose expertise and access to tools of the trade led them to make books for a kind of in crowd; in part by writers, taking the means of production into their own hands; and in part by artists, who saw the book as a means of circumventing the power system of the art world. The books they created, conceived as complete works of art in their own right, are given the name "artists' books," though the term is malleable, as we'll explore in this chapter. Such self-referential and self-aware objects have much to teach us about the changing nature of the book, in part because they highlight the "idea" by paradoxically drawing attention to the "object" we have come to take for granted. They disrupt our treatment of the book as a transparent container for literary and aesthetic "content" and engage its material form in the work's meaning.

Artist and theorist Johanna Drucker, one of the field's foremost scholars and practitioners, has called the artist's book the "twentieth-century art form par excellence"[1]—both because it threads its way through every artistic movement from Futurism onward, and because the principles with which it is bound up (collaboration, institutional critique, alternative economies, and the dematerialization of the work of art) reflect a suite of concerns that mark the period's artistic production. These works interrogate the codex, calling into question how books communicate and how we read, using every aspect of their structure, form, and content to make meaning. Engaging with the book as an idea brings its material form back into the conversation in ways that can be productive, exciting, perplexing, and at times problematic. When the aesthetic of bookness itself is fetishized to such a degree that it can be bought and sold (as cell phone cases, home safes, and printed sportswear, for example), we've come full circle to the commodification of the book object.

A book ... is not an inert thing that exists in advance of interaction, rather it is produced new by the activity of each reading. ... Thus in thinking of a book, whether literal or virtual, we should paraphrase Heinz von Foerster ... and ask "how" a book "does" its particular actions, rather than "what" a book "is."

—JOHANNA DRUCKER,
"THE VIRTUAL CODEX:
FROM PAGE SPACE TO E-SPACE"

Defining the Artist's Book

The term "artist's book" is a contentious one, and each theorist and maker feels the need to weigh in on its definition. I hew to Drucker's formulation of the artist's book as a "zone of activity"[2] by artists and writers who create books as original works of art that "integrate the formal means of [their] realization and production with [their] thematic or aesthetic issues."[3] By this definition, the artist's book is not a catalog, a book containing images of artworks, or a fine press production of a novel with illustrations by a celebrated artist, exquisitely tooled leather covers, and marbled endpapers. It *can* be one of those things, but only if those choices are interrogated and integrated into the way the work makes meaning. For instance, the book's producer may behave like an editor, archivist, or anthologist, collecting material and assembling it in book form, as artist Erik Kessels does in his series *In Almost Every Picture*, volumes of vernacular photographs arranged thematically—from photos of a family's black dog to images in which the anonymous photographer's finger has accidentally entered the frame.[4] As long as the impulse is to create an original work of art through the accumulation and juxtaposition of these materials, the work is within the zone.

The artist's book might have text, but it can be, like the works scholar Craig Dworkin adeptly discusses in his book *No Medium*, entirely blank.[5] It can also be purposefully illegible, its pages torn or carefully cut to make volumetric forms, as in Doug Beube's work. It can be a sculptural object, like Alisa Banks's altered book series *Edges* in which the artist treats the hardbound codex's fore-edge as hairline, gathering groups of pages with synthetic hair in *(Cornrow), (Lace Braid), (Thread Wrap),* and *(Twist)*—styles that celebrate the tradition of African braiding while commenting on the intolerance that shuts "others" out and pushes them to the margins.[6] It can be bound or unbound, like Yoko Ono's and Alison Knowles's event scores—typed on postcards—or Ray Johnson's *Book About Death* (1963–1965), whose thirteen loose pages the author mailed piecemeal to friends and offered for sale in the *Village Voice* classified section. It can be collaborative—like the books of the Russian Futurists, created with wallpaper and rubber stamps—a portable, ephemeral means of self-publishing. It can be editioned or unique, produced by hand or machine, as compact as a walnut or as large as a house. It can include sound art, video, tactile objects, and artifacts, like *Doc/Undoc: Ars Shamánica Perfomormática* (2014), a collaboration between Guillermo Gómez-Peña, Gustavo Vazquez, Zachary James Watkins, Jennifer A. González, and Felicia Rice that combines an altar and a cabinet of curiosities to provide readers with "a toolbox for self-transformation."[7] If the activating energy is to explore what a book can be or do, rather than to take advantage of a particular market, then it is in the zone.

When we trace the history of the artist's book, several flashpoints are often given, though the motivation to work with and against the codex arises simultaneously in a number of different twentieth-century art and literary movements. Still, for the purposes of essential knowledge, it is worth briefly noting these works and their makers. Rather than presenting these texts as the "lineage" of the artist's book, I mention them here as useful representatives of the energies motivating artwork in book form.

William Blake's "Illuminated Printing"

The works of Romantic poet and engraver William Blake (1757–1827) are often cited as precursor artists' books, since he undertook every stage of their production. Blake wrote, illustrated, printed, hand-colored, and sold his own books as a cost-saving measure, but also because he viewed each element as central to the work's expressive power. Bemoaning the "dark Satanic Mills" of eighteenth-century London that emitted toxic fumes, employed the poor and children in horrendous conditions, and made books into mass-produced commodities, he sought to return to an earlier idea of the book—one steeped in mystery, beauty, and visionary language that bears the marks of its creator's hand.[8] To do so, he invented a novel printing technique in 1788 that enabled him to print both text and illustration simultaneously.

Blake attributed his innovative approach to his beloved brother Robert, who, he claimed, appeared to him in a vision a year after his death to teach Blake "illuminated printing"—a method whose name references the illuminated manuscripts that intertwined calligraphic writing and visionary artwork in the codex book's early history. As he describes it in *The Marriage of Heaven and Hell*:

> This I shall do, by printing in the infernal method, by corrosives, which in Hell are salutary and medicinal, melting apparent surfaces away, and displaying the infinite which was hid.
>
> If the doors of perception were cleansed every thing would appear to man as it is: infinite.[9]

With this rich metaphor, Blake describes both his process and subject. Illuminated printing returned visionary power to the book and allowed him to fight back against the so-called Satanic Mills. He was not alone in this "infernal" endeavor; his wife Catherine worked alongside him until his death—proofing, printing, drawing, and coloring the works for which her husband is known.

An Aside on Printing Methods:
Intaglio and Relief Printing

Blake's innovation melded his experience as an engraver with the techniques of letterpress printing by "melting apparent surfaces away." In *intaglio* printing (his method of printing from engravings), the surface of a copper plate is treated with an acid-resistant coating or wax and the design scratched into this surface. When acid is applied, it etches the design into the plate, allowing for very fine line-work. A printer then removes the coating, applies ink to the plate, and wipes the excess away, leaving the etched lines filled. The printer then places dampened paper onto the inked plate, along with thick felt pads, and rolls the ensemble through a press that applies high pressure, forcing the ink up into the paper's fibers. The extreme force both transfers the image and leaves behind a slight indentation the size and shape of the plate.

In relief printing, such as letterpress, the image and text are raised rather than recessed, which requires less force to transfer to the paper and means the edges of the plate do not bite into it, as they do in etching. This allows for the clean, two-sided printing we associate with the codex; it can create a continuous reading experience across every turning. Blake's innovation was to treat his copper plates as relief surfaces, painting his designs and texts directly onto them using an acid-resistant varnish. Acid then "melt[ed] away" the exposed surface, and his designs and text were left behind.[10] For this technique to work, Blake must have been highly skilled at writing backward, since, as in printing from movable type, the art transferred to the page was a mirror image of the art on the plate.

This innovation had numerous benefits, both financial and artistic. It allowed Blake to use both sides of his engraving plates—since they were etched shallowly—and to print on both sides of the leaf, saving money on both copper and fine engraving paper. It also spared the expense of having texts letterpress-printed at another shop. Uniting manuscript tradition and mechanical reproduction, Blake's technique allowed for a more calligraphic writing style and a harmony between reading and looking, rather than relegating text and image to separate pages. By extension, it brought the hand back into the book, so his manual effort and artistry showed on every page. The Blakes worked together, hand-tinting each leaf with washes of color to create depth and complexity. Later, Blake applied colored inks directly to the plate, allowing variation each time it was printed.[11] Perhaps most importantly, illuminated printing allowed Blake to conceive of text and image simultaneously—creating what scholar W. J. T. Mitchell has called an "image-text," a design to be both read and looked at—and to work expressively with their merger.[12] Because he drew his designs directly on the plate, invention and fabrication became inseparable.

Blake's first two books created with this technique, *All Religions Are One* (1788) and *There Is No Natural Religion* (1788) used aphorisms to refute eighteenth-century rationalism, which sought a scientific basis for God through evidence in the natural world. These books are emblematic of Blake's relationship to print—he believed in the power of poetic genius, and in printing as a visionary art form with the capacity for social change. Blake was connected to many radical thinkers of his time, and the work he is best known for, *Songs of Innocence and of Experience* (1794), reflects his own critiques of eighteenth-century London through sweetly rhymed poems in his expressive handwriting surrounded by illustrations of the loss of innocence and destruction of the natural world. Much like an illuminated manuscript, Blake's illustrations fill the margins and negative space of each page, merging text and design, as when, for instance, the title grows out of a tree's gnarled trunk on the book's frontispiece (see figure 9). Incidentally, on that page, Blake refers to himself as "The Author & Printer W. Blake," making clear the union of creativity and craft in his work. Blake's engagement with the social issues of his day, and his use of book form to respond to child labor, urban squalor, and slavery, established an

Figure 9 The title page from William Blake's *Songs of Innocence and of Experience* (Yale Center for British Art, Bentley Copy L) demonstrating illuminated printing. Public domain image courtesy the Yale Center for British Art, Paul Mellon Collection.

Through my mis-education I have arrived at the conclusion that the book is a political tool.

—AMOS PAUL KENNEDY JR., "SOCIAL BOOK BUILDING"

important trend in both artists' books and independent publishing—the utility of the book as a means of spreading social justice.

Some might quibble with the notion of the Blakes as book artists, since they didn't actually bind their works but sold to collectors the unbound leaves enclosed in paper folios.[13] As a result, extant copies of some books can differ in their ordering of the prints, suggesting the arc of the collected poems was not integral to Blake's vision. He was, however, acting in accord with his time and the expectations of his buyers, who would have had their books bound to order. The eighteenth-century codex was a personal artifact, and a collection was made uniform with this finishing step so that the library reflected its reader rather than the whims of the publisher. Whether the page order was changed by the Blakes or the binders, these works were printed and conceived as "Illuminated Books" according to Blake's own 1793 prospectus advertising them for sale, and Blake produced an order list for the *Songs of Innocence and of Experience* for at least one buyer to facilitate the book's binding.[14] It would have been a huge leap for Blake to bind them himself, requiring great expense and making it significantly harder to find collectors.

One of the chief reasons Blake might be considered a progenitor of the artist's book, however, is his rationale for making books in the first place. The production and sale of the books did not make him wealthy (Blake worked as an engraver to support his family throughout his life), but it did disseminate his work more broadly than exhibition could. As he confided to one buyer: "The Few I have Printed and Sold are sufficient to have gained me great reputation as an Artist which was the chief thing Intended."[15] They were limited-edition books, labor-intensive to produce, through which he realized his vision for the best presentation of his subversive, visionary ideas.

Stéphane Mallarmé's Book as "Spiritual Instrument"

While Blake's artistry and control of each aspect of his books gives us a deep history of creators blurring the line between writer and bookmaker, some point to French poet Stéphane Mallarmé (1842–1898) the twentieth century's first true book artist for his thorough break from Victorian typographic tradition. In his 1897 book-length poem *Un coup de Dés jamais n'abolira le Hasard* (*A Throw of the Dice Will Never Abolish Chance*), the page is not a vessel, but an ocean; and the text, tossed on its waves, is a shipwreck in language that draws the reader's eye across its shimmering surface. In a way, Mallarmé continued Blake's work to return power to the idea of the book, but rather than taking the illuminated manuscript as a model, Mallarmé looked to a more widespread medium—contemporary newsprint—to revivify poetry.

Mallarmé was writing a century after Blake, at a time of greater typographic intensity. The late nineteenth century saw an explosion in signage, visible in photographs of the period depicting city streets crowded with signboards and advertisements pasted and painted on the sides of buildings.[16] The period also saw an increase in the availability and quantity of print, thanks in part to the advent of typesetting machines, which allowed compositors to set type using a keyboard, rather than hunting through the cases. From these machines came *hot metal typesetting*, which combined type casting and setting, vastly increasing the speed and efficiency of composition. The Linotype (1886), as its name homophonically implies, allowed compositors to produce a complete line of text that could be melted down and reused—no time-consuming distribution back to the cases required. Developed by Ottmar Mergenthaler for the *New York Tribune*, the machine sped up production so significantly—with a Linotype operator working five times as fast as a hand compositor[17]—that Thomas Edison reportedly called it the eighth wonder of the world. While Linotype was swiftly adopted for news, a slightly different system took hold in publishing. Monotype, invented by Tolbert Lanston in 1896, cast letters individually and composed them, giving book printers greater control of the look of each line and offering them a number of typefaces to choose from.

Seeing this proliferation of language in the landscape and in the pages of the daily newspaper, Mallarmé perceived what he called a "crisis in poetry."[18] The workmanlike columns of the newspaper made text available and accessible on a scale that he felt threatened the power of the book. It also made language a tool of commerce and mass culture, displacing its expressive power. In response to this crisis, he called for a poetry that would use the space of the page to bring mystery and expressivity back to type and to language, adopting the very techniques of that intrusive newspaper. He outlined this vision of the book's potential power in his essay "The Book, Spiritual Instrument," which advocated newsprint's large headings and use of uppercase: "a burst of grandeur, of thought or of emotion, eminent, a sentence pursued in large letters, one line per page, in a graduated arrangement—wouldn't this keep the reader in suspense throughout the whole book ... [while] all around, minor clusters ... explicatory or derivative—*an array of flourishes*."[19] This arrangement of eye-catching headings with smaller texts bubbling up around them would, he felt, charge the book with spiritual energy.

In *Un coup de Dés*, the book he was working on up to his death and that only appeared in its intended form posthumously, Mallarmé would realize this vision.[20] He planned each page carefully, scoring it as one might a piece of music, with words and phrases scattered fragmentarily across each spread. In his preface, he refers to these line breaks as "prismatic subdivisions of the Idea."[21] Eschewing the tradition of contained stanzas surrounded by white margins, he dispersed the text, allowing space to play an expressive role so "that it seems to sometimes accelerate and slow the movement, articulating it, even intimating it through a simultaneous vision of the page."[22] Dropping punctuation, using multiple type sizes to emphasize particular words, and interspersing phrases in all caps with those in lower case, he guides the reader's eye through the text, with special attention to the interaction between facing pages.

Mallarmé's was not the first visual treatment of poetry, since it was preceded by acrostics and shaped poems depicting crosses, seraphim, monks, and other figures known as "carmina figurata" in medieval codices from the ninth century onward. The use of such patterns for devotional poetry extends to Welsh poet George Herbert's seventeenth-century collection *The Temple* (1633), which includes an altar, a pair of wings, and other forms that illustrate the text. However, in these earlier works the visual design spoke to the content of a single poem, not the book as a whole. These shaped poems *imitated* their subject matter, while Mallarmé's text *enacted* it.

Even to readers of French, the free verse of *Un coup de Dés* is complex and hard to follow—some scholars believe we have yet to truly understand or explicate it. The text refuses narrative in favor of, in Mallarmé's words, "retreats, prolongations, flights."[23] He suggested that readers view *Un coup de Dés*—a complex poem whose imagery suggests shipwreck but whose language seems to refer to the act of writing itself—as a musical score, making the page into a stage on which language performs. Typeset in Didot, the early nineteenth-century font associated with literary publishing, the text disrupts the lyric expectations it sets up. Instead of a poem of individual experience voiced by a speaker recollecting and reflecting upon it, Mallarmé gives us a tumbling series of images suggesting a captain who goes down with his ship.

The lines' fragmentation forces one to read across the book's gutter in search of connection, so that one sees, for example, on facing pages, a "corpse by the arm" across from "detached from the secret it holds." Much as the text is likewise "detached" by the seam of the gutter where verso and recto meet, the ship going "into the storm / reopen[s] the seam and pass[es] proudly" into the unknown space suggested by that furrow—a whirlpool, a waterwall, a place where *there be dragons*.[24] The captain's body, too, is severed by that "seam," his arm gripping the helm as waves crash over (see figure 10a, b). Mallarmé's language animates the book and makes the reader complicit in this shipwreck. Our eye's movements back and forth, our hand turning the pages in crests that fall back

THE MASTER

arisen
    inferring

           from this conflagration

               that

         as one threatens

       the unique Number unable

             hesitates
          corpse by the arm

rather
   than play
      like a gray-haired maniac
         the game
       in the name of the waves

               a

        shipwreck this time

a.

       beyond ancient calculations
      where the maneuver forgotten with age

            of old he would grab hold of the helm

at his feet
      of the unanimous horizon

prepares itself
  is shaken and mixes
    in the fist that would grasp it
a fate and the winds

to be an other

      Spirit
        to toss it
           into the storm
            reopen the seam and pass proudly

detached from the secret it holds

breaks over the captain
flows through the submissive beard

straight from the man

    with no vessel
        any
           where futile

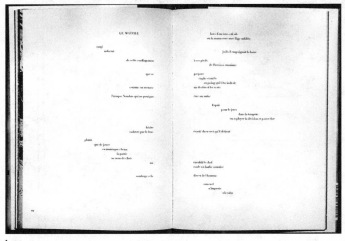

b.

Figures 10a (pages 130–131) and 10b (above) *A Roll of the Dice (Un coup de Dés)* by Stéphane Mallarmé, translation copyright 2015 by Jeff Clark and Robert Bononno. Reprinted with permission of the translator and Wave Books.

on the text, and the very sound of those pages fluttering and falling create the storm it describes. By the end of the text, we are holding the open book as a buoy or flotation device we hope will take us, as the penultimate line suggests, to "some final place of consecration."[25]

To translate *Un coup de Dés* requires not only a playful understanding of the text's swirling sense, but a sensitivity to Mallarmé's intent. The images presented here, from a collaboration between Robert Bononno and designer

Jeff Clark, reflect a thoughtful approach to the relationship between form and content. While the French text adheres to the specifications in Mallarmé's notes on the 1897 Vollard edition he was working on at his death, the English is set in Helvetica. This divergence is designed to strike contemporary eyes the way Mallarmé's evocation of newsprint shook his own readers. The ubiquitous font brings the voice of street signs, logos, and government forms into the text, rupturing the space of the page with public flotsam that drifts across its surface. The volume includes surreal black-and-white photographs that evoke the sea floor, the surface of the waves, and the cosmos in homage to three lithographs by Odilon Redon that were to be included in the 1897 printing. A modern interpretation, it translates not only the work's content but also its form for contemporary English readers.

When Mallarmé died, he was only beginning the experimentation suggested by his manifesto, a throw of the dice that would change poets' relation to the page forever. It would be up to the avant-gardes of the twentieth century, including the Futurists, Vorticists, Lettrists, and Concrete Poets, to continue his explorations of the page and book as spaces of play and visual communication. His establishment of the page as a musical score would go on to influence a range of practices, from Kurt Schwitters's Dada sound poetry to Charles Olson's typewritten projective verse. These later writers embraced the techniques of

Everything in the world exists in order to end up as a book.

advertising, incorporating it into and subverting it with their own works. In "The Book, Spiritual Instrument," Mallarmé suggested "everything in the world exists in order to end up as a book."[26] That proposition, in a less mystic formulation, would come to fruition in the middle of the twentieth century.

Ed Ruscha's Democratic Multiples

Unlike Mallarmé or Blake, Ed Ruscha (b. 1937) wasn't interested in language when he began making books, but in their capacity to serve as conceptual artworks. His artists' books of the 1960s and 1970s are deadpan photographic collections produced inexpensively and distributed, at least initially, outside of the bookstore and publishing system—inaugurating what Drucker refers to as "the artist's book as democratic multiple."[27] Producing a book as an artwork, in this case, was thought by artists of the 1960s to be "democratic" because it was inexpensive, allowed wider dissemination of the work, and bypassed the gallery system, severing the division between high and low culture such institutions were thought to represent. As curator, critic, and artist Lucy Lippard put it, the artist's book of the 1960s was conceived as "a portable exhibition ... considered by many the easiest way out of the art world and into the heart of a broader audience."[28]

As its title suggests, Ruscha's first book, *Twentysix Gasoline Stations* (1963), is a collection of photographs of filling stations on Route 66 between Los Angeles and Oklahoma City. The book is an exhibition between covers, one that requires no gallery, no commission, and no art-world reviews. As an artifact, it looks like a standard paperback, yet it plays with the codex's features—the opening, juxtaposition, sequence—drawing attention to the ways we read its form, even when we think we are reading the images or text within it.

Ruscha's black-and-white photographs look distinctly unimposing, and in some cases, unplanned. Signage is cut off by the frame's edge. The photographer casts a shadow on his subject. Some photos, taken at night, are blurry. And in others, the station itself is obscured by cars. The design, too, gives the impression of informality. Some stations take up a two-page spread, while others are confined to a half page, leaving significant white space in which a caption consisting of the station name and location floats free. The individual photographs are not presented as fine artworks. They must be read together to achieve the artist's intentionally cheeky effect.

Though Ruscha provides no framing text, in still after still he implies a kind of armchair travel. Where would one encounter so many different gas stations but on the road? Reading the book as travelogue, however, seems absurd, given the banality of these stops. The codex's inherent sequentiality (we can view only one opening at a time, and glimpse a second spread only in the process of turning the page) provides the metaphor of movement in spite of the static nature of the shots. If we mapped the cities named, we could seemingly track the absent photographer's path. In fact, these images were taken on a road trip Ruscha made to his parents' Oklahoma City home, but he has placed some out of order, troubling our assumptions about the relationship between sequence and temporality: to move forward in the book is not necessarily to move forward in space or time.

Ruscha would go on to explore travel more linearly in *Every Building on the Sunset Strip* (1966), an accordion-folded filmstrip-like document of one of LA's best known thoroughfares. The twenty-five-foot long book consists of panoramic portraits of the north and south sides of the street, stitched together from discrete images—a precursor to the Google Street View perspective to which we are now accustomed. As predigitally montages, Ruscha's photographs show their seams: sometimes cars are cut off or repeated, and occasionally misaligned shots do not precisely match. These cinematic strips run along the top and bottom of the page, facing one another, with numbers and cross-streets providing captions that locate us spatially. A generous swath of white space running horizontally through the book implies the reader's path—of our eyes moving forward through the planes of the book, and, metaphorically, of our imagined car, cruising past pharmacies and restaurants, billboards and phone poles as we head west down the boulevard.

In addition to *Twentysix Gasoline Stations*, Ruscha published a number of photographic artist's books in the sixties and seventies, including *Various Small Fires and Milk* (1964), *Some Los Angeles Apartments* (1965), and *Nine Swimming Pools and a Broken Glass* (1968), in each case playing with the page opening and our expectations regarding sequence. His use of declarative titles, typeset in three lines that lend each word extra emphasis, suggest the works' deadpan humor (see figure 11). These books, produced cheaply and distributed outside the gallery system, have become such important touchstones among artists that an entire anthology, *Various Small Books* (Cambridge, MA: MIT Press, 2013), has been devoted to the numerous artist publications riffing on his theme.

Four hundred signed and numbered copies of *Twentysix Gasoline Stations*, its first run, were sold for $3 each according to an ad in *Artforum*—democratic indeed. Yet anyone familiar with Ruscha's body of work will tell you that those cheaply produced books went through several printings in increasingly larger runs (as high as 3,000 in 1969), and are now out of print, with copies selling for thousands of dollars.[29] Ruscha intended to keep the book available in an open edition, but he eventually had to move on. The "democratic multiple" couldn't prevent the artist

Figure 11 Ed Ruscha's artists' books *Twentysix Gasoline Stations*, 1962
($7" \times 5\frac{1}{2}" \times 1\frac{9}{16}"$); *Various Small Fires and Milk*, 1964 ($7\frac{1}{16}" \times 5\frac{1}{2}" \times \frac{3}{16}"$); and
Some Los Angeles Apartments, 1965 ($7\frac{1}{8}" \times 5\frac{5}{18}" \times \frac{3}{16}"$). ©Ed Ruscha. Courtesy
of the artist and Gagosian.

from being absorbed back into the art world's celebrity system. Still, Ruscha's work, tied to art's dematerialization (to use Lucy Lippard's term for the conceptual art movement)—prioritizing idea over artifact and concept over craft—reflects the values of the moment in which it arose.

In each of these three cases, an artist took control of the bookmaking process to create a work of art in book form. Had they been produced as broadsides or gallery exhibitions, these books would have functioned differently, and their intervention into commerce would have been less apparent. Blake used his craftsmanship to develop the relationship between word and image. Mallarmé used the design of his text to resist the absorption of language into consumer culture. Ruscha used his books to create exhibitions outside the gallery setting. While the types of books they created were quite different from one another, as progenitors of artists' books, they shared a concern with the commodification of the codex.

The New Art of Making Books

The ubiquity of the book as a marketable artifact led Mexican author and artist Ulises Carrión (1941–1989) to write rebelliously in 1975, "A book may be the accidental container of a text, the structure of which is irrelevant to the book: these are the books of bookshops and libraries."[30] We have to imagine a long pause where that colon hinges the sentence together—one heavy with sarcasm. Carrión's tongue-in-cheek dig at the book as a commercial artifact reflects on the separation of form and content he perceived in the writing and publishing of his time. Carrión was not opposed to bookshops altogether, and in fact founded one himself, Other Books and So, in Amsterdam that same year. Specializing in artists' books and multiples, the shop was also an artist-run exhibition and event space that distributed the kind of work he wanted to see more of in the world: books conceived of as a whole, rather than "texts" bestowed by the author on a publisher for dissemination to a reading public. In an advertisement for the space, he called them "non books, anti books, pseudo books, quasi books, concrete books, visual books, conceptual books, structural books, project books, statement books, instruction books,"[31] a list suggestive of his vexed relationship with the marketplace. Ultimately, he would coin a new term to describe the kind of artists' publications he championed: *bookworks*. In part, Carrión's was a clarion call for authors to be more attuned to the book's materiality and impact on meaning, but it was also a demand for a breakdown of the system that privileged writing as intellectual labor and denigrated the physical aspect of book production.

Like Mallarmé, Carrión perceived a crisis in literature, and for him that crisis arose from its place in the publishing system. He knew this system firsthand, having achieved early success by winning the state prize for short stories in 1960, publishing work in periodicals, and ultimately releasing two successful story collections, in 1966 and 1970. Carrión had studied literature and philosophy at UNAM, and he gained enough acclaim to receive grants for graduate study in France, Germany, and the United Kingdom. While in England he began to envision a different approach to the book and publishing, thanks to Mexican artists Felipe Ehrenberg and Martha Hellion, whose Beau Geste Press (founded in 1970) introduced him to mimeographed books by members of *Fluxus*, a loose collective of artists interested in chance operations, ephemeral performances, conceptual practice, and participatory works that blur the line between art and life. When he moved to Amsterdam in 1972, Carrión began producing artists' books of his own, the first of which, *Sonnets*, provided forty-four iterations of Dante Gabriel Rossetti's "Heart's Compass." In the manner of Raymond Queneau's *Exercises in Style* (1947), Carrión played with his source text, rewriting it in different styles to amusing ends. It was in this context of experimentation with poetry, and a move from narrative toward conceptual art, that Carrión began to formulate the notion of the bookwork.

Demanding that writers take a more active role in the conceptualization of their books, he published "The New

Art of Making Books" (1975), a manifesto whose polemical tone served as a provocation that still irks some readers today. Originally written in Spanish and published in *Plural*, the magazine founded by Octavio Paz, it was aimed at a literary audience Carrión felt needed a jolt. Disavowing the novel as "a book where nothing happens," and proclaiming "there is not and will not be new literature anymore," he clearly hoped to ruffle feathers.[32] The novel, of course, is not dead, and it still serves an important expressive purpose, but Carrión's reenvisioning of the capacities of the book show us much about the ways artists' books have helped multiply its possibilities by treating the book as an intermedial space.

Like Mallarmé, Carrión saw the page's spatial potential. His manifesto opens, "A book is a sequence of spaces,"[33] a definition so porous as to allow for any number of objects or artifacts we might think of as books: a bound codex, a deck of cards, or a series of rooms. But his definition stretches still further:

Each of these spaces is perceived at a different moment—a book is also a sequence of moments.

· · · ·

A book is not a case of words, nor a bag of words, nor a bearer of words.

· · · ·

... A book is a space-time sequence.[34]

If a book is a space-time sequence, it is also a kind of film. It can be animated, rather than static. By the time Carrión penned this statement, creators of flip-books and their precursor, the nickelodeon, had exploited this aspect of the book's sequential potential for just over a century (the flip-book having been patented in 1868 by John Barnes Linnett as the kineograph). This notion, though, that the page is more than simply "a bag of words" suggests that writers must stop treating language as transparent, utilitarian, and direct. Only in the old art could one believe "the meanings of the words are the bearers of the author's intentions."[35] Clearly, Carrión's thinking bears the hallmarks of poststructural theory, which by this point had shaken up notions of meaning and authorship.

In lieu of such "boring" books "of 500 pages, or of 100, or even of 25 wherein all the pages are similar,"[36] Carrión called for books "conceived as an expressive unity," as he would write in a 1978 exhibition catalog.[37] While calling pages of justified prose "boring" sounds purposefully bombastic, we ought to consider the role page numbers and running heads play in facilitating reading and revisiting a work. These signposts help us navigate a text that looks the same from page to page, though its words may vary. "In a bookwork," by Carrión's definition, "the message is the sum of all the material and formal elements."[38] The bookwork, thus, engages in a critique of the book and an exploration of its affordances. It takes nothing at face value and asks the reader to remain attentive not only to the text but also to its physicality. As scholar Garrett Stewart writes, a bookwork is "not for normal reading, but for thinking about."[39] It represents a conceptual approach to bookmaking, and one that relies on the viewer's interaction with the object to make meaning. For this reason Carrión called such works "anti books"—because they refuse the book's function while interrogating its form, separating the idea of the book from the object.

In a 1986 video recorded in Olympia, Washington, where Carrión was to speak at The Evergreen State College, he professes a perspective common today, "I firmly believe that every book that now exists will eventually disappear." And true to form, he expresses little sadness over the loss: "And I see here no reason for lamentation. Like any other living organism, books will grow, multiply, change color, and, eventually, die. At the moment, bookworks represent the final phase of this irrevocable process. Libraries, museums, archives are the perfect cemeteries for books."[40]

Sounding a death knell for books that has since become a refrain, Carrión suggests that bookworks take on greater importance when the codex itself seems to be imperiled. This feels especially true at our current moment, when publishers are taking greater risks with artistic publications and conceptually inventive books like Jonathan

Safran Foer's die-cut erasure *Tree of Codes* (Visual Editions, 2010), Mark Danielewski's typographically complex *House of Leaves* (Pantheon, 2000), Anne Carson's accordion-bound *Nox* (New Directions, 2010), and Jen Bervin's collection of Emily Dickinson's envelope fragments, *Gorgeous Nothings* (New Directions, 2013), a volume that feels like a coffee-table book. As the material form of the codex threatens to disintegrate into the digital, works highly attuned to materiality give us a chance to think about and savor the physical artifact, precisely by asking us to reflect on the very immaterial "idea" of the book.

The Book's Ideas

So what do artists' books have to teach us about a path forward for the book? As close engagements with its material shape, they serve a dual purpose: first, they offer a great variety of formats that can carry the name "book," proliferating the objects to which we can apply the idea and reminding us of the deep history of formal experimentation with the material text; and, second, the features of the book they explore and exploit link them to digitally mediated books, which share many of the same concerns. Ironic though his polemics may have been, Carrión's manifestos outline several key themes that recur throughout artists' books of the twentieth century: spatiotemporal play, animation, recombinant structures, ephemerality, silence, and interactivity.

An examination of artists' books helps us understand the link between contemporary digital books and the historical forms we explored in chapters 1 and 2. They remind us that books are fundamentally interactive reading devices whose meanings, far from being fixed, arise at the moment of access. The commodification and industrialization of print creates the illusion of text's fixity and meaning's stability.[41] But books are always a negotiation, a performance, an event: even a Dickens novel remains inert until a reader opens it up, engaging its language and imaginative world. Artists' books continually remind us of the reader's role in the book by forcing us to reckon with its materiality and, by extension, our own embodiment. Such experiments present a path forward for digital books, which would do well to consider the affordances of their media and the importance of the reader, rather than treating the e-reader as a Warde-ian crystal goblet for the delivery of content.

Artists' books have taken myriad shapes over the years, so what follows are a series of examples that draw our attention to specific affordances of the book worth noting—along with historical precedents where appropriate. I would urge anyone interested in the book to seek out local university and museum collections, some of which are listed in Further Reading and Writing, because nothing

A book is a sequence
of spaces.

Each of these spaces
is perceived at a
different moment—
a book is also a sequence
of moments.

• • • •

A book is not a case
of words, nor a bag of
words, nor a bearer
of words.

—ULISES CARRIÓN,
"THE NEW ART OF MAKING BOOKS"

compares to spending several hours holding artists' books in your hands. They are, first and foremost, meant to be activated by a reader, and thus describing them in brief simply does not do them justice.

The Book as Virtual Reality

Carrión's initial definition of the book as a "sequence of spaces" sounds like an abstraction, but it can, in fact, be taken literally. Each opening of the codex is a unique space, and when we turn the page we leave that space and enter a new one. Book artists have explored this spatiality by creating virtual realities that puncture the two-dimensional plane of the page. The book is, after all, a volume, a term suggesting both sequence (volume 1, volume 2, etc.) and space.

We see the book's depth most readily in pop-up books, which unfold to fill each opening with material that pulls itself up off the page. One way book artists make us confront the voluminous potential of the book is through the tunnel binding style, also known as the *peep-show*, a form that originated during the Italian Renaissance. Familiar to anyone who has played with a cut-paper stage set as a child, the *tunnel book* developed from Leon Battista Alberti's (1404–1472) optical experiments, for which he built a peep-show box with a perspective scene inside.[42] By the seventeenth century, similar devices developed as traveling peep-shows invited viewers to look into boxes with layers of cut-out characters and landscapes depicting scenes from the Bible, mythology, and history. These theaters-in-a-box became increasingly complex, with strings the presenter could pull to animate the scene.[43] By the eighteenth century, such peep-shows were being printed on a smaller scale for sale to individuals, bound with paper accordions along both sides. They became popular in the mid-nineteenth century as souvenirs for events like the opening of the Thames Tunnel (1851), which ostensibly provides the name by which we now know them.

When fully extended and viewed through an opening in the cover, the tunnel book's superimposed flat planes create the illusion of depth—successive layers adding detail to the scene. Such books can include text around their borders, or they can be wordless. They can be printed or blank. They can even accommodate projection to animate their surfaces, as in artist William Kentridge's video installation *Preparing the Flute* (2005). Built as a working model for the Brussels Opera's production of Mozart's *Die Zauberflöte*, the series of charcoal, pastel, and pencil drawings frame a miniature stage, serving as backdrop for a series of animated films that deepen their illusion.

Another model of projection-animated pop-up structures might be found in *The Icebook* (2011) by Davy and Kristin McGuire. Described by its creators as "a miniature theatre show made of paper and light," the book uses projection mapping to play a fairy tale across a series of eleven blank pop-up pages. The projected video adds characters, detail, and lighting effects to a wooded landscape, a Victorian mansion, a lighthouse, a church, and other settings. Like Kentridge's miniature theater, *The Icebook* began as a maquette for stage performance, and its success has led the McGuires to collaborate with theater companies and advertisers to create paper/projection spectacles, including the rear projection–mapped *Theater Book—Macbeth,* a battery-powered cinematic pop-up book depicting scenes from the Scottish play, created with the Royal Shakespeare Company.

This theatrical component of the book has been realized on a much larger scale by Fluxus artist Alison Knowles, who creates books as sets activated by the viewer. The first of these installations, *The Big Book* (1967), was an eight-foot-tall codex described by Bill Wilson in *Art in America* as "a work of art to be lived in."[44] Knowles installed *The Big Book*, constructed with her spouse Dick Higgins and sculptor Masami Kodama, at Something Else Gallery, the exhibition space of Higgins's Something Else Press, on the first floor of their Chelsea brownstone. Something Else Press is notable as a pioneer of innovative small-press publishing, putting out books of Fluxus art and concrete poetry from 1963 to 1974 as an affordable means of disseminating this work and creating a community of practitioners.

A precursor to Carrión's *Other Books and So* bookshop, it joined a tradition of artist-run presses of the 1960s, which served as not only venues for distributing artwork but also gathering and exhibition spaces for experimental book forms.[45]

Critic Howard Junker praised Knowles's project, which he called a "Pandora's Book," as the realization of Mallarmé's dream and a response to McLuhan's admonitions about the "post-literate" age, writing in *Newsweek,* "Freed from the linearity of type and the one-at-a-time strictures of pages bound together, the book is again a contemporary medium."[46] A series of giant pages attached at a central hinge, the book didn't dispense with seriality so much as exploit it to remind us just how bound the codex is (we might say boundedness is one of the book's key characteristics). Some read the work as taking part in the feminist critique of the restrictive domestic sphere prevalent at the time. No matter how "big" the book is, its pathways are limited.

Visitors entering *The Big Book* pass through eight pages, with each opening immersing them in a different scene (see figure 12). To get from one to the next, one might crawl through a four-foot tunnel of grass, enter an open window, or climb a ladder. The scenes include a library, gallery, working kitchen, and even a chemical toilet. The "pages," made of bonded sheeting, are slightly translucent, allowing a preview of the opening to come.

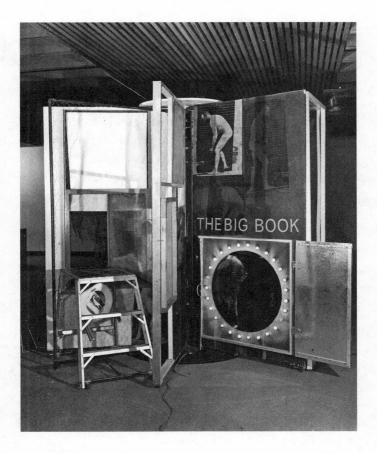

Figure 12 Alison Knowles, *The Big Book*, University Art Gallery, University of California San Diego, La Jolla, 1969. Image used with permission of the artist and the University Art Gallery.

Knowles's big book is bounded but offers everything the artist might need, including artifacts from her own home meant to nurture creativity (a typewriter, a gallery of work by her friends, and a kitchen for the sustenance to go on). Whether it revalues or critiques the domestic sphere, *The Big Book* turns it into a site of reading and interpretation, highlighting the way the codex structure uses sequence to make meaning.

Much of Knowles's work explores the intersection between the book and performance. She revisited the life-size book in her 1982 *Book of Bean*, another walk-through installation meditating on the bean's cross-cultural and personal significance. Built with artist Yoshi Wada and installed at avant-garde art space Franklin Furnace, the multisensory installation invites viewers traversing the sequence of spaces to read translations of the word *bean* across languages from Arabic to Swahili. They hear a soundscape that includes a poem composed of the names of every Bean in the phone book read alongside those of actual legumes, listen to a bean orchestra created by rattling beans inside different objects, exit through a window encircled by text about dreams and beans, and in the end are offered a dish of beans to eat.

Knowles's books, like her artistic practice, offer readers nourishment, reminding us that the book is an exchange, and one that is only completed when we arrive. In her own words: "You have to get right into it, as you do

You have to get right into it, as you do with any good book, and you must become involved and experience it yourself. Then you will *know* something and *feel* something. Let us say that it provides a milieu for your *experience* but what you bring to it is the biggest ingredient, far more important than what is there.

—ALISON KNOWLES,
THE BIG BOOK

with any good book, and you must become involved and experience it yourself. Then you will *know* something and *feel* something. Let us say that it provides a milieu for your *experience* but what you bring to it is the biggest ingredient, far more important than what is there."[47] Crawling through *The Big Book*, *Book of Bean*, or a new incarnation, *Boat Book* (2014), the visitor's body stands in for the reader's eye. As we traverse the pages, our experience is itself the text, which will be different for each viewer because of what we have seen before, between, and after these pages.

The book's virtual realities can also take digital shape, as they do in the works of Caitlin Fisher, founder of York University's Future Cinema Lab. Fisher has been working with digital media since 2000, when she published her dissertation on feminist theory in hypertext form. She has gone on to work in *augmented reality* (AR), which uses a computer or phone's camera to layer digital media onto live video, techniques at the intersection of performance, pop-up books, and installation art. Her AR installation *Circle* (2012) consists of an open suitcase whose family heirlooms—a teacup, Victorian postcards, and other ephemera—inspire us to imagine their history. When viewed through an iPad or iPhone using Fisher's app, the screen becomes a "magic looking glass" and short videos and animations spring from each piece, accompanied by haunting audio describing the memories of three generations of women embedded in these domestic objects.[48] The book, distributed across them, becomes a multimedia and multi-navigable space: a virtual reality layered onto our own. AR works can be more codex-like in shape, as with Carla Gannis's Lumen Award–winning *Selfie Drawings* (2016), a hardcover book of fifty-two AR portraits that animate and change when viewed through an app on one's smart device.[49] Like Knowles and Fisher, Gannis explores femininity and self-representation in her work, using AR to construct new worlds for the artist to inhabit.

The Book as Cinematic Space

The notion of the book as a sequence of spaces also implies its capacity for animation. When books consist of images, it is easy to picture them as little films—whether those illustrations depict vignettes from the text, as in Lewis Carroll's illustrations of Alice's adventures, or they comprise the text, as in a flip-book where image succeeds image, creating the illusion of movement. Flip-books, of course, were the precursor to cinema, with Victorian experiments in sequential photography by Edweard Muybridge and others creating proto-movies thanks to the persistence of vision.

The flip-book and peep-show box meet in the Mutoscope, an early cinematic technology for extremely short vignettes of about a minute each. Patented by Herman

Casler in 1894, the Mutoscope, whose name is a Latin borrowing that suggests "changing-views,"[50] was a box of standing height with a hooded glass lens. Viewers who turned the machine's crank were treated to a private show as a sequence of around 850 cards on a central reel flicked before their eyes. The book's role in the development of film adds a layer of irony to 1950s fears that books simply couldn't compete with cinema. Similar complaints arise with each new technology—will video games, the computer, the dramatic miniseries, streaming video, or the latest media consumption technology signal the death of the book? That question isn't as interesting, though, as the question of how each of these technologies has been, and will continue to be, part of the book's development.

Book artists have examined the page's potential for animation in a number of projects exploiting the codex's flippable structure. Michael Snow's *Cover to Cover* (1975), for instance, confronts the reader with a door through which, it seems, we are invited to enter the volume—a subtle reference to the architectural metaphors for the book that arose in the Renaissance.[51] The black-and-white world between these covers plays with verso and recto as the back and front of a single plane, so that we are continually seeing things from both sides in a manner that suggests movement, though we are, in fact, going nowhere. When we open the front door we find, on the inside cover, an image of its reverse, a black door against which the artist stands, in a neatly tucked collared dress shirt, with his back to us. Is he waiting for us to open the door? Is he trying to get out? At recto we find another door upon which are printed the artist's name and title. Opening that, we find yet another spread in which the artist has his back to us at verso and a door appears at recto. It feels like a funhouse, with each door leading only to another door.

Yet as we get deeper into the book, we realize that though we haven't moved, the artist is making progress. At verso he opens the door before him. At recto, the door is partly ajar. The book, we realize, is beginning to animate like a flip-book or GIF, and we're seeing on each verso the reverse shot of the recto image beside it. The book's conceit is revealed when the door opens fully and we find at recto an image of the photographer documenting the artist's verso departure. The magician reveals how his trick is done—simultaneous photographs taken from both sides of the door until the two camera operators face one another across the opening. Snow takes the viewer deeper down the rabbit hole as one photographer covers his camera with a piece of paper, which is in turn apparently documented by the other, whose page goes white. An image of the artist's finger partly obscuring the white page, however, reveals that what has passed for a space has in fact been a surface all along—a photographic print of the supposed photographer, which is then fed into a typewriter and processed into text. Over the course of the book, recto and verso appear to document a series of connected scenes, always from two angles: a record being placed on a phonograph, a window being obscured by branches, the artist leaving the house to go to a gallery, and periodically those hands, ghosted below our own, manipulating the pages. Confused? That's partly the pleasure of the book, which refuses to let us settle into any one space—like the Mutoscope, *Cover to Cover* keeps changing the view.

Animation is not, however, limited to images. Poet and artist Emmett Williams (1925–2007) animates text in several books published with Something Else Press (where he served as editor in chief from 1966 to 1970) in the 1960s. *Sweethearts* (1967), a beguiling book with Marcel Duchamp's last print, *Coeurs Volants*, on the cover, tells the story of HE and SHE, two characters whose appearance is made possible by the presence of the letters S, H, and E in the title. Printed in sans-serif lowercase type whose widely set letters are arranged in a grid, the book's text appears only at verso, requiring readers to start at the back and flip their way forward. On each page, words are formed from letters floating in an invisible net of SWEETHEARTS, simulating movement like letters flicking on and off in a neon sign. As Williams describes in the preface, "No single poem can be more than 11 letters wide or 11 letters deep" (see figure 13).[52] As we turn the pages, HE and SHE engage in a courtship full of innuendo composed from the letters of SWEETHEARTS in the order in which they appear.

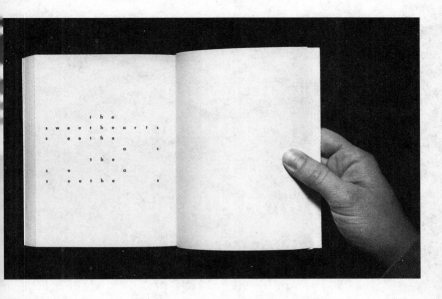

Figure 13 A page from Emmett Williams's *Sweethearts* (Berlin: Verlag der Buchandlung Walther König, [1967] 2010). Image used with grateful permission of Ann-Noël Williams.

They go to the SEA, they have a laugh (HA HA), they SEE THE STARS, pledge their HEARTS, and START A SWEET WAR getting WET on the shore, perhaps reenacting the wave-crashing scene in *From Here to Eternity*.[53] The book's cheeky humor and visual play connect it to the bawdy history of the Mutoscope and other Nickelodeon machines, which often featured risqué scenes with names like "From Show Girl to Burlesque Queen," "A Modern Sappho," and

A book, in its purest form, is a phenomenon of space and time and dimensionality that is unique unto itself. When we turn the page, the previous page passes into our past and we are confronted by a new world.

—DICK HIGGINS, "A BOOK"

"Her Morning Ablutions."[54] In addition to "girlie" films, the Mutoscopes traded on racist tropes, war propaganda, and by the 1920s and 1930s, newsreels and excerpts from popular films by Charlie Chaplin, Buster Keaton, and other silent "STARS." Williams refers to his constellations' animation as "a primitive cinematic effect," and because the book is meant to be not only read but watched, the pages go unnumbered: like a flip-book, the poems gain meaning in relation rather than stasis.

Williams's *A Valentine for Noël: Four Variations on A Scheme* (1973), dedicated to his wife, artist Ann Noël, includes a series of concrete poems that animate across the page. Among the best known, "Soldier" arose from a screenprint Williams created in protest of the Vietnam War, *DIE as in SOLDIER* (1970). In the poem, Williams draws our attention to the space of the page. Half an inch from the fore-edge, the word SOLDIER repeats over and over, aligned perfectly like a column of infantry that extends to the page's limit, suggesting that it stretches infinitely beyond our view. Printed in uppercase lettering in blue ink, the SOLDIERs are uniform, regimental, identical, and upright. Their column, though, is gradually infiltrated over the course of forty pages by red ink, highlighting the DIE in SOLDIER. Page by page, from top to bottom, the DIE turns red, cascading downward as one soldier after another falls, succumbing, it seems, to a fate predetermined in language. No longer "Sweet" or "wet," the term "war" at this historic moment could not be recuperated for Williams. His DIE/SOLDIER paragram is no joke, but a political commentary on "war as a killing machine," as publisher Zédélé, who reissued the book in 2015, puts it.[55]

Not only does Williams's work animate the page, it draws attention to the grid-like structure underlying it—from the screens used to mold the paper to the letterpress printer's chase. The letters that move across the page in *Sweethearts* can do so by virtue of the invisible grid of the word S W E E T H E A R T S, repeated over and over, which provides the lattice across which these letters climb. The word *page*, after all, comes from an Indo-European word root that means "to join or affix."[56] That root gives us the Latin *pagina*, which translates to "trellis," evoking the page as a fruitful space and training structure to which language is pinned. The SOLDIERs, too, are held in formation, and their advancing line evokes not only the battlefield but also the firing squad. A throw of the die cannot abolish the chance these soldiers will fall.

Williams's cinematic endeavors are presaged in the work of an early twentieth-century writer who, charmed by the advent of sound film, wanted to embrace the cinematic possibilities of the page. Rather than the flip-book, Robert Carlton (Bob) Brown (1886–1959) looked back to the scroll as a model for a continual moving text. In 1930, he published an article in the avant-garde literary journal *transition* describing "readies," a new textual form aided by machine: "a method of enjoying literature in a manner as up-to-date as the lively talkies."[57] In talking up his invention, he suggested it would reignite popular interest in reading and bring writing up to date as an "Optical Art." Unlike Warde, Brown saw the codex as an inadequate vessel: "Writing has been bottled up in books since the start. It is time to pull out the stopper."[58]

How to let the spirit out of the bottle? Brown devised a machine akin to microfiche or movieola—a narrow ribbon imprinted with tiny text that would be enlarged on an adjustable magnifying lens between it and the reader. The size could be adjusted by moving the lens closer or further from the ribbon, and the text could be sped up, slowed down, advanced, or retracted with the turn of a dial, giving one utmost control over the reading experience (see figure 14). In addition to the entertainment value of such a device, Brown touted the potential cost savings on paper, ink, and binding. His rapid-fire texts omitted connective words, created portmanteaus to speed up the pace of ideas, and used the em dash in place of full stops to score the text.[59] The claims he made in this manifesto and the subsequent fifty-two-page pamphlet *The Readies* (1930), published under his imprint Roving Eye Press, were intentionally hyperbolic in their assertions and belied the author's long-standing relationship with the codex. A collector of rare books, Brown himself had made a comfortable living publishing journalism, fiction and poetry,

Figure 14 A prototype of Bob Brown's Reading Machine constructed by Ross Saunders and Hilaire Hiler (1930–1931). Artwork by Elffin Burrill in Craig Saper's *Amazing Adventures of Bob Brown* (2016), based on a photograph glued into copies of *Readies for Bob Brown's Machine* (1931). Image used with permission of the artist and Craig Saper.

cookbooks, and pulp stories.[60] He collaborated with his wife and his mother on books about food and drink, including the popular post-Prohibition history *Let There Be Beer!* (Harrison Smith and Robert Haas, 1932), dedicated to fellow beer-lover H. L. Menken, whose blurb enjoins the reader to buy two copies: "one for himself and one for his pastor."[61]

Brown had begun making cartoonish visual puns 1912, one of which was published by Marcel Duchamp in *Blindman* in 1917. Duchamp would be a formative influence on his work, as would Guillaume Apollinaire, whose *Calligrammes* (1918), visual poems using shape and arrangement to make texts that mimicked their titles, also inspired him.[62] An American in Europe after the First World War, Brown befriended many expatriate writers, soliciting contributions from Gertrude Stein, William Carlos Williams, F. T. Marinetti, Eugène Jolas, and Paul Bowles, among others, for his 1931 anthology *Readies for Bob Brown's Machine*. A prototype machine was built that year, and a digital iteration has been published online by Craig Saper and K. A. Wisniewski, who have revived Roving Eye Press to reissue Brown's innovative works.[63] While the Reading Machine was perhaps more conceptual game than reading revolution, it presages contemporary speed-reading technologies like Spritz, a web app that helps readers quickly absorb texts using an optical system to feed them one word at a time.[64] Brown's readies, based on the technologies of his moment, used the paper scroll as an animated surface—one that unrolled before the reader's eyes in a merger of film and tickertape, turning readers themselves into a kind of machine for making meaning.

The Book as Recombinant Structure

While we might presume the ability to rearrange a book's parts is an affordance reserved for the digital realm, artists' books showcase several historical forms that turn the book into a recombinant structure, allowing readers to create new juxtapositions within it. Such interactivity is present already in the accordion book, which, as an intermediate point between scroll and codex, allows readers to open one spread at a time or unfold several, seeing across the folds' peaks and valleys to survey the text.

The ability to completely open this structure makes it especially useful for topographic work like Blaise Cendrars and Sonia Delaunay's 1913 collaboration *La Prose du Transsibérien et de la Petite Jehanne de France* (*The Prose of the Trans-Siberian and of Little Jehanne of France*), a vertical cityscape of colorful pochoir paintings and poetry where the eye's traversal of word and image suggest the simultaneity of a dark past and a vivid present for the poem's speaker as he recalls a railroad journey from Moscow to Harbin during the Russian-Japanese war of 1905; or like

Ruscha's *Every Building on the Sunset Strip*, which allows a kind of armchair tourism across the Los Angeles landscape. The form lends itself to exhibition for this reason—we can see more of its contents at a glance than a codex if the accordion is stood on end and extended, revealing every peak and valley, front and back. When the accordion's ends are attached to a cover, it creates a loop, potentially inviting us to start again. But the accordion need not be a linear or landscape experience. It also permits new juxtapositions by allowing readers to refold peaks into valleys and bring distant pages close to one another. Artists' books in accordion form remind us that the book is, as Stewart notes, "Western culture's first interactive medium."[65]

This recombinant quality of the book takes place not only across but within the page. The technique, in fact, appears in some of the earliest movable books, which use *volvelles*, turnable discs affixed to the page with a pin or piece of string, to facilitate calculation and navigation. The earliest volvelles, those of thirteenth-century Catalan mystic Ramon Lull, precede print, and the technique rose in prominence during the incunable period for its scholarly utility. The Regiomontanus *Kalendarium* (1476), whose frontispiece was discussed in chapter 2, for example, also included volvelles for astrological calculation.[66] Another important recombinant tool appears in the sixteenth and seventeenth centuries in the form of flap books or turn-up books composed of a printed page with a sequence of flaps that alter the narrative each time the reader lifts a hinge. Also known as transformation books or *Harlequinades*, for the London pantomime figure they often depict, such eighteenth-century novelty books were among the first marketed to children (by London bookseller Robert Sayer around 1765) offering morals and lessons through the transformations they depicted. The harlequinade's legacy continues in children's mix-and-match books that use sliced pages and a spiral binding to allow one to swap a face's features, create hybrid bodies, or otherwise interchange an image or text's parts.

The recombinant form lends itself to text as well. French author Raymond Queneau (1903–1976), inspired by such childlike "*têtes folles*"[67] and intrigued by the possibilities offered by a series of cut pages hinged along a spine, composed fourteen Petrarchan sonnets with the identical rhyme scheme, bound them, and sliced the lines apart. Published in 1961, *Cent mille milliards de poèmes* (*One hundred thousand billion poems*) offers the reader 10^{14} different poems, accessed by turning the lines one at a time to make new texts. To read them all, Queneau calculated, would take more than two hundred million years of devoted study.[68] The work is thus a conceptual one but also offers a pleasurable reading experience borne of the novelty inherent in using the author's text to generate new

My definition of a book grew until I realized, there can be none. To define anything limits it to your past resolutions with no room to expand.

—KEITH A. SMITH,
"STRUGGLING TO SEE"

poems. No wonder, then, that this work is popular with coders, whose digital implementations enact its computational potential. Such remediations, however, lack the tactile pleasure of the interlocking strips that compose the book. They also cannot replicate the sense of potential made palpable by seeing these strips in front of you, lifting themselves away from the spine of the open book and fluttering apart.

Queneau joined forces with a group of French writers in the 1960s who were interested in creating new literary forms based on scientific and mathematical principles, and this text is seminal to the movement. Dubbed Oulipo, short for Ouvoir de Littérature Potentielle (Workshop of Potential Literature), the group pioneered constraint-based writing, which set up a rigid conceptual basis for the production of a work, but one that could yield any number of potential results. *Cent mille milliards* is rife with potential, and the interactivity through which we activate that potential, while it gives some agency to the reader, also highlights Queneau's authorial genius. The task of composing interchangeable sonnets in the identical meter and rhyme scheme draws attention to his authorship, as does much Oulipo work, including Georges Perec's *La disparition* (Editions Denoël, 1969), a novel composed without the letter "e" that provides a parable for the disappearance of millions of Jews, including the author's own parents, during the Second World War; and Anne Garréta's *Sphinx*

(Grasset, 1986), which remains silent throughout about the gender of its protagonist. Members of Oulipo would go on to generate recombinant and computational poetry under the auspices of Alamo, short for Atelier de Littérature Assistée par la Mathématique et les Ordinateurs (Workshop for Literature Assisted by Mathematics and Computers), founded by Paul Braffort and Jacques Roubaud in 1981.[69]

Such game-like recombinant texts are not limited to artists' books, of course. Many of us enjoyed interactive books published for a mass audience in the 1970s and 1980s. These multisequential books, perhaps the best known being the Choose Your Own Adventure series, offered the reader a series of vignettes, each followed by a choice about what to do next. One path through the book led to the best of all possible endings, while the rest led to trouble, heartbreak, even death. These interactive books—while suggesting that there are many paths, but that we, like Robert Frost, cannot travel them and "be one traveler"[70]—actually allowed readers to pursue them all, thanks to the ability to bookmark the choice point with a finger or slip of paper and read each of the potential outcomes before moving on. One such book, *Inside UFO 54–40*, took advantage of readers' tendency to cheat by including a page spread inaccessible through any of the reading paths. To reach the miraculous planet Ultima it described, you had to break the rules.

The legacy of these multisequential books lives on in digital interactive fiction (IF), which was among the first game genres made possible by computing. IF, which can be presented on the web, in standalone apps, and even in print, presents readers with choices that alter their path through a work. Jason Shiga's *Meanwhile* (2010), a graphic novel boasting 3,856 possible readings, uses a print analogue to hypertext: pipes that extend from a sequence of panels off the edge of the page to create a kind of tabbed *thumb index* by which one can leap to other points in the book.[71] Designed to emulate what comic book artist and theorist Scott McCloud calls an "infinite canvas," *Meanwhile* also exists as an app in which all potential paths are available in an interface that scrolls in every direction.[72]

Interactive books come in other game-like forms, including Mad Libs, storytelling dice and decks, and magnetic poetry. Publishers and book artists have used the deck of cards as another playful model for the book that can be sequenced by the reader. John Cage's work with indeterminacy in the 1960s might be included among such works; as would French author Marc Saporta's *Composition No. 1* (Éditions du Seuil, 1961), a box of 150 leaves printed on only one side that the reader is instructed to shuffle at the outset; and B. S. Johnson's *The Unfortunates* (Panther Books, 1969), whose opening and closing quires enclose twenty-five sections that may be read in any order. This bracketing method, in which the story's opening and closing are set, was used by Robert Coover for "Heart Suit," a story in *McSweeney's Issue 16* (May 2005) printed on fifteen oversized heart-suited cards including a title card and a joker providing the tale's introduction and conclusion. Artist Christian Marclay, whose work focuses on found and appropriated materials, published a deck of cards called *Shuffle* in 2007 that, in Cagean fashion, presents the reader with seventy-five images of musical notation in situ (as a decorative element on mugs, jackets, murals, and the like), which are meant to be shuffled to create a playable score.

Artist Carolee Schneeman's *ABC—We Print Anything—In the Cards* (1977) is seminal in this regard. Consisting of 158 color-coded cards in a blue cloth box, the work was intended as a score that could be variously interpreted by the reader. Including dream and diary excerpts on yellow cards, quotes by characters A, B, and C (based on Schneeman; her soon-to-be ex, Anthony; and her new lover Bruce) on blue cards, and comments from friends on pink cards, the book suggests that as a relationship ends, it can feel as if every possibility were predetermined, or "in the cards." "We print anything," perhaps the slogan of a print shop or tabloid, tells us that this ABC, far from rudimentary schoolbook, is for an adult audience, and that it holds nothing back, just as Schneeman kept little off-limits in her body art and performance work. Black-and-white photographic cards intersperse images of her nude body, her domestic space, and erotic artwork as if to reinforce the fact that the book lays all her cards on the table.

What happens, though, when a book is boxed and unbound? Do we still recognize it as a book? Of course we do—the box acts like a familiar slipcase for a hardbound book. It presents a rectilinear volume that can be arrayed on a bookshelf, and it contains the pages or cards that come together in its content. Yet, while it looks like a codex from outside, the moment we open the box something changes. These pages can be "turned" in that they can be flipped over, creating two stacks of loose sheets facing one another. Is the space between them properly an "opening" as one finds in a codex or accordion book? Yes. And no. In an accordion or codex, the author and designer have conceived of the opening and the interplay between the facing pages. In an unbound book, that interplay will be different each time it is read, since we can shuffle and reorder them at will. If the cards or pages are not numbered, then the order is truly left up to the reader, and perhaps even the orientation—the page can now be rotated (though in some cases, this will render its text illegible without a mirror or Blake's skills).

Some of the loveliest works to play with this potentiality are Swiss-German poet Dieter Roth's (born Karl Dietrich Roth, 1930–1998) series titled simply *Bok* (*Book*) from the late 1950s and early 1960s. Born in Germany, Roth's parents sent him to Switzerland in 1943 for the duration of the war (his family reunited there in 1946) and there he trained as a graphic designer, met concrete poet Eugen Gomringer, and began experimenting with visual poems and artists' books. When he moved to Reykjavik in 1957, Roth created his own small press, forlag ed., and began to issue books in a variety of cut-paper formats. Famously playful with book form, his first publication, *Kinderbuch* (*Children's Book*), originated as a gift for his friend Claus Bremer's son and consisted of twenty-eight 32 × 32 cm pages letterpress-printed with red, yellow, black, and blue circles and squares in a variety of arrangements and sizes. The spiral-bound book was produced in an edition of one hundred, twenty-five of which also had die-cut shapes, which would become a technique of great interest to him.

That playful spirit continues in the *schlitzbücher* (slot-books) he began work on in 1959. These collections of loose cardstock pages, each around fifteen inches square with a smaller central square of hand-cut slots varying in width and orientation, have an immediately cheeky quality. Rather than titling them, each *bok* was given a number or double-letter designation. Minimalist in aesthetic, they consist of ten to twenty-four leaves of cardstock in two or three colors (black and white, red and blue, red and green, blue and orange, and in one case, red, green, and blue) encased in a portfolio. When stacked and turned by the reader, they alternately reveal and conceal portions of the pages below, creating a variety of optical effects and transformations. The portfolio format, here as in Blake's illuminated prints, reminds us that our definition of the book cannot rely on formal qualities alone—a book's meaning arises through use and through the apparatus set up to shape our interpretation of it.

Because they are unbound, each leaf of the slot-books can be oriented four ways (not all are symmetrically centered) as well as flipped, offering eight possible orientations for each sheet—which in turn are influenced by the arrangement of the pages below. These interactive works play with our notions of the book by presenting us with a space that references text (that central cut-out area evoking a prose block with ample margins), but that only becomes legible through flipping—rather than moving our eye to scan these lines, we move the page to make meaning from it. Though we can examine and appreciate an individual sheet as a work of op art, we must, in fact, look *through* it for juxtaposition with the page below, much as a single page of text gathers significance through its place in a book's sequence. One such recombinant book has been remediated by generative artist The55 into a visual simulation that allows us to layer the pages to our heart's content,[73] illuminating the extent and variety possible in the work, which must be activated by a reader to generate meaning, since, after all, the pages contain no text.

The Book as Ephemeral

Some artists have taken the act of cutting up the book to its logical conclusion: destruction, or perhaps less critically, deconstruction. Whether deforming and sculpting the book object to create something new or simply documenting its decomposition, such books draw attention to the format's ephemerality. Much as we love books, archiving them in libraries for future generations and exhibiting them behind glass as art objects, they are a vulnerable medium. Not only are their physical forms (including the tablet, scroll, codex, and variations) susceptible to decay, their power to spread ideas makes them vulnerable to censorship, defacement, and destruction, particularly motivated by ideological and political difference.[74] Some artists' books embrace this impermanence, inviting us to meditate on our fears that books might go up in smoke.

The resurgence of artists' books in the 1960s is concurrent with the dematerialization of the work of art, a turn away from the gallery system, and a broad artistic interest in the viewer's participation, decentering the artist. Unlike Oulipo, whose constraints provide opportunities for creative bravado, the instruction-based works of Fluxus artists provide opportunities for critiques of genius and for increased attention to the viewer. In 1968, artist Bruce Nauman created a conceptual artist's book that epitomizes the concurrent sense of the book's utility and ephemerality. His *Burning Small Fires* consists of photographs documenting Nauman burning each page of Ruscha's *Various Small Fires and Milk*, which he pulled out of the volume and scattered on his studio floor. The glass of milk, however, he spared.

Offset-printed on a single, large foldout poster, the fifteen time-lapse photographs are tipped into a folio whose cover is printed in bright red on white paper, classic Ruscha colors, save a gradient of red ink at the fore-edge that suggests the titular fire licking its way out of its enclosure. The title's stacked red lettering evokes Ruscha's typography as well, but plays with it by using lowercase letters and staggering, rather than centering, the words. This alignment breaks each word across the folio's spine, creating a subtle dig when we realize the front cover reads "urning all ires," homophonically suggesting Nauman expected an angry reaction to his gesture. Little did he know he would earn not "ire" but adulation. Ruscha, flattered and amused, acquired several copies for his own collection.[75] Nauman's book follows through on the implicit burning of Ruscha's book by not only actualizing it but also revealing the insufficiency of the final image, that cooling glass of milk Ruscha serves up as a comic non sequitur to douse the preceding flames. There's a lovely ouroboros-like quality to the self-reflexive gesture of extinguishing Ruscha's fires by setting them. In 2003, Jonathan Monk would chase the tail with *Small Fires Burning*, a 16mm film in which he burned Nauman's book.

Chinese artist Cai Guo-Qiang was thinking about the explosive power of books when he created *Danger Book: Suicide Fireworks* (Ivory Press, 2006), a series of nine unique oversized fifty-page books on handmade paper that contain drawings of fireworks explosions and columns of smoke executed in gunpowder and glue. A bundle of matches precariously adhered to a striking strip inside the book near its spine extends a bit of string from between the closed volume's pages. This bookmark, when pulled, sets the dangerous book ablaze.[76] The artist's statement warns, "Be careful of books. Be careful with books. Be careful or one can become a weapon-wielder. Be careful or one can become the victim."[77] Books are, as biblioclasts well know, highly combustible in both material form and content.

In spite of its vulnerability to flame, insects, water, and sun damage, the codex is, in fact, a wonderful archival medium. It requires no software updates, can hold up in hot and cold climates, and, if printed and bound with quality acid-free materials, can withstand the oil of readers' hands, the jostling of being taken up and put back down, and numerous openings and closings that gradually break its spine. But the codex is vulnerable to both political and market forces. As ideologies shift, as data is updated, and as libraries become more cluttered, books are deaccessioned, sold, and in some cases thrown away. In 2013, the Libraries of Fisheries and Oceans Canada underwent a massive digitization process before closing seven of its eleven branches to reduce operating costs. The digitization was never completed, however, and stores of ecological research from the nineteenth century forward were simply sold to third parties, given away, or tossed in landfills.[78] Libraries throughout the United States have, for the last decade, focused spending on creating comfortable social and collaboration spaces, providing access to computers and the internet, and facilitating meetings and events. In many cases stacks get hidden underground or off-site, limiting what we can easily access. We can't save all information forever, and writers can't necessarily presume their work will last through the ages. While we might assume that digital books will have a longer shelf life than print, the proliferation of reading devices coupled with the pace of technological development virtually ensures the obsolescence of e-books tied to particular software or hardware. Ephemerality is thus a concern shared by physical and digital books.

Libraries' practice of selling and discarding books has directly fed an important current in contemporary book arts, since artists can get their hands on "unwanted" tomes extremely affordably. The twenty-first century has seen a surge of interest in altered books and book sculpture, facilitated by the overarching notion that the book

From scroll to bound folio, books have indeed evolved. And like all things subject to evolution, they can face extinction.

—GARRETT STEWART,
BOOKWORK: MEDIUM TO OBJECT TO CONCEPT TO ART

is an artifact not long for this world, something Renaissance authors like Shakespeare sensed with their repeated punning on tome and tomb.[79] Artist Brian Dettmer, who carves away at encyclopedias, dictionaries, and old hardbound volumes to create visual palimpsests, talks about his practice as one of liberating books rendered outmoded by the digital age. His carefully scalpeled sculptures treat the book as a body—Stewart refers to such works as "vivisections,"[80] since these books are not, in fact, as dead as their destroyers would like to believe. In *Bookworks*, a thoughtful study of de-mediated or unreadable books, Stewart attributes the volume of altered bookworks to a popular belief that the book's information storage and retrieval function has been absorbed by digital media. Sculptures like Dettmer's turn codex books from conveyors of information back into objects. They draw our attention to the ephemerality of the codex and treat the book as material, like clay or stone, to be used in new ways. Inherent in this gesture, however, is the viewer's knowledge that the book before us is now inaccessible. It is given and taken away at once, and we can't see it outside the system of communication in which it normally functions.

Books' ephemerality, volatility, and potential to "self-destruct" have been activated by many book artists, perhaps first in Marcel Duchamp's *Unhappy Readymade* (1919), a perverse wedding gift to his sister Suzanne and her husband Jean Crotti, sent to them on their honeymoon in Buenos Aires. His piece consisted of instructions to hang a geometry textbook from strings on their balcony where the elements could gradually wear away at it. Duchamp's title suggests the piece is itself unhappy—a book mourning its own loss. His intent, however, in asking Suzanne to participate in the creation of the work was not sadness, but humor: "It amused me to bring the idea of happy and unhappy into readymades, and then the rain, the wind, the pages flying, it was an amusing idea."[81] All that remains of the work, which has been lost like most of Duchamp's original readymades, is Suzanne's painting of it—a book that can truly never be read.

Dieter Roth took a comic perspective on books' ephemerality in his series *Literaturwurst* (*Literature Sausage*, 1961–1970), for which he pulped books and magazines he disliked and cured them, using spices, fat, gelatin, and water to fit Marx, Hegel, and German tabloids into new casings. We ought to remember that a hardback is also known as a *case binding* because the covers are constructed separately and the book block glued into this case. We also commonly store books on bookcases, once more commonly known as "presses," perhaps for the way they enclose and contain our ever-expanding libraries.[82] His "processing" of these texts puns on our "consumption" of literature as well as our desire to "preserve" it, which changes its form entirely by encasing and drying it out. The book on the archival shelf is inactive, heavy, desiccated, unlike the vivid copy in the reader's hands. While Roth's intent appears to be preservation, the joke's on the archivist: unless refrigerated, the shelf life of a dried sausage is approximately six weeks, according to the USDA, and many of the artist's works are thus highly unstable.

Roth was also, it seems, punning on his own name (he adopted the spelling Diter Rot when he moved to Iceland)—the work would, he knew, undoubtedly decompose. As he famously wrote in his work *Snow* (1964–1965), "Wait, later this will be nothing,"[83] a phrase that would apply equally well to his sculptures made of chocolate, birdseed, and rabbit feces—organic materials making a humble claim for art and the artist's impermanence. Roth even planned an unrealized series of poems printed on rolling paper to be smoked—an idea that also occurred to Chinese artist Xu Bing, who in 2000 created *Tobacco Project*, a series of artworks exploring tobacco's cultural, economic, and historic significance in North Carolina, China, and Virginia. It includes *Red Book,* a red metal case of Zhonghua-brand cigarettes with quotes from Mao Zedong's *Little Red Book* stamped on them; *Traveling Down the River*, a thirty-foot-long cigarette laid on top of a reproduction of a twelfth-century pictorial scroll and burned; and *Tobacco Book*, whose pages of compressed tobacco leaves were consumed by beetles during the exhibition.

We might equate altered and ephemeral books with recycling—giving old materials new life. Roth frequently reused all kinds of printed matter, creating books from cut-up pages of the London *Daily Mirror*, discarded Make Ready proofs collected from print shop floors, and pages of comic books with die-cut holes like bubbles popping to reveal the page below. Newsprint and Make Ready are two materials intended to be discarded. The newspaper is relevant today but superseded tomorrow by an entirely new set of news, hence its name. Make Ready, the sheets used in offset production to proof a print before running hundreds of copies, also has a short life span—it is a precursor to the *real* print, a kind of dress rehearsal for the page's final performance. Make Ready sheets can be recycled or used for other purposes in the print shop, but they are, by definition, not yet *ready* for consumption. In bringing them together, Roth highlights the book as a container for even the flimsiest of propositions and makes us think about the status of completion conferred by the act of binding as well as the illusion of permanence it lends its content.

Impermanence need not be read only through the lens of loss. For those altered bookmakers and writers engaged in the poetic process of erasure, systematically obscuring words from a source text in order to draw the reader's attention to alternative texts embedded within it, destruction is a generative impulse—one that reveals the potentiality inherent in any text. Treating the page as a grid of language, as Williams does in *Sweethearts*, artists and writers like Tom Phillips, Jen Bervin, and Mary Ruefle unearth new texts that in some cases comment upon, subvert, or renew the books in which they appear.

The Book as Mute Object

Some artists' books, however, purposefully offer the idea of the book without providing any reading material whatsoever. While many theorists consider such illegible objects "anti books" or book sculpture, separating them from the artist's book because of their refusal of access, such works remind us that the book is a concept we have imbued with cultural capital and importance by virtue of the resources spent on its production and the prestige associated with authorship. Our contemporary concerns over the death of the book are as bound up in fear of the death of the author or the loss of our intellectual heritage, which books have come to symbolize.

Pamela Paulsrud makes this anxiety palpable with her *Touchstones*, contemporary codices sanded down into smooth oblong agates, their covers and text revealing bands of color within. We touch such stones to remember, rather than read, just as we keep books on our shelves to remind us who we once were and what mattered to us, even if only to run our fingers along their spines. If a book can be explosive, these rocks feel less dangerous and more elemental. Paulsrud suggests even the silent book might provide an important foundation.

Lisa Kokin takes a more cynical perspective on the mute weight of books, turning them into stones to comment on the ways they weigh us down. In her series *Room for Improvement*, the artist pulps self-help books and sculpts them into papier-mâché balls, silencing their advice. While they look weighty, these objects are featherlight, ironically revealing these books, which profit off our desire for "improvement," in fact lack substance. In these balls we catch glimpses of text, headbands, sometimes fragments of titles, but as books they are worth nothing more than the paper and glue they were once made from.

While these artists use stones to draw our attention to the book's materials, others play with the mute page to draw our attention to text's own materiality. Cuban artist Reynier Leyva Novo's *5 Nights,* from his series "The Weight of History," transfers the entire content of "revolutionary texts that constituted the basis of totalitarian regimes in the twentieth century"[84] into solid rectangular "pages" of ink painted directly on the gallery wall in dimensions equivalent to the ink used in their printing. All we can read are the titles and attribution for works by Hitler, Lenin, Castro, Mao, and Gadhafi with heavy ink above them shimmering like the blue-green surface of an oil slick. Referencing the influence of the written word and the heavy hand of censorship, Novo's silent texts become imposing monolithic commentaries on the book's power.

Ann Hamilton reflects on this power as well, but suggests it might heal, rather than wound us in her 1994 work *lineament*. For the piece, a performer peels text out of hardbound books whose pages are scored boustrophedon-style, allowing line after line to be lifted away in a single strand like an orange peel. These she winds into balls that turn the flat plane of the book into a three-dimensional object, evoking Wallace Stevens's notion in "The Planet on the Table" that worthy poems contain "some lineament or character ... / Of the planet of which they were a part."[85] Lines of text with all their characters intact are wound into planets in Hamilton's hands. The work reveals the volumetric quality of an object we presume to be flat, as the emptied pages form a well and the text accretes into a ball. The performance itself also draws attention to the text as a body, exhumed from that well. Touching it gently, as with liniment, the performer passes each ball through an opening in a small hospital screen to arrive like a patient "on the table" in a new form.

Like Hamilton, Buzz Spector silences the page to draw our attention to the language we use to construct the idea of the book. His *A Passage*, created the same year as Hamilton's *lineament*, consists of a hardbound codex whose pages have been incrementally torn such that the flyleaf is nothing more than a deckled strip extending from the spine, the next page is perhaps a millimeter wider, and so on, each page a plateau extending beyond the one above it. With its cover open, the result is a sloping form our eye descends. This traversal reveals the structure of the page: its fully justified prose block, uniform margins, running title, and page number are so symmetrical they align across each torn edge. One is reminded of Carrión's comments on the utter sameness of the page in mass-produced books. Not only does taking the pages apart draw attention to the codex's careful design, it reveals that the same text has been printed on every sheet: page 181 of a book titled *A Passage*, containing a self-reflexive anecdote about a Jewish scholar who knew the Talmud so well he could identify the letter printed on the reverse of any other in the text.

While the scholar's mental map implies intensive study and intimacy, the viewer has no hope of achieving such familiarity. The movement of our eyes provides no passage, keeping us in the same place, even as the volume is spent. We become bleary-eyed students reading and rereading the same selection without comprehension. It seems telling that the text refers to Spector's series of torn books as "wedge shapes," linking the reduced text to both cuneiform writing and the doorstop.[86] Perhaps Spector's self-effacing (literally, the anecdote begins with a friend visiting the artist's studio) book suggests that while the codex is a helpful structure for the support and transport of ideas, it is also temporary and transitional like the passage of time itself.

Perhaps no book form has been so superseded as the encyclopedia. The first of its kind, Denis Diderot's seventeen-volume folio-size *Encyclopédie,* published in 1751, was a massive undertaking that employed a workforce of thousands, from writers to printers and binders. Diderot both contributed and enlisted the greatest minds of the French Enlightenment, including Rousseau and Voltaire, to provide the most current philosophy, science, culture, and mathematics to the masses. Perhaps most astonishingly, the Encyclopédie was both profitable and popular—so much so that quarto and octavo editions were introduced to ensure the book would be affordable to a broad readership. Over the course of the eighteenth century, it sold almost twenty-five thousand copies across Europe.[87] The encyclopedia was just as popular in the 1950s. A mainstay of the modern home, where bookshelves were proudly devoted to displaying the series of identically bound volumes, such sets now serve mostly as visual filler in furniture showrooms.

With the advent of digital encyclopedias on CD-ROM in the 1990s, and on the web shortly thereafter, the static codex with its periodic revisions and updates gave way to a malleable, living text. The devalued, decommissioned collections of knowledge often find their way into artists' altered books, perhaps most poignantly in Scott McCarney's book sculptures, in which large volumes hang open, their contents cascading out like a hypertextual waterfall of interconnected ideas. The volume itself becomes a literal *Hanging Index* (1992), as its title implies—with pages shredded to interwoven ribbons. McCarney comments directly on the deaccessioning of unpopular books by libraries in *Never Read* (1988), a sculpture composed of stacked library discards that narrows as it ascends. In his pointed pillar, the artist transforms the "never red" into its opposite—an evergreen. Sited in his garden, the sculpture provides bird nests in springtime, a vine trellis in summer, mouse holes in fall, and a snow-bedecked conifer in winter. Books, for such artists, are perennial spaces of transformation and possibility. Even when their content is not to be trusted, the power with which we imbue them is undeniable.

Muted books take on a totemic significance. Because we can't "read" a book object or book sculpture, we see the idea of the book, a metaphor that has penetrated our culture so deeply it informs the language we use to describe ourselves. Though we're taught not to "judge a book by its cover," an honest person is "an open book" and a perceptive one can "read us like a book," while we might emulate either by "taking a page out of their book." "Bookworms" metaphorically consume books' ideas the way their namesake (actually not a worm but a kind of beetle larva) consumes their pages. Such bibliophiles might find themselves "marginalized." And we each carry an inner moral tome we consult before passing judgment on others with the phrase "In my book …" We book a trip because such voyages were once entered into a volume, though now such records happen mostly online. Likewise our bookkeeper "balances the books" even when using accounting software like Quickbooks to manage our finances. When studying for an exam, we "pound the books" until we're expert enough to say we "wrote the book" on the subject. The book looms large in English idiom, standing in for the law ("throw the book at 'em"), history ("one for the books"), and social norms ("by the book").

The language of the book as a space of fixity, certainty, and order reminds us that the book has been transmuted into an idea and ideal based on the role it plays in culture. Books are bedrock, and the rectilinear form has allowed us to envision them as the foundation of social order and self-actualization. Easily arrayed on shelves as a sign of erudition, capability, or wealth, the codex's shape props us up not only metaphorically but also quite literally— for instance, when used to raise uneven furniture. It can, itself, serve as a kind of furnishing, offering as it does, a storage and filing system between its pages, in which we might press flowers, copy recipes, keep photographs, or compile clippings—habits of Renaissance readers that continue today.[88] The book props up its neighbors, too, as we learn pulling books off the shelf and watching the adjoining volumes topple. It can take us down as well, since it's portability makes it a handy projectile when the moment arises. Defining the book involves consideration for its use as much as its form. Our changing idea of the book is co-constitutive of its changing structure.

THE BOOK AS INTERFACE

Book artists and their predecessors have used the codex and any number of inventive book-like forms to draw our attention to the assumptions we make about the book's fixity, authority, materiality, and permanence. As we have seen in the preceding chapters, the book is an idea we have of a bounded text, issued into the world through the power of publication, and able to take any number of physical forms, dependent upon the needs of its content and its reader or the whims of its author. It is, essentially, an interface through which we encounter ideas. Its materiality need have no bearing on its content, yet whenever we hold a codex book, we are subconsciously drawing on a history of physical and embodied interaction that has taught us to recognize and manipulate it. The codex has achieved such popularity because it has proven useful as a portable, resource-efficient physical support suited to the average human body. Its design allows us to rest it on a surface or hold it aloft, to extend it about a foot or two from our faces and see text or image, or to run our fingers across its braille surface. We may insert a digit or bookmark between pages to hold onto a passage of interest while flipping elsewhere to consult another. We can annotate the margins to talk back to the author, to subsequent readers, or to our future selves. The book accommodates us, and we accommodate to it.

We encounter interfaces continually—on computers, cars, televisions, vending machines—and, like the print codex, we tend to notice them only when they misbehave. A good interface, according to human-centered design principles, is like Warde's crystal goblet: a transparent vessel through which we access the information we want. This invisibility may be marketed as utility, but it is not necessarily in our best interest. As media archeologist and scholar Lori Emerson writes, the drive to make interfaces invisible limits our ability to understand and change their inner workings, "definitively turning us into consumers rather than producers of content."[1] Digital reading devices, by and large, have taken this approach to providing access to literature, reference material, and millions of "volumes" through interfaces that aim to create a seamless reading experience built on the affordances of the codex and the behaviors we have adapted from it. From annotation and bookmarking to black text on creamy "pages," interfaces

In many ways, it is the book form—the *combination* of the ability to scroll with the capacity for random access, enabling you to leap from place to place—that has provided the model which these other cultural technologies now seek to emulate.

—PETER STALLYBRASS,
"BOOKS AND SCROLLS: NAVIGATING
THE BIBLE"

like that of the Kindle borrow a number of the physical book's structures, *remediating* them in the digital environment while flattening the codex to the dimensions of a thin wax tablet. We refer to works read on such devices as "electronic books" or "e-books," though there is little that is codex-like about their physical form. Such nomenclature is evidence of the extent to which the term *book* has come to signify "content" and of the role of the *pagina*, as Bonnie Mak has shown (see chapter 1), in defining the object in our imagination.

The potential of digital devices to serve as book interfaces has been present since the early days of portable computing. Alan Kay's 1972 vision of the Dynabook, one of the earliest laptop computers, established the idea of the notebook computer with a polyptych-like clamshell hinge and the capacity to contain volumes of digital content. Indeed many contemporary laptops are approximately the same dimensions as a quarto. The appendage of bookishness to our portable computing devices persists because the codex itself is an exemplary portable storage and retrieval technology. As Peter Stallybrass has noted, it allows both sequential reading and random access, much like the computer.[2] It can be indexed and cross-referenced in a way that directs us outward to other sources, though following the trail is slightly more time-consuming than clicking a hyperlink. The book is a model, as scholar

Matthew Kirschenbaum points out, for the way we think about reading in electronic space.[3]

The book-like qualities of the notebook computer helped drive the development of the earliest e-books. When Voyager—publisher of the Criterion Collection, whose laser discs included bonus materials alongside seminal films—received an early Apple PowerBook 100, a member of the team rotated the device, turning the laptop's hinge into a spine, and the idea to design books exclusively for the Apple device took shape.[4] Voyager had already experimented with multimedia publishing in 1989, when it released a CD-ROM companion to Beethoven's Ninth Symphony with an educational HyperCard stack. While they didn't expect readers to turn their laptops 90 degrees to read them, Voyager began publishing hypertexts called Expanded Books in 1992. Released on floppy disks and boxed in packaging reminiscent of paperbacks, they let readers track their progress through the text, bookmark pages with a virtual dog-ear, type in marginal notes, and search the work's contents. Those Expanded Books set the tone for the early stage of e-books and e-readers by remediating print and taking advantage of digital storage to add extras to the text, a trend that continues in "enhanced e-books," book apps that include ancillary features like performances by well-known actors and related archival material.

Such *remediation,* to use a term coined by Jay David Bolter and Richard Grusin, has historically played a role in the book's development.[5] As we have seen, the codex emulated the narrow columns of the scroll, early typefaces copied manuscript hands, and the design of the Penguin paperback revisited the golden ratio of the medieval manuscript page. Evidence suggests that Andalusian papermakers mimicked parchment by adding faint stretch marks and sizing their paper with wheat starch to improve its receptivity to ink.[6] One might even consider the columnar orientation of Chinese writing a reinscription of the technique of *jiance* scrolls. While these remediations echo what came before, they also fundamentally change both reading and writing through their altered material supports. For example, as Ong's work has made clear, the shift from oral performance to written text was a remediation that fundamentally changed the shape of literature, dispensing with formulaic language in favor of complex sentences and narratives that enriched rhetoric and, some argue, facilitated the rise of the novel.

This volume is not, however, about the novel, poetry, autobiography, or any literary genre. It is about the material text—the portable supports through which we read that we think of as "the book." These supports have changed in the forty-five hundred years since the cuneiform tablet, and will certainly continue to do so, given the rapid development of communication technologies. As we begin to consider the relationship of e-books to their predecessors, we might examine the book as what scholar N. Katherine Hayles calls a "material metaphor" through which we interface with language and which in turn alters how we can do so.[7]

As Hayles suggests, "To change the physical form of the artifact is not merely to change the act of reading ... but to profoundly transform the metaphoric relation of word to world."[8] Before considering contemporary e-readers, we need to explore the development of the e-book they support, which changed the relationship of word to world by turning text into data, fundamentally altering its portability. Text's digital life untethers it from any specific material support, making it accessible through a variety of interfaces (including the computer, cell phone, tablet, and dedicated e-reader), each of which influences our reading. We will also consider contemporary approaches to digital reading that, rather than offering up a crystal goblet, invite us to trace our finger along text's rim and make it sing: drawing attention to the interface to explore and exploit the affordances of the digital. This is not a narrative of progress or the seductive conceit of "the upgrade path," as new media theorist Terry Harpold calls it.[9] My intention is rather to draw attention to the ways these approaches shape and are shaped by the needs of twentieth- and twenty-first-century readers who will shape the book to come.

We are not generally accustomed to think of the book as a material metaphor, but in fact it is an artifact whose physical properties and historical usages structure our interactions with it in ways obvious and subtle.

—N. KATHERINE HAYLES,
WRITING MACHINES

Talking Books

Some might cite a far more common remediated book as the e-book's predecessor—audiobooks on cassette, CD, and now digital download. Historian Matthew Rubery contends that the medium emerged to both reproduce the printed book and repair its shortcomings.[10] Its trajectory is similar to that of e-readers and digitized books. While the spoken word had been part of sound recording from its inception, with Thomas Edison recording a recitation of "Mary Had a Little Lamb" on a foil cylinder in 1878, the recording and distribution of complete books in audio form was not possible until 1932, when engineers at the American Foundation for the Blind, recognizing the potential of recently patented long playing record technology, created what they called the Talking Book to serve visually impaired readers. Among their earliest recording tests were Helen Keller's autobiography *Midstream* (Doubleday, 1929) and Edgar Allen Poe's sonorous poem "The Raven" (1845). The first records produced were public domain texts like The Declaration of Independence, and the book of Psalms, some of Shakespeare's plays and poems, and fiction classics by P. G. Wodehouse, Lewis Carroll, Rudyard Kipling, and others, though the Foundation would soon see the need for access to contemporary works. With grants from the Carnegie Corporation and benefactor Ada Moore, the Foundation set about not only recording books themselves, but engineering a new material in which to fabricate them, vinylite, that would be flexible, light, and easy to ship. They even developed two playback phonographs, one electric and one spring-driven, to accommodate homes with and without electricity. While twelve-inch, $33\frac{1}{3}$ rpm records would not be available to the public until CBS released them in 1948, visually impaired listeners would enjoy the medium from its inception.

To satisfy the demands of publishers and authors that these free long-playing records, the first of their kind, not compete with published books, the Foundation had to agree that they would only be distributed to the blind, would be kept off the radio, and would not be played publicly. Contracts with the Author's Guild and National Association of Book Publishers enabled the Foundation to create royalty-free recordings, paying a flat $25-per-title fee to issue each work. Stipulations like these about copyright and the legality of remediating published books have dogged those who make and sell such works ever since. By 1934, The Foundation began loaning record players and LPs of its twenty-seven Talking Books to the blind, and in 1935, they were hired by the Library of Congress, through funding from the newly formed Works Progress Administration, to manufacture Talking Books and players on a scale that would accommodate tens of thousands of Americans.

Thanking President Roosevelt for setting the project in motion, Keller wrote, "With a stroke of the pen you have released the blessing of the talking-book---the most constructive aid to the blind since the invention of braille which opened to them the doors of education."[11] Though she had initially resisted Talking Books as frivolous when the were being developed during the Great Depression, Keller had come around to see their benefits not only in providing access to literature but also in creating jobs for those with vision loss. In a report about the program in 1937, Executive Director Robert B. Irwin boasted that "forty sightless citizens, taken off relief" were working alongside sighted workers to manufacture record players at the WPA workshop in New York City.[12] This was not a moneymaking enterprise, but one for the public good—by 1951, the Library of Congress was loaning its thirty thousand devices to listeners through fifty-four local agencies across the United States. The technology evolved during the 1950s and 1960s to include reel-to-reel tape, and cassettes emerged in the 1970s, bringing the recorded book to a booming market of suburban commuters and busy homemakers through commercial audiobook publishers. By 2000, the American Foundation for the Blind, like most other audiobook producers, had shifted to digital. In the 1980s, at the height of audiobooks' popularity, many worried that they heralded the death of the printed book, but as we have seen, the two formats continue to exist side by side, each meeting the needs of different situations and embodiments that affect how we access text.

This wasn't humankind's first exposure to reading aloud—from the 1920s onward radio plays and serials offered stories over the airwaves, but these were largely written for their medium. Of course, literature emerged from an oral tradition that included bards, troubadours, filid, meddahs, and griots, among other literary performers. Yet such tales, as we have seen, were composed on the fly using a series of mnemonic devices, not recorded verbatim as readings of defined text. With audiobooks, the recording exists—and circulates—independently of its speaker, much as the written word does. When we listen to the nearly thirty-six hours of George Eliot's *Middlemarch*, we feel confident saying that we have "read" the book. The Talking Book, as a forerunner of the audiobook, was the first systematic recording of existing literature in a new medium, and the problems it faced from publishers, authors, and the reading public presaged those of the digital projects that followed.

Digital Affordances

A number of seminal projects have attempted to reconceptualize the book through different media, in each case updating the interface through which we encounter it based on new developments. Each offers some useful ways of thinking through how our metaphor can adapt to different materials. As anyone who has read a digital book can tell you, digitization facilitates many of the affordances already inherent in print. The codex is a storage and retrieval mechanism. A digital device can store vast quantities of books for retrieval. Books can be indexed and translated, and concordances of terms can be made to facilitate research. Digital books make this much less labor intensive, since the text is already data. Books might use notes to direct the reader to additional sources or intertextual references to allude to a network of texts that have informed their composition. Likewise digital hyperlinks can take us directly to those sources. As we saw in chapter 3, both physical and digital books can be interactive multimedia experiences, though our embodied experience of that interactivity will vary from device to device and person to person.

The earliest digital reading device, and perhaps the one that laid the foundation for the possibilities of digital books, was conceived in 1945, in the early days of computing, by Vannevar Bush, director of the Office of Scientific Research and Development. Having helped develop nuclear weapons for the military during the Second World War, Bush sought a more beneficent postwar role in which he might facilitate connection rather than destruction. Though never constructed, the Memex, described in Bush's oft-cited essay "As We May Think," envisioned a research device for retrieving and cross-referencing large collections of material. His desire to chart the connections between scholarly works via the researcher's own network of references prefigures the Google Books initiative and our own reliance on bookmark history and textual metadata.

The hypothetical Memex would be a desk equipped with rear-projection screens on which a researcher might examine books, magazines, photographs, or other media stored on microfilm (see figure 15). This device would be accompanied by an electronic "supersecretary" to take dictation, and a pair of microcamera-embedded glasses to facilitate data collection in the field. Already in 1945, Bush foresaw the coming of information saturation: "There is a growing mountain of research. ... The investigator is staggered by the findings and conclusions of thousands of other workers—conclusions which he cannot find time to grasp, much less to remember, as they appear."[13] The Memex would enable researchers to apply keywords to content (like the metadata with which we are familiar today), thereby connecting items by association. The network thus created, he imagined, would be of greater use than any library or catalog because data would be organized intelligently and could even include explanatory annotations made by the researcher on-screen. The Memex was never built, but adding metadata to book entries has become a key component of library science since digital

Figure 15 Vannevar Bush's Memex as illustrated by Alfred D. Crimi for *Life Magazine* (1945). Image used with grateful permission of Joan Adria D'Amico.

finding aids replaced card catalogs. In addition, individual researchers can now organize information based on self-defined keywords using numerous information-gathering and tagging tools on their personal computers.

Bush's prognostications are most often cited as an early vision of the internet, but the interface he chose for it is a telling one—that of a scholar's desk with multiple books open for simultaneous consultation. While the Memex is a bit more cumbersome than today's e-readers, as a remediation of the book through photographic reproduction it is a precursor to today's book scanning initiatives

A book is a knot.

—DIETER ROTH,
246 LITTLE CLOUDS

and, of course, to the desktop that is our primary metaphor for the computer's graphical user interface (for the time being). Scholars haven't changed much since the Renaissance, when they commissioned revolving lecterns and lazy Susan–like desks for their libraries to help them consult several texts at once (a practice that facilitated keeping one's commonplace book). Such wheels may originate in sixth-century China, where they were used in Buddhist temples to collate scripture.[14] The demand for a multivolume reading interface led one ingenious inventor, Agostino Ramelli, to design a wheel (also likely never built) with twelve angled shelves on which open codices could be arrayed, each brought before the reader's eyes with a gentle spin so one never had to leave one's chair or lose one's place (see figure 16). With the advent of digital media, the number of books a reader might access simultaneously would, of course, multiply, carried by the revolving wheel of the network.

Project Gutenberg (E-texts and E-books)

The first attempt to create a digital online library occurred on July 4, 1971, when student Michael S. Hart (1947–2011) typed up The Declaration of Independence, intending to send the 5K text file to all one hundred users on the University of Illinois computer network. Dissuaded from

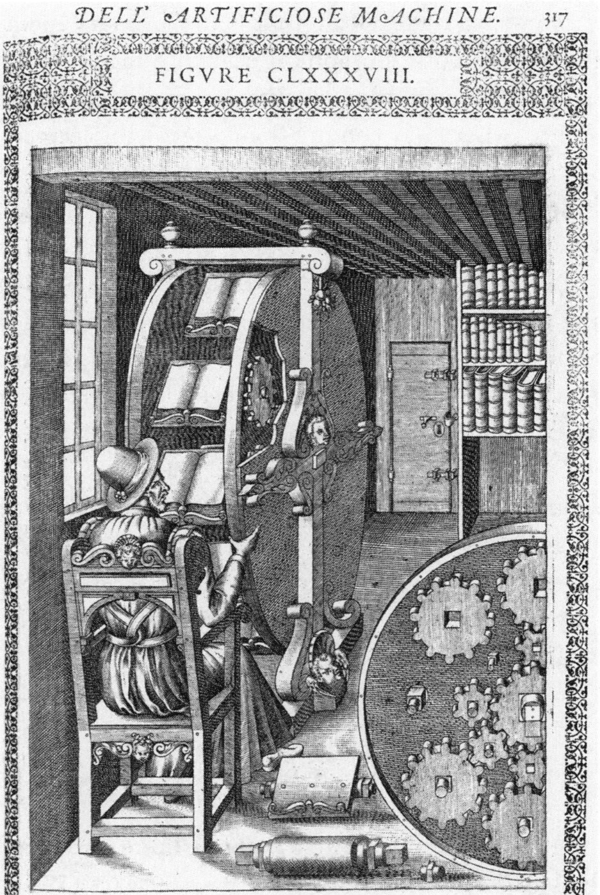

Figure 16 A bookwheel designed by Italian Engineer Agostino Ramelli, which appears under the title "Aux benins lecteurs" in his volume *Le Diverse et Artificiose Machine del Capitano Agostino Ramelli* (Paris: In casa del'autore, 1588).

doing so because the file would have crashed it, he instead sent out the directory address to the server on which the file was stored, and six people proceeded to download it. Hart, who had been granted $100 million worth of computer time, thanks, in part, to his friendship with the operators of the campus Xerox Sigma V mainframe, needed to find some way to use those resources. Rather than processing information, he saw the potential of computers for storage and retrieval as their true benefit.[15] Typing up texts like America's founding documents and other public domain books, he reasoned, would be a boon to libraries, enabling a single instance of a text to be shared simultaneously by readers all over the world. Inspired by the progenitor credited with making book replication possible, he called the initiative Project Gutenberg and proceeded to digitize, eventually with the help of volunteers, as much public domain literature as possible. As of this writing, Project Gutenberg has accumulated "over 54,000 free e-books,"[16] including "the world's great literature ... especially older works for which copyright has expired," reminding us that these books have attained "great" status through the vetting, intervention, and prestige conferred by print publishing and scholarship. This mission statement also, in a sense, reminds readers that though we encounter them in digital form, these books were once ensconced between covers, many of which can be previewed as JPG images on the site.

Because Project Gutenberg was founded to make books as accessible as possible, Hart and his collaborators prioritized sharing these e-texts in "Plain Vanilla ASCII," eschewing stylization for broad legibility as well as easy file storage.[17] Unlike Gutenberg with his metal type and attention to the dimensions of the page, the Project Gutenberg philosophy treats text as liquid that can reflow into the reader's mediating vessel of choice and encourages those readers looking to replicate print to use the e-text to generate these other forms. The digitization process, however, generally begins with scanning each page of a book and running *optical character recognition* (OCR) to generate a preliminary text for proofreading.

By reducing text to its bare minimum, Project Gutenberg intends to make these books searchable, indexable, and as archivable as possible, independent of changes to software and hardware over time. In an essay touting e-texts as "The Next Killer App," Hart suggested that they surpass print with their liquidity: "eTexts are never checked out when you need them, never in for rebinding, never sitting on a cart waiting to be reshelved or reshelved in the wrong location. Their pages are never missing—they are never lost or stolen—and the library is never closed."[18] While some might argue with his privileging of content over form, his perspective was forward-thinking in that this distribution format, with copies of the same text stored simultaneously on multiple servers and with volunteers actively correcting, translating, and generating additional texts, has significant long-term capacity. The site has since expanded to include free audiobooks recorded by volunteers and computer text-to-speech systems, improving accessibility, as well as cross-platform CD and DVD images containing e-book collections for download.

The Internet Archive

Several important digitization initiatives followed Hart's, born from a sense that the internet represents the future of libraries, and that digitizing text is a means of doing a public good. The Internet Archive, founded by MIT graduate Brewster Kahle in 1996 to archive the ephemeral pages of the World Wide Web, would seem to be far removed from the world of books. Best known for "The Wayback Machine," an interface that allows visitors to see earlier versions of any website that has been indexed—like a snapshot of the site from a previous year—the Internet Archive has, over time, become a clearinghouse of media, including film, audio, text, software, and magazines, with the goal of offering permanent future access to this work in digital format. The experience of archiving the unstable and boundless Internet gave the project's founders a fresh perspective on digitizing the book and, despite the company's digital origins, in 2005 the Internet Archive began scanning library books for posterity. Originally a partnership with Microsoft, which provided sophisticated scanners and data storage in the first three years of the project, the Internet Archive extended its digitization tools to public and private libraries worldwide in 2008 with the intent of archiving a single scanned copy of every book ever published.

This initiative was not simply an attempt to gobble up and digitize all printed matter—the team approached these artifacts with care. The Archive's Scribe book scanning system, designed by engineer Tom McCarty, uses a cradle and camera setup that has since become common. While previous methods involved slicing off a book's binding to facilitate auto-feed of its pages through a scanner (a technique some still use to save time), this approach preserves the codex. The resulting JP2000 images are provided on the website along with a PDF and a web-accessible version of the book with searchable content. In addition to out-of-copyright works, the Internet Archive's Open Library initiative aims to create a web-based finding aid for every book ever written, including a scan, if available. Open Library expands the Archive's offerings through a partnership with over one thousand international libraries that allows patrons to borrow scans of in-copyright works and contemporary e-books in those libraries' holdings.[19] Like their physical counterparts, only one patron can use a given e-book at a time, thus preventing copyright infringement while vastly expanding the number of texts to which readers have easy access.

The Internet Archive now runs more than twenty-eight scanning centers across the globe where libraries and other institutions pay nominal fees to have their collections scanned at a rate of one thousand books per day.[20] As of this writing, it has archived more than three million books online (that number goes up to eleven million counting e-texts). And in 2010, the Archive released over one million documents digitized in DAISY (Digital Accessible Information System), a special format that makes text accessible to readers with print disabilities, who can not only hear the text, but bookmark, search, and control its playback. Not only did the Archive prioritize not destroying the books they scanned, the process of handling so many, coupled with the constraints of copyright, led it to take the surprising step in 2011 of starting a physical archive for them. Seeing that libraries often did not want physical books returned or were storing them off-site because they were not in demand, and recognizing that holding a physical copy of each scanned book entitled the Archive to share the digital one, they initiated what Kahle called a "Physical Archive of the Internet Archive," housed in forty-foot climate-controlled shipping containers in Richmond, California, to maintain the books, records, and movies in their digital archive.[21]

This would be a Wayback Machine of an entirely different kind. The initiative is modeled on the Svalbard Global Seed Vault, which provides long-term storage of crop seeds from around the world in a bunker nestled into the permafrost of the Norwegian archipelago to ensure crop diversity in the event of a natural or human-made disaster. The Internet Archive's intentions are only slightly more modest—to provide copies for cross-reference with their digital editions, to rescue volumes being deaccessioned by libraries due to digitization, and to ensure long-term stable storage of these materials that will likely outlast the hard disks on which their digital copies are stored, which must be refreshed every three to five years. As an added precaution, the Internet Archive is backed up at the Bibliotheca Alexandrina, the modern Egyptian Library of Alexandria that opened to the public in 2002. Facing growing concerns about the stability and openness of the American Internet after the 2016 election, Kahle announced in 2017 that the Internet Archive would raise funds to create a backup in Canada as well.[22]

So committed is the Internet Archive to making books widely available that in 2002 the organization built a bookmobile, which, rather than carting books to neighborhoods without brick-and-mortar libraries, brought laptops, a satellite IP connection, a color laser and inkjet printer, a perfect binder, and a guillotine cutter on the road to help readers print and bind their own free copies of public

The book will not become obsolete with new reading platforms, but rather, will change and develop new incarnations and readerships; it will continue to serve certain kinds of literacy needs and literary desires— specifically, those related to its book-bound physicality and potentiality.

domain books.[23] The bookmobile's journey from Menlo Park to Washington, DC, was intended to raise awareness about the Supreme Court decision *Eldred v. Ashcroft* (2003), which would address the constitutionality of the 1998 Sonny Bono Copyright Term Extension Act (CTEA). While the decision upheld the CTEA and prevented many works from entering the public domain, the project successfully piloted a DIY book printing program for libraries and public schools at a cost of around $1.50 to $2.00 in materials for a 240-page book. It also paved the way for *print-on-demand* (POD) publishing and the Espresso Book Machine, an all-in-one paperback printer, binder, and point of sale released in 2007 and available at select American and international bookstores and libraries.

Google Books

One more large-scale book scanning project must be mentioned in this context, since it belongs to one of the biggest corporations of our time—Google. In 2004 at the Frankfurt Book Fair where, 550 years earlier, Gutenberg's 1,282-page Bible had debuted, the company announced Google Print, an initiative to add book contents to its search results. In partnership with major publishers, it would offer readers a preview of a given book with page limits and copy protection to preserve publisher and author rights. It would allow readers to discover books and search within them to find "snippets" pertinent to their research, and it would give them links to buy the book or find it in a local library. The project seemed part and parcel of Google's overarching intent "to organize the world's information and make it universally accessible and useful."[24] In 2007, Jeffrey Toobin estimated in a *New Yorker* article that scanning all the world's books, or at least the 32 million then in WorldCat's database, would cost the company around $800 million, a cost few institutions could afford.

The corporation soon expanded its scanning to include the Google Print Library Project, which would add over fifteen million volumes in the collections of Harvard, the New York Public Library, Oxford, Stanford, and the University of Michigan, marking an important contribution to the digital distribution of public domain works and archival material. Google had actually been working with Michigan since 2002, developing the project as a gift to co-founder Larry Page's alma mater. The Library Project would be free to partners, who would receive e-books of their entire collections. These initiatives became Google Books in 2005, and the project has gone on to digitally archive more than twenty-five million books, both in and out of copyright.[25] Public domain works account for only around 7 percent of available books, with the emphasis on copyright-protected works, available in small samples, whose accessibility is dictated by publishers through the so-called Partner Program. The Google Books interface lets readers save books to a virtual "bookshelf," share excerpts, and download EPUB and PDF files of public domain works.

Though Google Books launched in 2004, the corporation's self-narrative places digital books at the company's inception. Back in 1996, while still in graduate school at Stanford, co-founders Page and Sergey Brin developed a web crawler called BackRub intended to analyze connections between books and help readers find the most relevant materials for their research. Part of the Stanford Digital Library Technologies Project, this crawler would provide the foundation for Google's PageRank algorithm, pricking out the page for the Alphabet of Google initiatives to come. Google began researching book scanning in 2002 under the codename "Project Ocean,"[26] inspired in part by Project Gutenberg and the Internet Archive, among other mass digitization programs. It is worth acknowledging that Google hasn't tried to corner the market on digitization and has supported others, for example, by making its scanner technology open-source and by donating $3 million to the Library of Congress toward its World Digital Library, which makes scans of multilingual primary materials from around the world available freely online.

Google's book scanning process is a far cry from both Michael S. Hart typing The Declaration of Independence one letter at a time into a terminal and Internet Archive volunteers carefully photographing each page of a tome with the Scribe camera. The project began manually in 2002, with Page and Marissa Mayer, a vice president at the company in charge of books, timing the duration it took to flip through a three-hundred-page volume and determining they would need to improve scanning technology to reduce the forty minutes to a more manageable time frame.[27] By 2015, that figure had jumped to six thousand pages an hour thanks to Google's proprietary technology, which uses a motorized cradle, four cameras, a foot-pedal trigger, and software that compensates for the curvature of the page. Most of Google's public scans focus on the text itself and are compressed to grayscale images to reduce file size and optimize OCR. They are also watermarked in the lower-right corner with the phrase "Digitized by Google" for scanned works and "Copyrighted material" for Partner works. Incidentally, the term *watermark* itself originates in papermaking as a design, visible when a page is held up to the light, that identifies its manufacturer.

Although it is high-tech, the scanning process at Google is not fully automated, since the variety of shapes, sizes, and archival states necessitates careful treatment of the library books with which the corporation has been entrusted. These include untrimmed volumes from Oxford's Bodleian Library, whose folded leaves have to be slit before scanning, and other rare books whose contents would otherwise be available only to a coterie of scholars with time and access. Because the hand cannot be fully removed from the scanning process, it leaves its traces on the page, as artist Andrew Norman Wilson discovered while working for Google in 2008. Wilson, on contract as a documentary filmmaker for the company, noticed a group of workers on the Mountain View campus who were isolated from the rest of the company's employees. They received none of the perks enjoyed by other staffers (like free shuttles to work and access to cafeterias, bikes, and massages), and were relegated to a single building from which they exited en masse at 2:15 p.m. each day. Curious about the caste system to which these workers, predominantly people of color, were subject, he proceeded to shoot an homage to Auguste and Louis Lumière's first film, *Sortie des Usines Lumière à Lyon* (*Workers Leaving the Lumière Factory*, 1895), recording their departure and then trying to interview them. Though this intervention got him fired, Wilson released his film, *Workers Leaving the GooglePlex*, in 2011 and has published images found among Google's books that include the hands or fingers of these invisible scanners— a reminder of the relationship between the manual and the digital. A number of artists have made collections of similar errors that draw attention to the scanning process, reminding readers that the text is not liquid pixels, in spite of our displays, but a deeply mediated image of a physical object.

Like the American Foundation for the Blind, Google faced significant resistance to its scanning initiative when

Books don't simply mediate a meeting of minds between reader and author. They also broker (or buffer) relationships among the bodies of successive and simultaneous readers—or even between one person who holds the book and others before whose gaze, or over whose dead body, she turns its pages.

—LEAH PRICE,
*HOW TO DO THINGS WITH BOOKS
IN VICTORIAN BRITAIN*

the Author's Guild and several major publishers—all of whom are partners in the Google Books project—filed suit in 2005 for copyright infringement. While they took no umbrage with Google's scanning of public domain works or helping publishers sell copyright works in print, they argued that the library project, which scans numerous copyright—but out-of-print—works, was illegal, and that Google needed to pay royalties for these books. While Google cited its digitization as fair use because it transforms its sources, offering readers the ability to search within texts but not read them in their entirety, the situation is complicated because this transformation happens not at the level of the text, like an author quoting a source or a DJ building a track out of samples, but at the level of the code. In 2015, after a prolonged series of lawsuits, a Second Circuit court sided in Google's favor, ruling its snippets of out-of-print copyright works (known as *orphan books*) legal. The judge in the case, Pierre Leval, who played a critical role in establishing fair use doctrine in 1990, determined: "Google's unauthorized digitizing of copyright-protected works, creation of a search functionality, and display of snippets from those works are noninfringing fair uses. The purpose of the copying is highly transformative, the public display of text is limited, and the revelations do not provide a significant market substitute for the protected aspects of the originals."[28]

Each of these three initiatives, Project Gutenberg, the Internet Archive, and Google Books, views its massive digitization effort as a public good, but their approaches to the book itself differ in important ways. Project Gutenberg's focus on ASCII renderings of public domain works aims to make the text as accessible and fluid as possible, ignoring its former materiality. This aligns it with Google, which also emphasizes text in the interest of indexing, searchability, and easy access. Offering images of the text at a reduced file size, it reminds us that the book is an object, but deemphasizes its particulars—the ultimate goal of Google's book scanning initiative remains fattening its search engine. The Internet Archive has it both ways—it treats the book as an object, providing high-resolution color scans that show the nuances of the page's surface and include foldout images and marginalia to replicate the book as closely as possible, but it also makes the same book available in multiple digital formats to meet the needs of different readers. With high-resolution scans for download or online use, EPUBs for use with e-readers, and DAISY talking-book format for the visually impaired, the Internet Archive is committed to serving as a digital public library. It has even incorporated more than 1.2 million volumes from Google Books[29] into its collection with the help of super-users who download and upload them to the site (behavior Google's legal disclaimer discourages).[30]

E-readers

Such scanned and digitized books, as well as the e-book editions of popular works by major publishers, are remediations of print, whose content can be accessed across multiple devices depending on their format, whether PDF, EPUB, MOBI, TXT, HTML, or Apple's proprietary iBAC (iBooks Author). The use of the term e-book to apply to digital content read on screens blurs the boundary between content and form, much as our use of the word "book" to refer to both a specific object and a general idea allows one to be subsumed by the other. The very existence of such digital books, however, precisely because they allow content to be poured into any crystal goblet available, gave rise in the 1990s and 2000s to e-readers—dedicated devices designed specifically for book reading. Technological innovations in microprocessing, solid state drives, and *E Ink* have all facilitated the development of portable, handheld computers with an immense capacity for storage of not only text, but also audio, video, and, in some cases, interactive animation. Such machines had been imagined as early as Bob Brown's readies and Vannevar Bush's Memex, but the design of those two early projects imagines stationary devices that lack the portability for which the book was originally developed. The Amazon Kindle, launched in 2007, is one of the most popular dedicated e-readers precisely because the single, paperback-sized device, with its high-resolution E Ink screen, can store thousands of books, allowing readers to take an entire library with them on the go.

Ideas for portable digital readers precede contemporary devices as well. One of the earliest was that of Galician schoolteacher Ángela Ruiz Robles, who patented a mechanical book in 1949 that would use electricity and compressed air to create an illuminated interactive page. While the project was never realized, Robles continued to develop the idea, patenting and prototyping her *Enciclopedia Mecánica* (*Mechanical Encyclopedia*), its successor, in 1962 to condense the number of textbooks young students would have to carry.[31] In 1985, Texas Instruments filed a patent for a device developed for the US Department of Defense that housed a portable electronic maintenance manual in a briefcase. Neither of these resembles current e-readers, in part because they lack the truly handheld size necessary for such a gadget to catch on.

The first e-readers to be mass-produced were, like the cuneiform tablet, quite small. Franklin Electronics, which had put out a compact digital spelling checker in 1985, issued the Bible on a pocket-sized device called the Bookman in 1989. Its small, rectangular screen displayed three lines of text at a time, which the reader navigated with a QWERTY keyboard and directional arrows. Readers could swap out reference works using a cartridge slot on the back of the device, making it truly a handheld library (see figure 17). Sony followed suit, releasing its Data Discman in 1990—a PDA-like reader aimed at students, whose high price at the time prevented it from reaching a wide audience. The Palm Pilot, appearing in 1996, would usher in the age of smartphones, increasing the prevalence of multipurpose digital devices for reading text.

These early devices had small, low-resolution screens and rather minimal design, their flat gray cases echoing laptops and calculators of the era. There were, however, a few e-readers whose physical forms were more attuned to the reader's hand. While they shared other early e-readers' disregard for the typography and page design central to the development of the codex, they used their materiality to hearken back to some of its earlier affordances. In 1992, Italian architectural students Franco Crugnola and Isabella Rigamonti prototyped a floppy disc e-reader called Incipit, which emulated a scroll unrolled in both hands, its thick curved sides surrounding a screen with the dimensions of a paperback book. Buttons positioned beneath the reader's thumbs would allow one to progress from page to page, and a keyboard at the bottom of the screen offered numeric buttons and playback keys.[32] The NuvoMedia Rocket eBook and the SoftBook, both released in 1998 and considered the first e-readers dedicated to emulating the physical book, are notable for their handedness—each rectangular device has one thicker, rounded side that evokes the curved spine of a paperback whose front cover

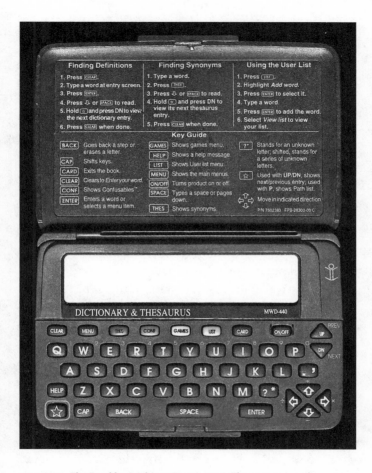

Figure 17 The Franklin Bookman Dictionary & Thesaurus, an early e-reader. Collection of the author.

has been curled in the reader's hand. The SoftBook even included a soft leather cover that turned the device on and off, boasting, "Just like a book, the SoftBook becomes 'ready to read' by simply opening the leather cover."[33] These simulations attempt to naturalize the e-reader's single-page display—a fundamental difference from the codex's "sequence of spaces" or openings. The design makes every page in these readers a recto (or verso, in the case of the Rocket, which adapts to either hand), awkwardly drawing attention to the interface it is trying to hide. If we were to bend back the cover of a paperback in that way, then the thick spine would pass from hand to hand as we turned the pages, or we would open the spread to read each verso before folding the cover back again.

Such affordances are not merely familiar but also useful. Curling the cover helps us grip and balance a paperback in one hand, which is especially important to readers on the go, a trait shared by users of both paperbacks and e-books. While these ergonomics disappeared from the next wave of e-readers, Amazon has returned them to its 2016 Kindle Oasis, whose case features a slightly thicker back along one side and corresponding buttons on the front, like the Rocket's, that can be used to turn the page with one's thumb in lieu of tapping the screen. Embracing readers' handedness, the device uses an accelerometer to rotate the page onscreen depending upon its orientation, allowing the virtual spine to be held in either hand, an update that adapts to the reader and the affordances of the digital.

A number of e-readers appeared in the late 1990s and early 2000s, but none really made an appreciable impact on the book market until the Kindle (see figure 18). This lightweight tablet, with its six-inch plain text E Ink screen framed by buttons for scrolling, page-turning, and text entry sold out within six hours of its 2007 release. Carrying a wide range of titles sold by Amazon, the device's chief drawback was its proprietary digital rights management system, which prevents readers from moving titles between devices. The year 2007 also saw the release of Apple's iPhone, which introduced portable touchscreen computers to a mass market. The smartphone paved the way for the iPad two years later, which would set the standard for color tablets that double as e-readers, loading books in a variety of formats. Kindle, Kobo, Nook, and other e-book sellers in turn have issued iOS apps to keep their readers in the fold while using Apple devices, reinforcing the book as content and commodity and the reader as its consumer (see figure 18). The Kindle Fire (2011), with its color touchscreen, brought Amazon more directly in competition with Apple, since it allows readers access to all their Amazon content (across books, music, and video) in the cloud. The major e-readers have by now incorporated Wi-Fi, and in some cases 3G and Bluetooth to compete with the iPad.

a. b.

c. d.

Figure 18   (a) Barnes and Noble's Nook Glowlight, 6.5" × 5.0" × 0.42" (2013), from Barnes & Noble, https://www.barnesandnoble.com/h/nook/media-kits; (b) Rakuten's Kobo Glo HD, 6.18" × 4.5" × 0.4". (2015), courtesy Rakuten Kobo Inc., http://news.kobo.com/media-library; (c) Amazon's Kindle Oasis, 5.6" × 4.8" × 0.13–0.33" (2016) from Amazon, http://phx .corporate-ir.net/phoenix.zhtml?c=176060&p=irol-imageproduct52; (d) Apple's iPad Pro, 9.4" × 6.6" × 0.29" (2017), courtesy Frmorrison at English Wikipedia, https://commons.wikimedia.org/wiki/File:IPad_2017 _tablet.jpg.

As e-readers proliferate, their features continue to remediate those that developed with the print codex. Lightweight and portable, with nonreflective grayscale E Ink screens, e-readers have dimensions that approximate a thin paperback. Most enable highlighting and annotation, simulate both page-turning and virtual bookmarking, and hold one's place, a necessary feature since they treat text as liquid, and thus pagination can alter from one device to another and depending on one's chosen font size. The Onyx company's Boox line, built on the Android operating system, adds audio recording and stylus-based annotation to the standard e-reader features—the former drawing on a unique affordance of digital media and the latter facilitating a more familiar note-taking experience. E Ink itself, developed at MIT in the late 1990s, proved pivotal to the development of e-readers, providing a paper-like surface that can display text without requiring internal illumination. The technology uses an electric charge to reconfigure black-and-white microparticles on the screen, an energy-efficient, high-contrast approach to rendering legible text that has become the industry standard.

The design of such readers has gradually streamlined to minimize buttons and dials, heightening the sense that they are simply interfaces for engaging with text and perpetuating the myth of digital disembodiment. They let readers change type size and typeface, illuminate the screen in low light, and, on some devices, use built-in text-to-speech functions to play their books aloud. These accessibility features mark an important distinction from the fixed interface of print and would not be possible without digitization. Not only can such devices carry thousands of titles, they last weeks between chargings, and in some cases provide waterproofing for those who want to read in the tub or at the beach. Like those cheap Victorian books that were instrumental in the shift toward thinking of the book as content rather than object, e-readers dispense with design for the most part, and some even include advertisements to capture more of their captive audience's dollars.

E-books remain tremendously popular, though in 2016, sales dropped in both the United States and the United Kingdom.[34] Some attribute the drop to "digital fatigue," while others argue Amazon's pricing influences whether consumers opt for a paperback, hardcover, or e-book. Despite their popularity, print book sales in the United States actually rose 3.3 percent over the preceding year. The breakdown is telling: hardcovers were up 5.4 percent; trade paperbacks, 4 percent; and children's board books, 7.4 percent. Parents, apparently, see the benefit of these tactile objects for learning and developing motor skills.[35] The categories currently slipping, mass market paperbacks and audio on CD and cassette, see direct competition from digital downloads because they are somewhat form-agnostic and don't provide much in the way of a material experience.

Bookish Paratexts

The e-book market, however, is not merely the purview of major publishers. Self-published authors can upload and distribute their work through a number of e-book stores that serve these devices, in many cases earning significant value for their labor. Given that anyone can become an author thanks to Amazon, it bears considering how we might differentiate between a digital file on a home computer and a "book." The document on the computer consists of text that can be treated as content and read on-screen, pasted into an email, posted to a discussion board, or printed. But is it a book? Even if we have a capacious definition of the term—one that can include both Alison Knowles's *The Big Book* and Aldine editions—most of us would answer no. Perhaps for this reason, when someone introduces themself as a writer, the first question most people ask is "Have you published anything?"

The act of publication—of making public—is central to our cultural definition of the book. Publication might presume cultural capital: some editorial body has deemed this work worthy of print. It might also presume an audience: a readership clamors for this text. But on a fundamental

It can be contended that the running paratext *defines the book itself* and as such, experiments are not trivial. The paratext point of view, rather than intellectual scope, narrative flow, character portrayal, literary grace, logic of plot, magical insight or a thousand other characteristics of bookish achievement, makes the book a book.

—GARY FROST,
FUTURE OF THE BOOK: A WAY FORWARD

level, publication presumes the appendage of a number of elements outside the text that help us recognize it as a book, even when published in digital form. Book historian Gérard Genette coined the term "paratexts" to refer to these framing devices, including the title page, index, running heads, covers, and other features outside the text that influence the ways we interface with it.[36] As we have seen, these elements arose as the readership of books shifted from monasteries to universities, in response to the need to use books differently—not for prayer or performance, but for argumentation and dialogue.[37] Book conservator and book art educator Gary Frost considers these appurtenances the true measure that "makes the book a book," since they help us see it as one.[38] Given that these extratextual supports arose partly in response to the changing needs of a reading public and the changing materiality of the book itself, it stands to reason that the contemporary book would also respond to current usage and expectation.

A good example of the way such *paratexts* might adapt to e-readers is the ISBN, or International Standard Book Number, a unique number that facilitates a book's sale and distribution. Developed in Britain in 1966 to standardize tracking, the ISBN is a complex code that includes information about a book's country of origin, publisher, and title/edition (multiple editions and bindings of the same title each require a different ISBN). Each cluster of digits in the original ten-digit number (the thirteen-digit ISBN arose in 2007, in response to the dwindling number of available ten-digit codes) provides part of this picture, and a final digit (or the letter x standing in for the number 10) serves as a check to ensure the code is valid.[39] The ISBN was initiated in the United States in 1967, though its gradual adoption was not complete until 1979. The addition of a scannable bar code in 1986 simplified book tracking and changed the face (or rather back) of books forever; the machine-readable European Article Number (EAN) code has been conventionalized to such a degree since its adoption that we instinctively see it as a kind of colophon.

The ISBN developed to help manage the vast quantity of books being produced and to catalog them in a central database, which enables them to be bought and sold through distributors and bookshops. Authors and publishers pay for the privilege of entering this database, and the ISBNs are issued by different agencies around the world and at different rates. In the United States, R. R. Bowker has the exclusive right to sell ISBN numbers to authors and publishers, using a cost structure based on volume. While a single ISBN will set buyers back $125, a package of ten costs $295 and one thousand drops the cost to only $1.50 per unit. This situation benefits major publishing houses, which put out hundreds of books each year, but the cost can seem prohibitive to authors seeking to self-publish their work. While most bookstores and distributors require them, and while Bowker touts the "bibliographic immortality" their codes confer,[40] e-book stores, including Amazon, Google Play, Kobo, and others, have dispensed with the ISBN, since their books are tracked digitally already. In 2016, 43 percent of e-book sales went to books lacking an ISBN,[41] reflecting the number of self-published authors who see no benefit to buying into the system.

The artist Fiona Banner has long played with the ISBN as a paratext that signifies commodity, publishing herself in 2009 by tattooing "ISBN 0-9548366-7-7" on her lower back.[42] She has engraved an ISBN number into stone under the title *Reclining* (2009); let the sun bleach one into paper left outside her studio under the title *Summer 2009* (2009); and printed one on mirrored cardstock as part of her series *Book 1/1* (2009), an edition of sixty-five one-page books each containing a unique ISBN on its reflective surface. Inviting viewers to see themselves as part of the highly individual, one-off works, Banner's *Book 1/1* suggests the one-to-one relationship of both ISBN to book and book to reader. The series of one-of-a-kind objects and ephemeral performances described above each used actual ISBN numbers and were "published" under the artist's imprint, Vanity Press.[43] The issuance of the unique codes triggered both copyright law and the UK's Legal Deposit Libraries Act, which requires publishers to submit a copy of every work to the British Library within a month of publication. To satisfy the Legal Deposit department, which contacted her requesting copies she simply couldn't provide, Banner produced a book documenting these ISBN works, including photographs of each piece along with relevant correspondence with the British Library to frame the book's contents. She titled her book *ISBN 978-1-907118-99-9*.

Interactivity and the Digital Book

Our current moment appears to be much like the first centuries of movable type, a cusp. Just as manuscript books persisted into the Gutenberg era, books currently exist in multiple forms simultaneously: as paperbacks, audiobooks, EPUB downloads, and, in rare cases, interactive digital experiences. While some e-books are simply liquid text, a number of authors and artists are using the medium to create immersive cinematic and game-like reading experiences that take advantage of the digital space opened up by this technology and demand a more expansive definition of the book. These projects provide opportunities for a new kind of attention that, while it will not replace the "deep reading" whose loss literary critic Sven Birkerts bemoaned more than two decades ago in his *Gutenberg Elegies*,[44] is markedly spatialized and embodied, and draws us below the screen's surface.

Since the advent of personal computers, authors have been making work specifically for the digital environment that takes advantage of its capacity for multimedia and multi-sequentiality. Rather than remediating print books, early e-book publishers created interactive, media-rich, and nonlinear works, such as Voyager's Expanded Books or Eastgate Systems' hypertext authoring system Storyspace, launched publicly in 1987 with Michael Joyce's *afternoon, a story*. With the rise of the web, electronic literature in the form of hyperlinked websites extended these postmodern structures into cyberspace, and Adobe Flash soon allowed animation and video-based interactive works. These works of "electronic literature," like artists' books, interrogate their formal structure (including code and interface) as part of their content, drawing on the affordances of their media.

While digital reading interfaces like the Kindle and Nook aim to pour texts written for print into digital vessels, some writers are developing books specifically for the affordances of networked, screen-based devices, incorporating video, sound, animation, and complex layouts. Because e-readers are limited in the kinds of files they can accept, and the kinds of interactivity those files facilitate are also circumscribed, these writers work directly with tablets, creating app-based books for Apple and Android that play with the material metaphor of its interface, integrating it into the work. The iPad, for example, is a touch interface that recognizes specific gestures hard-coded into the operating system: currently tap and double-tap, 3-D press, drag, flick, swipe, pinch, touch and hold, shake, and multi-finger gestures. These gestures are so ingrained into users' expectations of the iPad and iPhone, Apple's developer rules mandate their use and restrict alternative mappings of these behaviors to promote the company's ethos of intuitive interfaces and accessibility.[45] This brings us back to where we began, with *Pat the Bunny*, a book that teaches us how to read and how to touch. In exploring haptic modalities of reading, these digital books, too, foreground the reader's role in bringing a book to life—whatever its physical form.

Samantha Gorman and Danny Cannizaro's novella *Pry* (Tender Claws, 2014), for example, uses the affordances of iOS to create a cinematic reading experience in which touch drives the narrative.[46] Dispensing with the succession of page to page, it offers discrete chapters that each immerse us in a different cognitive space, integrating video, digital animation, sound, and interactivity that incorporate the iPad's repertoire of gestures into a narrative that explores the inner workings of the human mind. The story centers on James, a veteran of the first Gulf War whose experiences there haunt him and prevent him from fully engaging in civilian life. The subconscious mind is rendered in text: in one chapter as an accordion that can be unfolded again and again, revealing new lines that nuance the story; in another as an infinite canvas—a scroll extending in every direction that thwarts our desire for the page's fixed boundaries. As we flick rapidly across the tablet's surface, finding only more of the same, images of childhood mementos spring up from the darkness behind the text, suggesting they have been triggered by his mental map. Consciousness itself serves as a thin membrane that can be torn. While video footage of James's daily life as a demolitions expert or one of his night terrors plays, we can see through them to his repressed thoughts by touching two fingers to the screen and drawing them away from one another. Like a voyeur prying open a venetian blind, we pull his memories apart.

Each of seven chapters invites us to piece together James's traumatic past while keeping us, like him, in the dark (see figure 19). The connection between the gestural interface and his vision is integral to the narrative—he is gradually losing his eyesight, for reasons that become clear over the course of the book. Both nonlinear and game-like, *Pry* explicitly requires the reader's interaction to make meaning. Rather than taking the touchscreen for granted, it integrates it into the narrative in a profoundly moving way.

As with artists' books, when digital books make the interface a visible and integral part of the narrative, we begin to see the extent to which any book is a negotiation, a performance, a dynamic event that happens in the moment and is never the same twice. Filmmaker and programmer Erik Loyer, who develops graphic novels for iOS, has been experimenting with the ways touch can give readers

Culture is linked to
the book. The book
as repository and
receptacle of knowledge
is identified with
knowledge. The book
is not only the book
that sits in libraries—
that labyrinth in which
all combinations
of forms, words and
letters are rolled up in

volumes. The book is the Book. Still to be read, still to be written, always already written and thoroughly penetrated by reading, the book constitutes the condition for every possibility of reading and writing.

—MAURICE BLANCHOT,
"THE ABSENCE OF THE BOOK,"
IN *THE INFINITE CONVERSATION*

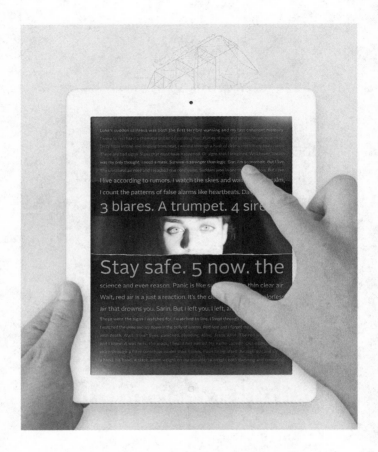

Figure 19 The reader pries open the protagonist's subconscious in Samantha Gorman and Danny Cannizaro's *Pry* (Tender Claws, 2016). Image used with permission of Tender Claws, LLC.

a sense of agency. His *Strange Rain* (Opertoon, 2011), like *Pry*, uses the touchscreen to create an immersive first-person reading experience that combines sound, video, and text. The app takes advantage of the glass screen and rectangular shape of the iPhone and iPad, turning it into a skylight. Reclining with the device overhead heightens the realism of the video we encounter: a cloudy sky with raindrops falling toward us that dissipate in rings on the glass. We hear the drops tapping the screen, and if we tap back, words and phrases become superimposed on that darkened sky—the protagonist's inner monologue manifesting in the exterior world, accompanied by an eerie melody timed to our touch. In this first-person perspective, we can control his meditative state, progressing rapidly between thoughts in an anxiety-producing rush, or slowly pressing deeper into his feelings as he grapples with a family emergency (see figure 20). We literally collect his thoughts to help him reach the emotional and psychological catharsis that will allow him to deal with the present moment.

In addition to supporting first-person works, the parallax of the screen and its potential for three-dimensional illusions lends it to motion comics as well, a subject Loyer has explored extensively. His *Ruben & Lullaby* (Opertoon, 2009) presents readers with a quarreling couple on a park bench whose argument we can not only witness but influence. Illustrated by Ezra Clayton Daniels, the interactive graphic novel progresses wordlessly as we tip our phone

Figure 20 The screen as skylight in Erik Loyer's *Strange Rain* (Opertoon, 2013). Image used with permission of Erik Loyer.

left to bring Ruben into focus, and right to see Lullaby's reaction. The visuals take advantage of the phone's motion sensor: the characters in the foreground appear sharp, while the park behind them recedes into a blur that responds to each movement of the device. Our actions influence the unfolding spat: stroking the screen to placate the characters adds a calming blue hue, shaking the phone to exacerbate the situation tints their world red, and the free jazz soundtrack ebbs and crescendos in response to each tilt, touch, and agitation. Through this interface, we must work at the couple's relationship to reach the conclusion we want for them. Loyer has gone on to work extensively in touch-interactive comics that use music, text, and motion to create a hybrid of graphic novel and film, taking advantage of parallax, responsive sound, and animation that are among the iOS's affordances.

These works go hand in hand with the trend in contemporary independent publishing to create works whose visual form and textual content are intertwined. One such publisher, Visual Editions, reissued Marc Saporta's long out-of-print *Composition No. 1*, described in chapter 3, in 2011, issuing an iPad app simultaneously that remediates the work to facilitate the project of shuffling the text. The publisher has since gone on to establish a separate imprint, in collaboration with Google, to create born-digital, web-based works that play with interactivity and the bounds of the screen. Editions at Play intends "to allow writers to create books which change dynamically on a reader's phone or tablet using the internet, and to engage the next generation of readers on their phones as well as in print."[47] These books could not be printed and work in quite the same way as they do in digital form—much like an artist's book that has to have some reason for the form it takes, they use the affordances of the web and mobile devices (including networks, algorithms, time stamps, geolocation, and sensor-responsiveness, to name a few) as part of their structure. The interactive experiences they create invite us to interrogate, or at least consider, the ubiquitous devices that structure our daily lives but that we tend to treat as invisible. One way these books respond directly to the unbound (though certainly not infinite) nature of such narrative is by measuring length in "read time" (sic), rather than pages, adopting a common e-reader metric since the page's paratexts don't apply in this context. In interactive narrative that dispenses with order or that gives the reader navigational control, we can't know how much we have or haven't seen, nor do we necessarily need to read every word. Duration, like a video game's progress bar, gives us a sense of where we are. Written in HTML, these works can be accessed on the web and mobile devices, as well as through Google Play, and they adapt to the dimensions of the screen. Some are free (subsidized by advertisements), while others cost a small fee.

The recently released *A Universe Explodes* (2017) by Tea Uglow, for example, uses blockchain to assign an owner to one of a hundred copies of the limited-edition digital work, each of whom must edit the text before passing it on to another reader, such that the book is gradually reduced to only one word per page. Nonowners can read any of these copies, seeing how they develop over time and how the story, of a parent making breakfast and meditating on the nature of family, time, and space, changes and degrades in parallel with its plot, which centers on loss. While some works in the series are more successful than others, the initiative, like those of Opertoon and Tender Claws, attempts to use the affordances of the digital rather than treating it as a crystal goblet. Such works consider both how we read and why we might choose to do so in this mediated way, given the availability, stability, and beauty of print books, which continue to tell us important stories.

Colophon or Incipit?

As we have seen, artists' books provide a useful touchstone for thinking about digital books because they are fundamentally interactive, tactile, and multisensory: the reader must manipulate them to experience their full effect. These works draw attention to the book's subversive and propagandistic potentials. They reflect on the circulation

So what is beyond the book is still the book.

—EDMOND JABÈS,
"SAND," IN *THE LITTLE BOOK OF
UNSUSPECTED SUBVERSION*

of such objects as well as their silencing. They remind us that the book has volume and sequence, sometimes by upending our expectations of order, and sometimes by exploiting it to animate the page. By bringing its interface into focus, they draw our attention to a deeper history of mutation and play with book form. Dick Higgins coined the term "intermedia" to describe such works, a word that sounds to contemporary ears like a description of an augmented reality or touchscreen reading experience. *Intermedia* works, by his definition, involve "a conceptual fusion" of the elements that constitute them.[48] For him, the artist's book is intermedial because its "design and format reflect its content—they *inter*merge, *inter*penetrate. ... The experience of reading it, viewing it, framing it—that is what the artist stresses in making it."[49] Intermedia are about the moment of their reception. They do not pretend to be the same book when arrayed behind glass as they are in a reader's (sometimes gloved, sometimes bare) hands. And they never take for granted their form as an integral element of the reader's meaning-making experience.

All books, I hope this volume suggests, arise in the moment of reception, in the hands, eyes, ears, and mind of the reader. The boundary-pushing cases of the artist's book and e-book reveal the plasticity of the term and the diverse range of interfaces to which we apply it. There will continue to be readers for whom the Kindle's utility is of chief concern—who want to read text with as little encumbrance as possible, just as Aldus Manutius and his fellow scholars did. Seeing that interface as a structuring mechanism, whose paratexts and affordances present us with possibilities that shape the meaning we make as readers (and writers) returns some agency to us in the face of the closed interface. Consumers of books have never been passive, as I hope these exemplars from history forward have suggested. Both we and the texts we read have bodies, and it is only when they come together that a book takes shape.

The process of the book's adaptation to its readers is not yet over, though the printed codex has had a stable life for over five hundred years. Some scholars consider this period of textual fixity and enclosure the Gutenberg parenthesis, rather than the Gutenberg era, suggesting that we are returning to a culture that values orality and ephemerality, no longer needing ideas bound between covers or owned in quite the same way.[50] While reading on digital devices is not going away, one technology clearly does not supersede the other. Rather, the simultaneity of these modes of reading, if the past is any indication, suggests our changing ideas about authorship, ownership, archives, scholarship, and leisure will continue to change our ideas about and expectations of the book. The term's slipperiness, far from a liability, proves its greatest asset. It is a malleable structure through which we encounter ideas. Object, content, idea, and interface, the book changes us as we change it, letter by letter, page by page.

CHRONOLOGY

An approximate timeline of the book's technologies
and of technologies that have shaped the book

BCE

3500:	Clay bullae (Sumer)
2800:	Clay tablet with cuneiform writing (Mesopotamia)
2600:	Papyrus with hieroglyphic writing (Egypt)
2500:	Oldest known khipu (Peru). Most date from the fifteenth century
2500:	Writing on leather (Egypt)
2300:	Inanna poems (Enheduanna)
2100:	Gilgamesh
1900:	Prisse Papyrus, the oldest written papyrus scroll
1600:	Bamboo scroll/*jiance* (China)
1600:	Parchment
1500:	Phoenician alphabet (consonants only)
1400:	Oracle inscriptions in animal bones and shells (China)
1300:	Wax tablet
700:	Earliest silk documents (China)
668–612:	King Ashurbanipal's library
300:	Library of Alexandria
200:	Palm leaf sutra/*pothī* (India and Sri Lanka)
200:	Introduction of punctuation by Aristophanes (Rome)
200–200 CE:	Composition of Hebrew Torah
197:	Library of Pergamum (Turkey)
170:	Perfection of parchment production in Pergamon (Turkey)
100:	Hemp paper (China)
55:	Roman parchment notebooks/pugillares membranae
39:	First public library in Rome

CE

65–150:	Composition of New Testament
105:	Invention of paper in China attributed to Cai Lun
150:	Codex
400–1300:	Preservation and reproduction of Greek writings in Byzantium, Islam, and the Christian world (fuels Renaissance)
600–1000:	Flourishing of intellectual arts and book production in Islam
600–1200:	Monastic manuscript production
675:	Word separation (Ireland)
700:	Accordion books (China)
750:	Paper mill at Samarkand
859:	Founding of Khizanat al-Qarawiyyin, library, mosque, and university, by Fatima Al-Fihiri. Considered the world's oldest continually operating library
868:	Woodblock printing (China, *Diamond Sutra*)
1041:	Wood and clay movable type in China (Bí Sheng)
1050:	*The Dresden Codex*, oldest surviving book printed in the Americas (Yucatan)
1078:	First European paper mill (Sativa, Spain)
1377:	*Jikji* printed from copper type (Korea)
1420:	Block-books (Europe)
1437:	Peepshow box (Leon Battista Alberti)
1450:	Printing press, metal type, and oil-based ink (Johannes Gutenberg)
1450–1501:	Incunable period in Europe
1456:	Gutenberg Bible
1522:	Wittenberg Bible
1501:	Aldine editions
1709:	Statute of Anne establishes copyright (England)
1725:	Stereotyping (William Ged)
1751:	*Encyclopédie* (Denis Diderot)
1765:	Metamorphosis books/harlequinades (Robert Sayer)
1774:	*Donaldson v. Beckett* strikes down perpetual copyright (England)
1788:	Illuminated printing (William Blake)
1790:	First U.S. Federal Copyright Act
1798:	Lithography (Alois Senefelder)
1798:	Papermaking machine, continuous roll paper (patented by Nicolas Robert)

1800:	Cast iron printing press (Charles Stanhope)
1807:	Fourdrinier papermaking machine (John Gamble, Henry and Sealy Fourdrinier)
1810:	Steam-powered printing press (Frederich König)
1816:	Photography (Nicéphore Niépce)
1830:	Flatbed cylinder press (Frederich König)
1838:	Typecasting machine (David Bruce)
1833:	Photographic print from negative (William Henry Fox Talbot)
1868:	Kineograph/flip-book (John Barnes Linnett)
1878:	Photogravure (Karel Válclav Klič)
1878:	Foil cylinder recording (Thomas Edison)
1879:	Stitched-binding machine (David M. Smyth)
1884:	Mimeograph (Thomas Edison and Albert Blake Dick)
1886:	Linotype (Ottmar Mergenthaler)
1886:	Berne Convention on Copyright
1894:	Mutoscope (Herman Casler)
1896:	Monotype (Tolbert Lanston)
1897:	*Un coup de Dés jamais n'abolira le Hasard* (Stéphane Mallarmé)
1903:	Lithographic offset press (Ira Rubel)
1912:	Intertype
1913:	*La Prose du Transsibérien et de la Petite Jehanne de France* (Blaise Cendrars and Sonia Delaunay)
1919:	*Unhappy Readymade* (Marcel Duchamp)
1930:	*Readies* (Bob Brown)
1932:	Audiobooks on LP (*The Talking Book*)
1938:	Xerography (Chester Carlson)
1945:	Memex (Vannevar Bush)
1949:	*El libro mecánico* (Ángela Ruiz Robles)
1950:	Intertype Fotosetter photocompositing machine
1951:	Inkjet printer (Siemens)
1955:	Universal Copyright Convention
1959:	Xerox 914 commercial photocopier
1961:	*Literaturwurst* (Dieter Roth)
1961:	*Composition No. 1* (Marc Saporta)
1961:	*Cent mille milliards de poèmes* (Raymond Queneau)
1962:	*Enciclopedia Mecánica* (Ángela Ruiz Robles)
1963:	*Twentysix Gasoline Stations* (Ed Ruscha)
1967:	Hypertext (Ted Nelson and Andries van Dam)
1967:	*The Big Book* (Alison Knowles)

1967:	*Sweethearts* (Emmett Williams)
1967:	ISBN introduced in United States
1971:	Project Gutenberg (Michael S. Hart)
1972:	Dynabook (Alan Kay)
1975:	"The New Art of Making Books" (Ulises Carrión)
1975:	*Cover to Cover* (Michael Snow)
1977:	*ABC—We Print Anything—In the Cards* (Carolee Schneeman)
1984:	Digital Domesday Project
1985:	CD-ROM introduced
1986:	Franklin Spelling Ace
1987:	Storyspace, Eastgate Systems (Jay David Bolter, Michael Joyce, and John B. Smith)
1992:	Voyager Expanded Books
1992:	Sony Data Discman
1992:	Incipit e-reader (Franco Crugnola Varese and Isabella Rigamonti)
1994:	*lineament* (Ann Hamilton)
1994:	*A Passage* (Buzz Spector)
1996:	The Internet Archive (Brewster Kahle)
1997:	ePaper/E Ink Corporation (Joseph Jacobson)
2000:	The first mass-market e-book for encrypted download (Stephen King's novella *Riding the Bullet* [Simon and Schuster])
2000:	*Tobacco Project* (Xu Bing)
2003:	First *keitai shousetsu*, or cell phone novel (*Deep Love*, by Yoshi)
2004:	Sony Librie e-reader
2004:	Google Print announced
2006:	Espresso Book Machine
2006:	Sony Reader
1006:	*Danger Book: Suicide Fireworks* (Cai Guo-Qiang)
2007:	Apple iPhone
2007:	Amazon Kindle
2009:	Barnes and Noble Nook
2010:	Apple iPad
2011:	The Physical Archive of the Internet Archive
2013:	Digital Public Library of America

Sources

Febvre, Lucien, and Henri-Jean Martin. *The Coming of the Book: The Impact of Printing, 1450–1800*, trans. David Gerard. London: Verso, 1976.

Howard, Nicole. *The Book: History of a Technology*. Baltimore: Johns Hopkins University Press, 2009.

Howsam, Leslie. *The Cambridge Companion to the History of the Book*. Cambridge: Cambridge University Press, 2015.

Kilgour, Frederick G. *The Evolution of the Book*. Oxford: Oxford University Press, 1998.

Manguel, Alberto. *A History of Reading*. New York: Penguin, 1996.

Norman, Jeremy. BookHistory.net (web).

Suarez, Michael, and H. R. Woodhuysen. *Oxford Companion to the Book*. Oxford: Oxford University Press, 2010.

Tsien, Tsuen-Hsuin. *Written on Bamboo and Silk: The Beginnings of Chinese Books and Inscriptions*. Chicago: University of Chicago Press, 2004.

Accordion/concertina/sutra-folded book
Chinese books made by folding paper back and forth on itself and adhering thick paper or boards to the outer pages. This pleated fold is also used as the basis for several contemporary book structures, in which case it becomes the spine to which pages are sewn or adhered.

ASCII
Abbreviation for American Standard Code for Information Interchange. This computing standard, developed in the 1960s from telegraph code, converts characters into seven-bit integers that are computer-readable.

Augmented reality (AR)
Technologies that augment physical space with digital media, viewable through a webcam, smartphone, or headset. AR differs from virtual reality in that it uses the lived environment, rather than immersing the viewer in an entirely computer-generated one.

Block-book
A medieval European book printed from carved woodblocks (xylography). Such publications featured religious images with descriptive text provided in captions, scroll-like speech bubbles, or on facing pages. Block-books likely played a role in the development of movable type and continued to be printed and sold widely through the fifteenth century.

Book block
The body of a book's collated and stacked sheets, folios, or signatures.

Book of hours
A medieval illuminated prayer book for private devotion that guides readers in the Hours of the Virgin.

Bookplate
A printed label pasted inside a book's cover to identify its owner.

Boustrophedon
Writing in which the direction reverses in each line, named for the method of ploughing fields in zigzag fashion.

Bulla/bullae (pl.)
Clay envelopes used by the Sumerians as receipts for goods. These round balls were impressed with tokens, which were then sealed inside. The tokens mark an important stage in the development of writing.

Carolingian
A rounded minuscule hand developed during the reign of Charlemagne (ca. 742–814 CE) as part of his initiatives to standardize manuscript writing. Fifteenth-century humanists based their chancery script on this hand, believing it closer to classical Rome.

Case binding
A binding in which the book block is adhered to a separately manufactured cover made of fabric or leather-wrapped boards.

Catchword
A word included at the end of a page or a signature in a manuscript or print codex that indicates the first word on the next page. Catchwords helped printers lay out *formes* on the press and facilitated collation during codex binding.

Chapbook
Inexpensive printed books, generally in the form of a signature folded down from a larger sheet. Sold by traveling peddlers called *chapmen* from the sixteenth to the nineteenth century. The format now plays a significant role in the distribution of contemporary poetry through chapbook publishers and self-published works.

Chase
Metal frame in which type formes are locked up for printing.

Codex
A block of pages bound on one side between covers. The name derives from the Latin *caudex* (tree trunk) because Romans used the term to describe gatherings of wax wooden tablets or pugillares.

Collate/collation
The process of arranging a book's sections or quires in sequence.

Colophon
A description of a book's production, often including details about typography, design, and materials. The term comes from the Greek for "finishing stroke" and refers to its position at the back of a book.

Commonplace book
Personal collections of literary quotations, bon mots, facts, and other information transcribed from one's reading.

Composing stick
A width-adjustable tool in which type is set. The stick can accommodate several lines, which are built up by the compositor with a piece of lead between them for spacing. Type is set upside down and from right to left in the stick to create a mirror image of the finished text.

Cordiform book
A heart-shaped book whose pages have been inscribed or printed, and cut such that when the book is opened, it forms a heart. Some examples form a double heart—one on either side of the spine. The Bibliothèque nationale de France holds two interesting examples: the *Chansonniere de Jean de Montchenu* (1470, scanned on the library's website), a collection of love songs, and the fifteenth-century *Book of Hours of Amiens Nicolas Blairie*.

Cuneiform
The writing system of ancient Mesopotamia, created by using the edge of a reed stylus to make combinations of impressions in wet clay. The name comes from the Latin *cuneus* for the wedge-like shapes of which it consists.

Deckle
A deckle edge is the uneven edge on a sheet of paper. While it can be simulated by tearing the paper, the term refers to an effect unique to paper-making in which some of the pulp seeps under the edge of the mold when being screened.

Dos-à-dos
A binding in which two books are joined by a shared back cover, and each opens in the opposite direction. The name comes from French, meaning

"back-to-back." Not to be confused with *tête-bêche* (from the French meaning "head-to-toe") books, in which the rear book is upside down relative to the one in front.

E Ink (electronic ink)
A display that simulates paper by using an electric charge to reconfigure black-and-white micro-particles. Such screens use reflected light rather than internal illumination.

Endsheets
A folio adhered to a book's side-cover (called the pastedown) and the joint of its first page (called the flyleaf). Often decorative, the endsheet also invites the reader into the book by pulling on the first page when the cover is opened.

E-reader (electronic reader)
A specialized digital storage device for reading, which can access text in several digital formats and store large quantities of documents locally or in the cloud.

Exemplar
An original text from which copies are made.

Fluxus
A loose collective of artists interested in chance operations, ephemeral performances, conceptual practice, and participatory works that blur the line between art and life. The ideals and techniques of Fluxus emerged from an experimental composition workshop led by John Cage at the New School for Social Research in 1958.

Folio
A sheet of paper or parchment folded in half to create two leaves/four pages.

Font
A collection of type in a single face/style that has been cast from molten metal. The terminology was adopted in digital media, where it refers to a line of type for purchase (as distinct from typeface, which refers to an idea, but not a product).

Fore-edge
The edge of a bound book opposite its spine.

Forme
A column of text arranged for printing by a typesetter. This text reads upside down and from right to left, with spacers between words and lines to hold them tightly in place, creating a mirror image of the text it will produce. A forme might be thought of as a page of text, arranged and ready for printing.

Frisket
A frame placed over paper before printing to protect the page's borders from wayward ink.

Galley
The tray on which type formes are stored.

Girdle book
A book whose block is stitched to an oversized leather cover with soft flaps that can be looped over one's belt. Popular among pilgrims and monks during the Middle Ages, the format continued to be produced through the Renaissance.

Gothic
Lettering based on the handwriting of medieval manuscripts, also referred to as *blackletter*. Gutenberg developed his Gothic typeface from Textura, the standard calligraphic style of fifteenth-century German books. The term was applied to such letterforms by Renaissance humanists who saw it as unrefined.

Grain
The direction in which a sheet of paper's fibers align. Most American paper is "grain long," meaning the fibers align in the same direction as the sheet's longest side. While harder to detect in machine-made paper than handmade paper, there is nonetheless an appreciable difference in the way a page reacts to folding with and against the grain.

Hand
The term used for different calligraphy styles. The terms *font* and *typeface* derive from movable type.

Harlequinade
Also known as metamorphoses, flap-books, and turn-up books, these lift-the-flap books began to be mass-produced for children in the late eighteenth

century. A series of flaps along the top and bottom of the page change the illustration and the narrative as they are raised.

Headband
Threads sewn at the head and foot of a codex book's spine developed in the Middle Ages to protect the text block from wear. Though still in use, they predominantly serve a decorative purpose.

Hieratic
An adaptation of hieroglyphics into a script.

Hieroglyphics
Ancient Egyptian pictographic writing system whose illustrations could represent both objects and sounds. The name comes from the Greek and refers to the sacredness attributed to these written forms: *hieros* (sacred) + *glyphein* (to carve).

Historiated initial
A miniature painting inside the initial letter of a passage in an illuminated manuscript. Such letters were made much larger than the lines around them and helped readers navigate a text.

Hot metal typesetting
Machines that incorporate type casting and setting, which allows lines of type to be produced as needed for a given job. Rather than placing prefabricated letters one at a time into a composing stick, a compositor could type out a line, which would be justified and then fabricated by the machine. The Linotype and Monotype are the best known such devices, but others were made as well.

Ideogram
A picture or symbol that stands in for an idea but not for a word.

Illuminated manuscript
A manuscript book in which handwritten text is embellished with decorative elements and miniature illustrations, often incorporating gold or silver leaf. Such illumination occurs in Hindu and Buddhist palm leaf manuscripts, Islamic manuscripts, and medieval European manuscripts.

Incipit
A stand-in for a work's title, often consisting of the work's opening phrase. The word *incipit* was used by scribes to open their texts and means "here begins" in Latin.

Incunabula/incunables
Codex books printed in Europe before 1501, the "cradle" period of print.

Insular
A term referring to styles of writing and manuscript decoration that originate in Ireland in the seventh century. The name refers to the source of these techniques, which include letters based on uncial forms, elaborate illumination, and complex interlocking shapes we might think of as Celtic, in the British Isles. Irish Christians spread the style to England, and from there it was distributed across Europe in the eighth century.

Intaglio
A printing method in which an image is carved into a hard surface, rubbed with ink, then wiped clean. The image is transferred to another surface under high pressure to draw the ink up out of the grooves.

Intermedia
Term coined by Fluxus artist and publisher Dick Higgins for a work of art that fuses multiple art forms, all of which are conceptually integrated into the way it makes meaning.

Italic type
Type developed in the fifteenth century in Venice that mimicked the cursive handwriting Italian Renaissance humanist scholars used in their notebooks.

Jiance
Chinese scrolls made by binding narrow, flat bamboo slips and inscribing them from top to bottom. The name comes from *jian* (bamboo strip) + *ce* (volume).

Khipu/quipu
Andean record keeping system using knots in cord that dates as early as 2500 BCE, though most extant examples come from the Inka civilization between 1400 and 1532 CE.

Leaf/leaves (pl.)

A sheet consisting of two pages: *recto* and *verso*. When a larger sheet of paper is folded down, it produces multiple leaves, each of which is two-sided.

Logogram

A symbol, character, or picture that represents a word or concept it does not directly depict.

Majuscule

Uppercase letterforms.

Manicule

A typographical mark consisting of a first with its index finger extended. Used first in manuscript, then by scholars annotating their books, the figure was normalized by typographers and began to be used for printing in the fifteenth century.

Manuscript

A book or document written by hand. The term comes from the Latin *manus* (hand) + *scriptus* (from *scribere*, to write).

Marginalia

Written commentary in the margins of books, usually in the form of notes by a reader indicative of their close engagement with the text, but also including doodles, love letters, scribal complaints, and any number of marginal forms.

Membrana/pugillares membranae

Roman parchment notebooks thought to be an important precursor to the codex book. They were likely made by folding a single sheet into a handy portable size for note-taking and drafting.

Minuscule

Lowercase letterforms.

Octavo

A folding that generates eight leaves (sixteen pages) from a larger page.

Opening
Two facing pages bound together, including a verso at left and recto at right. The term presumes a designed experience, but some book structures, like the accordion, can offer unexpected openings if the pages are refolded.

Optical character recognition (OCR)
A technique for converting images of text (optical characters) into machine-readable text. This involves recognizing and processing the characters in the image prior to digitization.

Orphan books
Books that are still in copyright, but whose copyright holder is unclear or unavailable

Pagina/paginae (pl.)
The columns of writing with which Greeks and Romans inscribed most of their papyrus and parchment scrolls. Some scrolls were written top to bottom, rather than held horizontally, in *transversa charta*.

Papyrus
Paper made from pressed strips of the *cyperus papyrus* plant. Formed from overlapping strips of the plant's stalk in two layers, perpendicular to one another, which are beaten to fuse them, the resulting paper has a natural grain that runs horizontally on the writing side and vertically on the reverse.

Paratext
Elements outside the text that help frame the work as a book. These include the title page, index, running heads, covers, pagination, typography design, and other features that help us identify and navigate a text.

Parchment
Writing surface made from animal hide which is cleaned, stretched, and treated for durability.

Peep-show/tunnel book
A book that provides a perspective view into a scene using a series of frames joined by a paper accordion or enclosed in a box.

Perfect binding
Glue-based binding most common in paperback books.

Phonogram
A character used to represent a sound, several of which are strung together to represent words.

Pictogram/pictographic
A drawing that symbolizes the object it depicts.

Polyptych
A grouping of wax tablets bound together with loops of leather through their wooden frames. Romans referred to a polyptych bound to a central hinge as a *codex*, an important source of our term for the codex book.

Pothī/palm leaf manuscript
A book structure of narrow, oblong pages bound between wooden boards with one or more strings passed through them. Originally written on specially treated palm leaves as a form of devotion and to disseminate the Buddha's teachings.

Print-on-demand (POD)
The ability to print books to order, rather than printing an entire run of a title up front. Facilitated by advances in digital printing and automated binding in the 1990s, POD publishers began cropping up in the early twenty-first-century catering to consumers interested in self-publishing at low cost.

Pugillares
The Roman name for wooden boards that have been hollowed and filled with wax, which were also used by Mesopotamians and Greeks. These wax tablets could be joined to create dyptychs (two tablets), triptychs (three tablets), or polyptychs (several tablets), which would be joined with leather thongs tying them end-to-end like an accordion or along one end, a format given the name *codex*.

Punch/punchcutter
The punchcutter manufactured punches from which type was made. A punch consists of a steel rod with a backward letter carved into its tip. This punch would be pressed into a piece of copper to create a right-reading indentation that could be fitted into a matrix and filled with molten metal to create type.

Quarto
A folding that generates four leaves (eight pages) from a larger sheet.

Quaternion
A gathering of four sheets, folded and sewn into a quire.

Quire
A gathering of pages made by folding a larger sheet into nested folios.

Recto/verso
The two sides of a leaf in a gathering: a *recto* (the front) and *verso* (the back). In a codex opening, the recto is always the right-hand page, while the verso always a left.

Remediation
A term coined by Jay David Bolter and Richard Grusin in 1999 to describe the process of give-and-take between media forms as they develop. New media can borrow older media forms, as when Apple's interface uses skeuomorphic icons to represent the camera and phone apps, and older media can borrow from new media, as when books are printed with conductive ink to create interactive circuits on the page.

Roman type
Developed in contrast to the Gothic blackletter types of Northern Europe, which Italian humanists felt were mired in the Gothic Middle Ages, this typeface used majuscules based on Roman inscriptions (copied from building facades) and minuscule based on the Carolingian hand. Humanists adopted this style believing it more properly fit the texts of classical Rome.

Rubrication
The addition of labels and markings in red ink to highlight important passages in a text. Rubrication is found in Egyptian manuscripts, was adopted by Greek and Roman scribes, and persisted into medieval manuscripts. The practice was incorporated into early printed books.

Saddle stitch
A sewn or stapled binding that pierces the fold of a gathering of folios.

Scriptio continua

The Greek and Roman method of writing in continuous script without spaces, capitalization, or punctuation to distinguish words. Scriptio continua came into being with the advent of the consonant-vowel alphabet and was meant to be read aloud.

Scriptorium

A dedicated space in Christian monasteries for manuscript production by monks (and some nuns) with the aid of select laymen. The scriptorium could hold from three to twenty monks, with twelve being the average number, though some monasteries employed many more.

Scroll

A rolled length of material used for writing. Scrolls were made of papyrus, leather, parchment, paper, silk, bamboo strips, and linen. Their use persisted from around 2000 BCE to around 700 CE.

Signature

A gathering of nested folios for binding as part of a book block. Used in book layout, the term refers to page numbers, an outgrowth of the history in which the gatherings of a codex were labeled with an alphanumeric signature to help the binder keep them in order.

Sorts

Individual pieces of type, including letters, punctuation, and spacing.

Stereotyping

The process, in use as early as the seventeenth century, of creating a papier-mâché mold from hand-set type and using this to cast a page form, allowing the type to be redistributed and the text to be continually reprinted. This was especially useful before the advent of hot metal typesetting.

Stylus

An inscription tool. The stylus used with clay tablets was formed from a wedge-shaped piece of reed whose tip and side could be impressed in clay to form characters and lines. The stylus used for wax tablets had a point on one end for writing and a flat end on the other to revise one's work. The term is also used to describe pointers used with touchscreen interfaces that similarly inscribe without ink.

Thumb index
A finding aid in which rounded cut-outs on a book's fore-edge are labeled. Most common in alphabetized works, like dictionaries and encyclopedias, or works with a detailed structure, like Bibles and religious works.

Titulus
The label of a scroll including a colophon and description of its content, which was attached to one end for easy access when scrolls were stored, either upright in bins or horizontally in cubbyholes.

Tympan
A piece of parchment on which paper is placed before being run through a printing press.

Uncial
A rounded uppercase (majuscule) hand based on roman lowercase (minuscule) letters used in manuscripts from the fourth to the ninth century CE.

Vellum
Treated calfskin used in writing and bookbinding, considered superior to parchment made from goat- and sheepskin.

Volumen
The Romans' term for scroll. The Latin word is the source of our "volume," which refers to bound pages, or a codex.

Watermark
A decorative imprint in paper made by a design in the screen on which it is made. Originating in thirteenth-century Italian papermaking, watermarks continue to be used in both handmade and machine-made paper. The term has also come to refer to a digital marker providing copyright information about a file.

Xylography
Printing from carved wooden blocks with a raised image.

NOTES

Preface and Acknowledgments

1. Leah Price, "Dead Again," *The New York Times*, August 10, 2012, accessed July 17, 2017, http://www.nytimes.com/2012/08/12/books/review/the-death -of-the-book-through-the-ages.html.

2. "codex, n.," OED Online, Oxford University Press, June 2017, accessed July 17, 2017, www.oed.com/view/Entry/35593.

3. *Reading at Risk: A Survey of Literary Reading in America*, National Endowment for the Arts, June 2004, accessed July 17, 2017, https://www.arts.gov/ sites/default/files/ReadingAtRisk.pdf.

1   The Book as Object

1. Frederick Kilgour, *The Evolution of the Book* (New York: Oxford University Press, 1998), 9.

2. Denise Schmandt-Besserat and Michael Erard, "Writing Systems," in *Encyclopedia of Archaeology*, vol. 3, edited by Deborah M. Pearsall (Oxford, UK: Academic Press, 2008), 2222–2234, Gale Virtual Reference Library, accessed July 20, 2017, doi: 10.1016/B978-012373962-9.00325-3.

3. Ibid.

4. Walter J. Ong, *Orality and Literacy: The Technologizing of the Word* (New York: Routledge, 2002), 85.

5. Jean-Jacques Glassner, Zainab Bahrani, and Marc Van De Mieroop, *The Invention of Cuneiform: Writing in Sumer* (Baltimore: Johns Hopkins University Press, 2003), 112.

6. Betty De Shong Meador, *Inanna, Lady of the Largest Heart: Poems of the Sumerian High Priestess Enheduanna* (Austin: University of Texas Press, 2000), 134.

7. Ibid., 69–70.

8. Alberto Manguel, *A History of Reading* (New York: Penguin, 1996), 181.

9. Lucien X. Polastron, *Books on Fire: The Destruction of Libraries throughout History*, trans. Jon E. Graham (Rochester: Inner Transitions, 2007), 3–4.

10. Kilgour, *The Evolution of the Book*, 20–21.

11. "The Flood Tablet," The British Museum Collection Online, accessed July 17, 2017, http://www.britishmuseum.org/research/collection_online/ collection_object_details.aspx?objectId=309929&partId=1.

12. Kilgour, *The Evolution of the Book*, 24.

13. Schmandt-Besserat and Erard, "Writing Systems," 2229.

14. Douglas C. McMurtrie, *The Book: The Story of Printing & Bookmaking* (New York: Covici-Friede, 1937), 15.

15. Adam Bülow-Jacobsen, "Writing Materials in the Ancient World," *Oxford Handbook of Papyrology*, (Oxford: Oxford University Press, 2011), Oxford Handbooks Online, accessed July 17, 2017, doi: 10.1093/oxfor dhb/9780199843695.013.0001.

16. Leila Avrin, *Scribes, Script, and Books: The Book Arts from Antiquity to the Renaissance* (Chicago: The American Library Association, 1991), 84.

17. Ibid., 85–86.

18. Toni Owen, "Papyrus: Secret of the Egyptians," Brooklyn Museum, June 23, 2010, accessed July 17, 2017, https://www.brooklynmuseum.org/community/blogosphere/2010/06/23/papyrus-secret-of-the-egyptians.

19. John H. Taylor, *Journey through the Afterlife: The Ancient Egyptian Book of the Dead* (Cambridge: Harvard University Press, 2010), 55.

20. Ibid., 267.

21. Avrin, *Scribes, Script, and Books*, 91.

22. Colin H. Roberts and T. C. Skeat, *The Birth of the Codex* (London: Oxford University Press, 1983), 49.

23. Henry Petroski, *The Book on the Bookshelf* (New York: Alfred A. Knopf: 1999), 24.

24. Kilgour, *The Evolution of the Book*, 39.

25. Bonnie Mak, *How the Page Matters* (Toronto: University of Toronto Press, 2011), 12.

26. Avrin, *Scribes, Script, and Books*, 145.

27. John Willis Clark, *The Care of Books; an Essay on the Development of Libraries and Their Fittings, from the Earliest Times to the End of the Eighteenth Century* (Cambridge: Cambridge University Press, 1901), 28.

28. Petroski, *The Book on the Bookshelf*, 25.

29. Laurent Pflughhaupt, *Letter by Letter*, trans. Gregory Bruhn (New York: Princeton Architectural Press, 2007), 14.

30. Avrin, *Scribes, Script, and Books*, 146.

31. Liu Guozhong, *Introduction to the Tsinghua Bamboo-Strip Manuscripts*, trans. Christopher J. Foster and William N. French (Leiden: Brill, 2016), 2.

32. Ibid., 4.

33. Keith A. Smith, *Non-Adhesive Binding: Books without Paste or Glue*, vol. 1, revised and expanded ed., 5th printing (Rochester, NY: Keith Smith Books, 2007), 45.

34. Tsuen-Hsuin Tsien, *Written on Bamboo and Silk: The Beginning of Chinese Books and Inscriptions*, 2nd ed. (Chicago: The University of Chicago Press, 2004), 204; Guozhong, *Introduction*, 5.

35. Guozhong, *Introduction*, 5.

36. Tsien, *Written on Bamboo and Silk*, 204.

37. Ibid., 108–109.

38. Ibid., 130.

39. J. S. Edgren, "The Book beyond the West—China," in *A Companion to the History of the Book*, ed. Simon Eliot and Jonathan Rose (Malden, MA: Blackwell Publishing, 2007), accessed July 17, 2017, doi: 10.1002/9780470690949.ch7.

40. Guozhong, *Introduction*, 7.

41. Kilgour, *The Evolution of the Book*, 59.

42. Ibid., 67.

43. Michael Albin, "The Islamic Book," in *A Companion to the History of the Book*, ed. Simon Eliot and Jonathan Rose (Malden, MA: Blackwell Publishing, 2007), accessed July 17, 2017, doi: 10.1002/9780470690949.ch12.

44. Gary Urton and Carrie Brezine, "What Is a Khipu?," *Khipu Database Project*, August 2009, accessed July 17, 2017, http://khipukamayuq.fas.harvard.edu/WhatIsAKhipu.html.

45. Charles C. Mann, "Unraveling Khipu's Secrets," *Science* 309, no. 5737 (August 12, 2005): 1008–1009, accessed July 17, 2017, http://science.sciencemag.org/content/309/5737/1008.

46. Cecilia Vicuña, "Knotations on a Quipu," in *Threads Talk Series*, ed. Steve Clay and Kyle Schlesinger (New York: Granary Books; Victoria, TX: Cuneiform Press, 2016), 82.

47. From *Instruction Manual and Orientation to Various Meanings*. See "*Chanccani Quipu* by Cecilia Vicuña," Granary Books, accessed July 17, 2017, http://www.granarybooks.com/book/1150/Cecilia_Vicuna+Chanccani_Quipu.

48. Urton's theory of the Khipu as 7-bit array is outlined in *Signs of the Inka Khipu* (Austin: University of Texas Press, 2003).

49. John V. Murra, "Cloth and Its Functions in the Inca State," *American Anthropologist* 64, no. 4 (1962): 710–728.

50. "role, n.," OED Online, Oxford University Press, June 2017, accessed July 17, 2017, www.oed.com/view/Entry/166971.

51. Om Prakash Agrawal, "Care and Conservation of Palm-Leaf and Paper Illuminated Manuscripts," in John Guy, *Palm-Leaf and Paper: Illustrated Manuscripts of India and Southeast Asia* (Melbourne: National Gallery of Victoria, 1982), 84–85.

52. Calvert Watkins, *American Heritage Dictionary of Indo-European Roots*, 3rd ed. (Boston: Houghton Mifflin Harcourt, 2011), 92; Peter Stoicheff, "Materials and Meanings," in *The Cambridge Companion to the History of the Book*, ed. Leslie Howsam (Cambridge: Cambridge University Press, 2015), 75.

53. Edgren, "The Book beyond the West," 104.

54. Anne Burkus-Chasson, "Visual Hermeneurics and the Act of Turning the Leaf: A Genealogy of Liu Yuan's *Lingyan ge*," in *Printing and Book Culture in Late Imperial China*, ed. Cynthia J. Brokaw and Kai-wing Chow (Berkeley: University of California Press, 2005), 373, Oxford University Press Ebooks, accessed July 17, 2017, doi: 10.1525/california/9780520231269.001.0001.

55. Ibid., 374.

56. Ibid., 100–101.

57. Edgren, "The Book beyond the West," 101.

58. Dorit Symington, "Late Bronze Age Writing-Boards and Their Uses: Textual Evidence from Anatolia and Syria," *Anatolian Studies* 41 (1991), 112.

59. Roberts and Skeat, *The Birth of the Codex*, 4.

60. Kilgour, *The Evolution of the Book*, 51.

61. Ibid.

62. Frederic G. Kenyon, *Books and Readers in Ancient Greece and Rome* (Oxford: Clarendon Press, 1932), 91.

63. *Collected Biblical Writings of T. C. Skeat*. (Leiden: Brill Academic Publishers, 2004), 45.

64. Kenyon, *Books and Readers*, 90.

65. Roberts and Skeat, *The Birth of the Codex*, 20.

66. Kilgour, *The Evolution of the Book*, 53.

67. Avrin, *Scribes, Script, and Books,* 174; Bülow-Jacobsen, "Writing Materials," 23; and William A. Johnson, "The Ancient Book," in *The Oxford Handbook of Papyrology*, ed. Roger S. Bagnall (New York: Oxford University Press, 2012), 265.

68. Avrin, *Scribes, Script, and Books*, 84.

69. Martin Andrews, "The Importance of Ephemera," in *A Companion to the History of the Book*, ed. Simon Eliot and Jonathan Rose (Malden, MA: Blackwell Publishing, 2007), doi: 10.1002/9780470690949.ch32.

70. Roberts and Skeat, *The Birth of the Codex*, 37.

71. Alan Cowell, "Grave Yields Psalms: World's Oldest?," *New York Times*, December 24, 1988, accessed July 17, 2017, http://www.nytimes.com/1988/12/24/arts/grave-yields-psalms-world-s-oldest.html.

72. Manguel, *A History of Reading*, 48.

73. Peter Stallybrass, "Books and Scrolls: Navigating the Bible," in *Material Texts: Books and Readers in Early Modern England*, ed. Jennifer Andersen and Elizabeth Sauer (Philadelphia: University of Pennsylvania Press, 2001), 43.

74. Henri-Jean Martin, *The History and Power of Writing* (Chicago: University of Chicago Press, 1994), 121.

75. McMurtrie, *The Book*, 78.

76. Florence Edler de Roover, "The Scriptorium," in *The Medieval Library*, ed. James Westfall Thompson (New York: Hafner Publishing, 1939), 604–606.

77. Kilgour, *The Evolution of the Book*, 71.

78. Avrin, *Scribes, Script, and Books*, 213.

79. Some excellent photographs of parchment imperfections in medieval manuscripts have been collected by Associate Curator Eric J. Johnson on the Ohio State University–University Libraries blog: "Scarring, Tears, Veins and Hair: The Imperfections of Medieval Parchment," *The Ohio State University–University Libraries*, December 1, 2008, accessed July 17, 2017, https://library.osu.edu/blogs/rarebooks/2008/12/01/107/.

80. David Finkelstein and Alistain McCleery, *An Introduction to Book History* (New York: Routledge, 2005), 45.

81. Kilgour, *The Evolution of the Book*, 38.

82. Keith Houston, *The Book: A Cover-to-Cover Exploration of the Most Powerful Object of Our Time* (New York: W. W. Norton, 2016), 170.

83. A scan of the book is available through the Trinity College Dublin website: "Book of Kells," Digital Collections, Trinity College Dublin, 2012, accessed July 17, 2017, http://digitalcollections.tcd.ie/home/index.php?DRIS_ID=MS58_003v.

84. "The Book of Kells," The Library of Trinity College Dublin, accessed July 17, 2017, https://www.tcd.ie/library/manuscripts/book-of-kells.php.

85. Martyn Lyons, *Books: A Living History* (Los Angeles: Getty Publications, 2011), 43.

86. Kilgour, *The Evolution of the Book*, 68–80.

87. Paul Saenger, *Space between Words: The Origins of Silent Reading* (Stanford: Stanford University Press, 1997), 9.

88. William A Johnson, "Bookroll as Media," in *Comparative Textual Media: Transforming the Humanities in the Postprint Era*, ed. N. Katherine Hayles and Jessica Pressman (Minneapolis: University of Minnesota Press, 2013), 106.

89. Ong, *Orality and Literary*, 59.

90. Plato, *Phaedrus* (section 275c), *Plato in Twelve Volumes*, vol. 9, trans. Harold N. Fowler (Cambridge, MA: Harvard University Press, 1925), Perseus Digital Library, accessed July 17, 2017, http://data.perseus.org/citations/urn:cts:greekLit:tlg0059.tlg012.perseus-eng1:275c.

91. Ong, *Orality and Literacy*, 9.

92. M. B. Parkes, "Reading, Copying and Interpreting a Text in the Early Middle Ages," in *A History of Reading in the West*, ed. Guglielmo Cavallo and Roger Chartier (Amherst: University of Massachusetts Press, 1999), 94–99.

93. Saenger, *Space between Words*, 124–129.

94. Kilgour, *The Evolution of the Book*, 74–75.

95. Lucien Febvre and Henri-Jean Martin, *The Coming of the Book: The Impact of Printing, 1450–1800*, trans. David Gerard (London: Verso, 1976), 19–21.

96. Saenger, *Space between Words*, 259–261.

97. David C. Lindberg, *The Beginnings of Western Science* (Chicago: The University of Chicago Press, 1992), 203. See also Johanna Drucker, "The Virtual Codex: From Page Space to E-space," The Book Arts Web, April 25, 2003, accessed July 17, 2017, http://www.philobiblon.com/drucker.

2   The Book as Content

1. Eric Jager, *The Book of the Heart* (Chicago: University of Chicago Press, 2000), 83–85.

2. Kai-wing Chow, "Reinventing Gutenberg: Woodblock and Movable-Type Printing in Europe and China," in *Agent of Change: Print Culture Studies after Elizabeth L. Eisenstein*, ed. Sabrina Baron, Eric Lindquist, and Eleanor Shevlin (Amherst: University of Massachusetts Press, 2007), 180.

3. John Man, *Gutenberg: How One Man Remade the World with Words* (New York: John Wiley and Sons, 2002), 185.

4. Febvre and Martin, *The Coming of the Book*, 56.

5. Ibid., 51.

6. Ibid., 50.

7. Blaise Agüera y Arcas, "Temporary Matrices and Elemental Punches in Gutenberg's DK Type," in *Incunabula and Their Readers: Printing, Selling and Using Books in the Fifteenth Century*, ed. Kristian Jensen (London: The British Library, 2003), 11.

8. McMurtrie, *The Book*, 237–238.

9. Febvre and Martin, *The Coming of the Book*, 62–63.

10. "Gutenberg Bible: Making the Bible—How Many," *British Library Treasures in Full—Gutenberg Bible*, accessed July 17, 2017, http://www.bl.uk/treasures/gutenberg/howmany.html.

11. "Fast Facts," *Harry Ransom Center—Gutenberg Bible*, accessed July 17, 2017, http://www.hrc.utexas.edu/exhibitions/permanent/gutenbergbible/facts/#top.

12. Man, *Gutenberg*, 144.

13. Chow, "Reinventing Gutenberg," 189.

14. Adrian Johns details the international jockeying by early bibliographers over the invention of type in *The Nature of the Book: Print and Knowledge in the Making* (Chicago: University of Chicago Press, 1998), 324–379.

15. Joseph Dane, *What Is a Book?: The Study of Early Printed Books* (Notre Dame: University of Notre Dame Press, 2012), 8.

16. Walter Benjamin, "The Work of Art in the Age of Its Technological Reproducibility," in *Selected Writings, Volume 4: 1938–1940*, ed. Howard Eiland and Michael W. Jennings (Cambridge, MA: Belknap Press, 2003), 254.

17. Richard Ovenden, "Bookplate," in *The Oxford Companion to the Book*, ed. Michael F. Suarez and H. R. Woodhuysen (Oxford: Oxford University Press, 2010), Oxford Reference, accessed July 17, 2017, doi: 10.1093/acref/9780198606536.001.0001.

18. Febvre and Martin, *The Coming of the Book*, 84.

19. Petroski, *The Book on the Bookshelf*, 26–28.

20. Margaret M. Smith, *The Title-Page, Its Early Development, 1460–1510* (London: British Library, 2000), 27.

21. Febvre and Martin, *The Coming of the Book*, 84.

22. McMurtrie, *The Book*, 562–563.

23. Roger Chartier, "The Printing Revolution: A Reappraisal," in *Agent of Change: Print Culture Studies after Elizabeth L. Eisenstein*, ed. Sabrina Alcorn Baron, Eric N. Lindquist, and Eleanor F. Shevlin (Amherst: University of Massachusetts Press: 2007), 401.

24. William H Sherman, "On the Threshold: Architexture, Paratext, and Early Print Culture," in *Agent of Change: Print Culture Studies after Elizabeth L. Eisenstein*, ed. Sabrina Baron, Eric Lindquist, and Eleanor Shevlin (Amherst: University of Massachusetts Press, 2007), 79.

25. Andrew Piper, *Book Was There: Reading in Electronic Times* (Chicago: University of Chicago Press: 2012), 29.

26. Dane, *What Is a Book?*, 22.

27. Smith, *The Title-Page*, 56.

28. Petroski, *The Book on the Bookshelf*, 150.

29. Ibid., 121–123.

30. Houston, *The Book*, 311.

31. Rowan Watson, "Some Non-textual Uses of Books," in *A Companion to the History of the Book*, ed. Simon Eliot and Jonathan Rose (Malden, MA: Blackwell Publishing, 2007), doi: 10.1002/9780470690949.ch35.

32. Finkelstein and McCleery, *An Introduction to Book History*, 53.

33. McMurtrie, *The Book*, 313–315.

34. Lyons, *Books: A Living History*, 75.

35. Stallybrass, "Books and Scrolls," 45.

36. Bradin Cormack and Carla Mazzio, *Book Use, Book Theory: 1500–1700* (Chicago: University of Chicago Library, 2005), 14–15.

37. William H. Sherman, *Used Books: Marking Readers in Renaissance England* (Philadelphia: University of Pennsylvania Press, 2008), 37.

38. Cormack and Mazzio, *Book Use, Book Theory*, 23.

39. Robert Darnton, *Case for Books* (New York: Public Affairs, 2009), 150.

40. Johnson, "Bookroll as Media," 114.

41. Chartier, "The Printing Revolution," 398.

42. Houston, *The Book*, 318.

43. Lyons, *Books: A Living History*, 115.

44. Nicholas Barker, *Aldus Manutius and the Development of Greek Script and Type in the Fifteenth Century* (New York: Fordham University Press, 1992), 114–116.

45. "The Aldine Republic of Letters," *Aldines at the Edward Worth Library*, accessed July 17, 2017, http://aldine.edwardworthlibrary.ie/apud-aldum/the-aldine-republic-of-letters/.

46. M. J. C Lowry, "The 'New Academy' of Aldus Manutius: A Renaissance Dream," *Bulletin of the John Rylands Library* 58, no. 2 (1976): 409.

47. Anthony Grafton, "The Humanist as Reader," in *A History of Reading in the West*, ed. Guglielmo Cavallo and Roger Chartier, trans. Lydia G. Cochrane (Amherst: University of Massachusetts Press, 1999), 180.

48. McMurtrie, *The Book*, 213; Dane, *What Is A Book?*, 125.

49. Martin Davies, *Aldus Manutius: Printer and Publisher of Renaissance Venice* (Tempe: Arizona Center for Medieval and Renaissance Studies, 1999), 37.

50. Richard Altick, "From Aldine to Everyman: Cheap Reprint Series of the English Classics 1830–1906," *Studies in Bibliography* 11 (1958): 5.

51. Ibid., 8.

52. Febvre and Martin, *The Coming of the Book*, 162.

53. Elizabeth Armstrong, *Before Copyright: The French Book Privilege System 1498–1526* (Cambridge: Cambridge University Press, 1990), 1–2.

54. Mark Rose, "The Author as Proprietor," *Representations* 23 (Summer 1988): 57.

55. Elizabeth Judge, "Kidnapped and Counterfeit Characters: Eighteenth-Century Fan Fiction, Copyright Law, and the Custody of Fictional Characters," in *Originality and Intellectual Property in the French and English Enlightenment*, ed. Reginald McGinnis (New York: Routledge, 2009), 14.

56. Ibid., 52–53.

57. Finkelstein and McCleery, *An Introduction to Book History*, 63.

58. "Copyright Timeline: A History of Copyright in the United States," *Association of Research Libraries Website*, accessed July 17, 2017, http://www.arl
.org/focus-areas/copyright-ip/2486-copyright-timeline#.VKMKJmTF9J0.

59. "Copyright Basics," *The United States Copyright Office*, May 2012, accessed July 17, 2017, https://www.copyright.gov/circs/circ01.pdf.

60. Lyons, *Books: A Living History*, 105.

61. Peter Shillingsburg, "Three- or Triple-Decker," in *The Oxford Companion to the Book*, ed. Michael F. Suarez and H. F. Woudhuysen (Oxford: Oxford University Press, 2010), Oxford Reference, accessed July 17, 2017, doi: 10.1093/acref/9780198606536.001.0001.

62. Altick, "From Aldine to Everyman," 15.

63. Jeffrey S. Anderson, "Bindings," *Collecting Everyman's Library*, May 5, 2008, accessed July 17, 2017, http://everymanslibrarycollecting.com.

64. Louis Menand, "Pulp's Big Moment: How Emily Brontë Met Mickey Spillane," *New Yorker*, January 5, 2015, accessed July 17, 2017, http://www.new
yorker.com/magazine/2015/01/05/pulps-big-moment.

65. Lyons, *Books: A Living History*, 173.

66. Jan Tschichold, *The New Typography: A Handbook for Modern Designers*, trans. Ruari McLean (Berkeley: University of California Press, 1995).

67. Richard Doubleday, "Jan Tschichold at Penguin Books—A Resurgence of Classical Book Design," *Baseline*, no. 49 (2006): 13–20.

68. Jost Hochuli, ed., *Jan Tschichold, Typographer and Type Designer, 1902–1974*, trans. Ruari McLean, W. A. Kelly, and Bernard Wolpe (Edinburgh: National Library of Scotland, 1982), 35, quoted in Doubleday.

69. Beatrice Warde, "The Crystal Goblet, or Printing Should Be Invisible," in *The Crystal Goblet: Sixteen Essays on Typography* (Cleveland: World Publishing Company, 1956), Typo-L Listserv, accessed July 17, 2017, http://gmunch
.home.pipeline.com/typo-L/misc/ward.htm.

70. Ibid.

3   The Book as Idea

1. Johanna Drucker, *The Century of Artists' Books* (New York: Granary Books, 1994), 1.

2. Ibid.

3. Ibid., 2.

4. Kessels's volumes can be seen at Kesselskramer Publishing, accessed July 17, 2017, http://www.kesselskramerpublishing.com/in-almost-every-picture/.

5. Craig Dworkin, *No Medium* (Cambridge, MA: MIT Press, 2013).

6. "Books," *Alisa Banks*, accessed July 17, 2017, http://www.alisabanks.com/artwork/books/.

7. "Press Release," Doc/Undoc, accessed July 17, 2017, https://docundoc.com/2014/07/06/press_release/.

8. William Blake, "Milton: A Poem in 2 Books," in *The Complete Poetry and Prose of William Blake*, ed. David V. Erdman (Berkeley: University of California Press), 95. This edition is also available online at *The William Blake Archive*, along with plates from his illuminated works, accessed July 17, 2017, http://erdman.blakearchive.org/.

9. Ibid., 39.

10. Robert N. Essick and Joseph Viscomi, "An Inquiry into William Blake's Method of Color Printing," *Blake: An Illustrated Quarterly* 35, no. 3 (Winter 2002): 96.

11. "Illuminated Printing," *The William Blake Archive*, accessed July 17, 2017, http://www.blakearchive.org/staticpage/biography?p=illuminatedprinting.

12. W. J. T. Mitchell, *Picture Theory: Essays on Verbal and Visual Representation* (Chicago: University of Chicago Press, 1994), 89.

13. "Illuminated Printing," *The William Blake Archive*.

14. William Blake, *The Complete Poetry and Prose*, 692–693.

15. Ibid., 771.

16. Simon Morley, *Writing on the Wall: Word and Image in Modern Art* (Los Angeles: University of California Press, 2003), 23.

17. Gary Frost, *Future of the Book: A Way Forward* (Coralville: Iowa Book Works, 2012), n.p.

18. Stéphane Mallarmé, "The Crisis in Poetry," in *Modernism: An Anthology of Sources and Documents*, ed. Vassiliki Kolocotroni, Jane Goldman, and Olga Taxidou (Chicago: University of Chicago Press, 1998), 126.

19. Stéphane Mallarmé, "The Book, Spiritual Instrument," trans. Michael Gibbs, in *The Book, Spiritual Instrument*, ed. Jerome Rothenberg and David Guss (New York: Granary Books, 1996), Granary Books, 2001, accessed July 17, 2017, http://www.granarybooks.com/books/rothenberg/rothenberg5.html.

20. A scan of the 1914 printing is available vie the Bibliothèque nationale de France at http://gallica.bnf.fr/ark:/12148/bpt6k71351c/.

21. Stéphane Mallarmé, *A Roll of the Dice*, trans. Jeff Clark and Robert Bononno (Seattle: Wave Books), 2.

22. Ibid.

23. Ibid.

24. Ibid., 8–9.

25. Ibid., 23.

26. Mallarmé, "The Book, Spiritual Instrument."

27. Drucker, *The Century of Artists' Books*, 69.

28. Lucy Lippard, "The Artist's Book Goes Public," in *Artists' Books: A Critical Anthology and Sourcebook*, ed. Joan Lyons (Rochester, NY: Visual Studies Workshop, 1985), 45.

29. Janis Ekdahl, "Artists' Books and Beyond: The Library of the Museum of Modern Art as a Curatorial and Research Resource," *Inspel* 33, no. 4 (1999), 244.

30. Ulises Carrión, "The New Art of Making Books," in *Second Thoughts* (Amsterdam: VOID Distributors, 1980), 7.

31. Carrión, quoted in Guy Schraenen, "A Story to Remember," in *Dear Reader. Don't Read* (Madrid: Museo Nacional Centro de Arte Reina Sofia, 2015), 17.

32. Carrión, "The New Art of Making Books," 10, 13.

33. Ibid.," 7.

34. Ibid.

35. Ibid., 14.

36. Ibid., 25.

37. Ulises Carrión, "From Bookworks to Mailworks," in *Second Thoughts* (Amsterdam: VOID Distributors, 1980), 25.

38. Ibid.

39. Garrett Stewart, *Bookwork: Medium to Object to Concept to Art* (Chicago: University of Chicago Press, 2011), xiv.

40. Ulises Carrión, "Bookworks Revisited," Bill Ritchie and Lynda Ritchie family Seattle Art Gallery, accessed July 17, 2017, http://www.seanet.com/~ritchie/vtbookw.html.

41. Ong, *Orality and Literacy*, 129.

42. Clare Ford-Wille, "Peepshow Box," in *The Oxford Companion to Western Art* (Oxford: Oxford University Press, 2001), accessed July 17, 2017, doi: 10.1093/acref/9780198662037.001.0001.

43. Ralph Hyde, *Paper Peepshows: The Jaqueline & Jonathan Gestetner Collection* (Woodbridge, Suffolk, England: Antique Collectors' Club, 2015), 6.

44. Bill Wilson, "The Big Book," in *The Big Book*, Alison Knowles (Leipzig: Passenger Books, 2013), 44. Wilson's article appeared originally in *Art in America* (July–August) and was also published in 1968 in the *Journal of Typographic Research*.

45. Steven Clay and Rodney Phillips track these presses in *A Secret Location on the Lower East Side: Adventures in Writing, 1960–1980* (New York: NYPL and Granary Books, 1998).

46. Junker, quoted in Nicole L. Woods, "Object/Poems: Alison Knowles' Feminist Archite(x)ture," *X-TRA: Contemporary Art Quarterly* 15, no. 1 (2012): 8.

47. Bruce Reed, "Unpublished review (1967)," in *The Big Book*, Alison Knowles (Leipzig: Passenger Books, 2013), 37. Unpublished draft for an article to appear in the *Toronto Telegram* (1967), presumably by Bruce Reed.

48. Caitlin Fisher, "Artist's Statement," *ELO 2012 Media Art Show*, accessed July 17, 2017, http://dtc-wsuv.org/elit/elo2012/elo2012/Fisher.html.

49. The Selfie Drawings, accessed July 17, 2017, http://theselfiedrawings .com.

50. "The Mutoscope," *San Francisco Call* 84, no. 159 (November 6, 1898), California Digital Newspaper Collection, accessed July 17, 2017, https://cdnc.ucr. edu.

51. Michael Snow, *Cover to Cover* (Halifax, Nova Scotia/New York: Nova Scotia College of Art & Design/New York University Press, 1975). For those who can't access a physical copy, a video documenting each spread perfectly animates the text, revealing the conceit and its playful conclusion: https://vimeo .com/88029485.

52. Emmett Williams, *Sweethearts* (Berlin: Verlag der Buchandlung Walther König, [1967] 2010).

53. The text's maneuvers have been digitized by designer Mindy Seu at "sweethearts," accessed July 17, 2017, http://sweetheartsweetheart.com.

54. Howard Lamarr Walls, *Motion Pictures, 1894–1912* (Washington, DC: Library of Congress Copyright Office, 1953).

55. "Soldier," *Editions Zédélé*, accessed July 17, 2017, http://www.editions -zedele.net.

56. Watkins, *Indo-European Word Roots*, 63.

57. Bob Brown, "The Readies," in *In Transition: A Paris Anthology: Writing and Art from* Transition *Magazine 1927–1930* (New York: Anchor, 1990), 59.

58. Ibid.

59. Craig Saper, "Introduction," in *The Readies by Bob Brown*, ed. Craig Saper (Baltimore: Roving Eye Press, 2014), ix.

60. Craig Saper, *The Amazing Adventures of Bob Brown: A Real-Life Zelig Who Wrote His Way through the Twentieth Century* (New York: Fordham University Press, 2016), 58.

61. Andrew F. Smith, "Brown, Bob, Cora, and Rose," in *The Oxford Encyclopedia of Food and Drink in America*, vol. 2, ed. Andrew F. Smith (New York: Oxford University Press: 2013), 218.

62. Saper, "Introduction," xii.

63. "The Reading Machine," Readies, accessed July 17, 2017, http://www.readies.org.

64. *Spritz Inc.*, accessed July 17, 2017, http://spritzinc.com/.

65. Stewart, *Bookwork*, 83.

66. A digitized 1476 edition is available through the University of Oklahoma Libraries, *History of Science*, accessed July 17, 2017, https://hos.ou.edu/galleries//15thCentury/Regiomontanus/1476/. Scholar Whitney Trettien's wonderful study of volvelles and combinatorial writing is written in a generative structure and available to read at *Computers, Cut-Ups, & Combinatory Volvelles: An Archaeology of Text-Generating Mechanisms*, accessed July 17, 2017, http://whitneyannetrettien.com/thesis/.

67. Raymond Queneau, "Instructions for Use," in *One Hundred Million Million Poems,* trans. John Crombie (France: Kickshaws Press, 1983), n.p.

68. Ibid.

69. Digital iterations of Queneau's book are available online in several translations, facilitating the process of reading the text's iterations. See "Cent mille millards de poèmes," *Magnus Bodin—Psykologisk Illusionist*, 1997, accessed July 17, 2017, http://x42.com/active/queneau.html.

70. *The Poetry of Robert Frost: The Collected Poems Complete and Unabridged* (New York: Henry Holt, 1979), 105.

71. The book is no longer available on the artist's website, but as a printed book through Amazon. Details on other graphic novels and forthcoming interactive work can be found at Shiga Books, accessed July 17, 2017, http://www.shigabooks.com.

72. Andrew Plotkin and Jason Shiga, "Meanwhile," accessed July 17, 2017, http://zarfhome.com/meanwhile/.

73. "Dieter Roth Interactive Composition Generator," The55, accessed July 17, 2017, http://www.the55.net/_13/sketch/dieter_roth_a#.WDOf8KIrLMU.

74. Rebecca Knuth, *Libricide: The Regime-Sponsored Destruction of Books and Libraries in the Twentieth Century* (Westport: Praeger, 2003), 49.

75. Edward Ruscha, interviewed by Christophe Cherix, The Museum of Modern Art Oral History Program, January 24, 2012, accessed July 17, 2017, https://www.moma.org/momaorg/shared/pdfs/docs/learn/archives/transcript_ruscha.pdf.

76. Documentation of the artist constructing and exploding the book in 2017 can be seen at vimeo.com/18052124.

77. "Cai Guo-Qiang, Danger Book: Suicide Fireworks," Ivory Press, accessed July 17, 2017, http://www.ivorypress.com/en/editorial/cai-guo-qiang.danger-book-suicide-fireworks.

78. Peter G. Wells, "Managing Ocean Information in the Digital Era—Events in Canada Open Questions about the Role of Marine Science Libraries," *Marine Pollution Bulletin* 83, no. 1 (2014): 1–4.

79. Thomas Fulton, "Gilded Monuments: Shakespeare's Sonnets, Donne's Letters, and the Mediated Text," in *Comparative Textual Media: Transforming the Humanities in the Postprint Era*, ed. N. Katherine Hayles and Jessica Pressman (Minneapolis: University of Minnesota Press, 2013), 225.

80. Stewart, *Bookwork*, 18.

81. Pierre Cabanne, *Dialogues with Marcel Duchamp* (New York: Da Capo Press, 1987), 61.

82. Petroski, *The Book on the Bookshelf*, 31.

83. Reproduced in *Wait, Later This Will Be Nothing: Editions By Dieter Roth*, ed. Sarah Suzuki (New York: The Museum of Modern Art, 2013), 87.

84. Museum label for Reynier Leyva Novo, *5 Nights*, from the series "The Weight of History," Smithsonian Institution Hirschhorn Museum and Sculpture Garden, Washington, DC, "Masterworks from the Hirshhorn Collection," June 9, 2016–September 4, 2017.

85. Wallace Stevens, "The Planet on the Table," *Collected Poetry and Prose* (New York: Library of America, 1997), 450.

86. Buzz Spector, "On the Fetishism of the Book Object," in *Threads Talk Series*, ed. Steve Clay and Kyle Schlesinger (New York: Granary Books; Victoria, TX: Cuneiform Press, 2016), 59.

87. Rietje van Vliet, "Print and Public in Europe 1600–1800," in *A Companion to the History of the Book*, ed. Simon Eliot and Jonathan Rose (Malden, MA: Blackwell Publishing, 2007), doi: 10.1002/9780470690949.ch18, 253.

88. The ways in which Renaissance readers "used" their books as a kind of furniture are beautifully cataloged and analyzed in Jeffrey Todd Knight's "Furnished for Action," *Book History* 12, no. 1 (2009): 37–73.

4   The Book as Interface

1. Lori Emerson, *Reading Writing Interfaces* (Minneapolis: University of Minnesota Press, 2014), 2.

2. Stallybrass, "Books and Scrolls," 46.

3. Matthew Kirschenbaum, "Bookscapes: Modeling Books in Electronic Space," paper presented at the Human Computer Interaction Lab 25th Annual Symposium, College Park, MD, May 29, 2008.

4. Michael E. Cohen, "Scotched," *The Magazine* #32 (December 19, 2013), accessed July 17, 2017, http://the-magazine.org/32/scotched.

5. Jay David Bolter and Richard Grusin, *Remediation: Understanding New Media* (Cambridge, MA: MIT Press, 1999).

6. Mark Kurlansky, *Paper: Paging Through History* (New York: W. W. Norton, 2016).

7. N. Katherine Hayles, *Writing Machines* (Cambridge, MA: MIT Press, 2002), 22.

8. Hayles, *Writing Machines*, 23.

9. Terry Harpold, *Ex-foliations: Reading Machines and the Upgrade Path* (Minneapolis: University of Minnesota Press, 2009), 3.

10. Matthew Rubery, *The Untold Story of the Talking Book* (Cambridge, MA: Harvard University Press, 2016), 31.

11. Frances A. Koestler, *The Unseen Minority: A Social History of Blindness in the United States* (New York: American Foundation for the Blind, 2004), accessed July 17, 2017, http://www.afb.org/unseen/book.asp.

12. "200 Years: The Life and Legacy of Louis Braille," *American Foundation for the Blind*, 2009, accessed July 17, 2017, http://www.afb.org/LouisBrailleMuseum/braillegallery.asp?FrameID=156.

13. Vannevar Bush, "As We May Think," in *The New Media Reader*, ed. Noah Wardrip-Fruin and Nick Montfort (Cambridge, MA: MIT Press, 2003), 37.

14. Petroski, *The Book on the Bookshelf*, 115; Harpold, *Ex-foliations*, 214.

15. Marie Lebert, *Project Gutenberg (1971–2008)*, 2008, accessed July 17, 2017, http://www.gutenberg.org/cache/epub/27045/pg27045-images.html.

16. *Free ebooks—Project Gutenberg*, accessed July 17, 2017, https://www.gutenberg.org/.

17. Michael S. Hart, "The History and Philosophy of Project Gutenberg," August 1992, accessed July 17, 2017, http://www.gutenberg.org/wiki/Gutenberg:The_History_and_Philosophy_of_Project_Gutenberg_by_Michael_Hart.

18. Michael S. Hart, "How eTexts Will Become the 'Killer App' of the Computer Revolution," November 22, 2006, accessed July 17, 2017, https://www.gutenberg.org/wiki/Gutenberg:How_eTexts_Will_Become_the_%22Killer_App%22_of_the_Computer_Revolution_by_Michael_Hart.

19. Open Library books are accessible both through the Internet Archive and a dedicated website, Open Library, accessed July 17, 2017, https://openlibrary.org.

20. "About the Internet Archive," The Internet Archive, accessed July 17, 2017, https://archive.org/about.

21. Brewster Kahle, "Why Preserve Books? The New Physical Archive of the Internet Archive," Internet Archive Blogs, June 6, 2011, accessed July 17, 2017,

http://blog.archive.org/2011/06/06/why-preserve-books-the-new-physical
-archive-of-the-internet-archive.

22. Brewster Kahle, "Help Us Keep the Archive Free, Accessible, and Reader Private," Internet Archive Blogs, November 29, 2016, accessed July 17, 2017, https://
blog.archive.org/2016/11/29/help-us-keep-the-archive-free-accessible-and
-private.

23. "Internet Archive: Bookmobile," The Internet Archive, accessed July 17,
2017, https://archive.org/texts/bookmobile.php.

24. "Google Books History," Google Books, accessed July 17, 2017, https://
books.google.com/intl/en/googlebooks/about/history.html.

25. Tim Wu, "Whatever Happened to Google Books," New Yorker, September 11, 2015, accessed July 17, 2017, http://www.newyorker.com/business/
currency/what-ever-happened-to-google-books.

26. James Somers, "Torching the Modern-Day Library of Alexandria," The Atlantic, April 20, 2017, accessed July 17, 2017, https://www.theatlantic.com/
technology/archive/2017/04/the-tragedy-of-google-books/523320/.

27. "Google Books History."

28. "Docket Item 230 from the case The Authors Guild v. Google, Inc.," United
States Courts Archive, October 16, 2015, accessed July 17, 2017, https://www
.unitedstatescourts.org/federal/ca2/13-4829/230-0.html.

29. The Internet Archive's trove of Google Book scans is available at "Google
Books," The Internet Archive, accessed July 17, 2017, https://archive.org/
details/googlebooks.

30. Mary E. Murrell, "The Open Book: Digital Form in the Making" (PhD diss.,
UC Berkeley, 2012), 89.

31. Mar Abad, "Ángela Ruíz Robles: la Española que vislumbró la era digital
edn los años 40," Yorokobu, accessed July 17, 2017, http://www.yorokobu.es/
angela-ruiz-robles/.

32. "Incipit 1992," Divisare, accessed July 17, 2017, https://divisare.com/
projects/185708-franco-crugnola-incipit-1992.

33. "The SoftBook System," SoftBook, December 2, 1998, accessed July 17,
2017, http://web.archive.org/web/19981202200925/http://www.softbook
.com:80/softbook_sys/index.html.

34. Sian Cain, "Ebook Sales Continue to Fall as Younger Generations Drive
Appetite for Print," The Guardian, March 14, 2017, accessed July 17, 2017,
https://www.theguardian.com/books/2017/mar/14/ebook-sales-continue-to
-fall-nielsen-survey-uk-book-sales?CMP=twt_books_b-gdnbooks.

35. Jonathan Segura, "Print Sales Stay Hot: Unit Sales of Print Books Rose
3.3% in 2016 over the Previous Year, Making It the Third-Straight Year of Print
Growth," Publishers Weekly 264, no. 2 (2017): 4.

36. Gerard Genette, *Paratexts: Thresholds of Interpretation*, trans. Jane E. Lewin (Cambridge: Cambridge University Press, 1997), 1–3.

37. Drucker, "The Virtual Codex."

38. Frost, *Future of the Book*, 68.

39. Ted Striphas provides a thorough breakdown of the history and implementation of the ISBN in *The Late Age of Print: Everyday Book Culture from Consumerism to Control* (New York: Columbia University Press, 2009), 92–95.

40. "ISBN US," Bowker, accessed July 17, 2017, http://www.bowker.com/products/ISBN-US.html

41. Susan Lulgjuraj, "DBW '17: Why Are Print Sales Up?," TeleRead, accessed July 17, 2017, https://teleread.org/2017/01/17/dbw-17-print-books-ebooks.

42. Fiona Banner, "Legal Deposit," *Bomb Magazine* 112 (Summer 2010), accessed July 17, 2017, http://bombmagazine.org/article/3553/legal-deposit.

43. An image is available at the artist's website: "Vanity Press," Fiona Banner, accessed July 17, 2017, http://www.fionabanner.com/vanitypress/isbnbook/index.htm.

44. Sven Birkerts, *The Gutenberg Elegies* (New York: Faber and Faber, 1994), 146.

45. "Human Interface Guidelines: Gestures," *Apple Developer*, accessed July 17, 2017, https://developer.apple.com/ios/human-interface-guidelines/interaction/gestures/.

46. The novella must be purchased through The App Store, but documentation is available at the Pry website, accessed July 17, 2017, http://prynovella.com.

47. "About Us," Editions at Play, accessed July 17, 2017, https://editionsatplay.withgoogle.com/#/about.

48. Dick Higgins and Hannah Higgins, "Intermedia," *Leonardo* 34, no. 1 (2001): 53.

49. Dick Higgins, "A Preface," in *Artists' Books: A Critical Anthology and Sourcebook*, ed. Joan Lyons (Rochester, NY: Visual Studies Workshop Press, 1985), 11.

50. "The Gutenberg Parenthesis Research Forum," Southern Denmark University, 2007, accessed October 22, 2017, https://www.sdu.dk/en/om_sdu/institutter_centre/ikv/forskning/forskningsprojekter/gutenberg_projekt/glog.

BIBLIOGRAPHY

Agrawal, Om Prakash. "Care and Conservation of Palm-Leaf and Paper Illuminated Manuscripts." In *Palm-Leaf and Paper: Illustrated Manuscripts of India and Southeast Asia*, ed. John Guy, 84–90. Melbourne: National Gallery of Victoria, 1982.

Agüera y Arcas, Blaise. "Temporary Matrices and Elemental Punches in Gutenberg's DK Type." In *Incunabula and Their Readers: Printing, Selling and Using Books in the Fifteenth Century*, ed. Kristian Jensen, 3–12. London: The British Library, 2003.

Albin, Michael. "The Islamic Book." In *A Companion to the History of the Book*, ed. Simon Eliot and Jonathan Rose, 165–176. Malden, MA: Blackwell Publishing, 2007. Accessed July 17, 2017. doi: 10.1002/9780470690949.ch12.

Altick, Richard. "From Aldine to Everyman: Cheap Reprint Series of the English Classics 1830–1906." *Studies in Bibliography* 11 (1958): 3–24.

Andrews, Martin. "The Importance of Ephemera." In *A Companion to the History of the Book*, ed. Simon Eliot and Jonathan Rose, 434–450. Malden, MA: Blackwell Publishing, 2007. Accessed July 17, 2017. doi: 10.1002/9780470690949.ch32.

Armstrong, Elizabeth. *Before Copyright: The French Book Privilege System 1498–1526*. Cambridge: Cambridge University Press, 1990.

Avrin, Leila. *Scribes, Script, and Books: The Book Arts from Antiquity to the Renaissance*. Chicago: The American Library Association, 1991.

Barker, Nicholas. *Aldus Manutius and the Development of Greek Script and Type in the Fifteenth Century*. New York: Fordham University Press, 1992.

Benjamin, Walter. "The Work of Art in the Age of Its Technological Reproducibility." In *Selected Writings, Volume 4: 1938–1940*, ed. Howard Eiland and Michael W. Jennings, 251–283. Cambridge, MA: Belknap Press of Harvard University Press, 2003.

Birkerts, Sven. *The Gutenberg Elegies*. New York: Faber and Faber, 1994.

Blake, William. *The Complete Poetry and Prose of William Blake*. Ed. David V. Erdman. Berkeley: University of California Press, 2008.

Blanchot, Maurice. *The Infinite Conversation*. Trans. Susan Hanson. Minneapolis: University of Minnesota Press, 1993.

Bolter, Jay David and Richard Grusin. *Remediation: Understanding New Media*. Cambridge, MA: MIT Press, 1999.

Brantley, Jessica. "The Prehistory of the Book." *PMLA: Publications of the Modern Language Association of America* 124, no. 2 (2009): 632–639.

Brown, Bob. "The Readies." In *Transition: A Paris Anthology: Writing and Art from* Transition *Magazine 1927–1930*, 59–64. New York: Anchor, 1990.

Bülow-Jacobsen, Adam. "Writing Materials in the Ancient World." In *Oxford Handbook of Papyrology*, ed. Roger S. Bagnall, 3–29. Oxford: Oxford University Press, 2011. Oxford Handbooks Online. Accessed July 17, 2017. doi: 10.1093/oxfordhb/9780199843695.013.0001.

Burkus-Chasson, Anne. "Visual Hermeneutics and the Act of Turning the Leaf: A Genealogy of Liu Yuan's Lingyan ge." In *Printing and Book Culture in Late Imperial China*, ed. Cynthia J. Brokaw and Chow Kai-wing, 371–416. Berkeley: University of California Press, 2005. Oxford University Press Ebooks. Accessed July 17, 2017. doi: 10.1525/california/9780520231269.001.0001.

Bush, Vannevar. "As We May Think." In *The New Media Reader*, ed. Noah Wardrip-Fruin and Nick Montfort, 35–48. Cambridge, MA: MIT Press, 2003.

Cabanne, Pierre. *Dialogues with Marcel Duchamp*. New York: Da Capo Press, 1987.

Carrión, Ulises. "The New Art of Making Books." In *Second Thoughts*, 6–22. Amsterdam: VOID Distributors, 1980.

Carrión, Ulises. "From Bookworks to Mailworks." In *Second Thoughts*, 24–31. Amsterdam: VOID Distributors, 1980.

Cavallo, Guglielmo, and Roger Chartier, eds. *A History of Reading in the West*. Trans. Lydia G. Cochrane. Amherst: University of Massachusetts Press, 1999.

"*Chanccani Quipu* by Cecilia Vicuña." Granary Books. Accessed July 17, 2017. http://www.granarybooks.com/book/1150/Cecilia_Vicuna+Chanccani_Quipu.

Chartier, Roger. "The Printing Revolution: A Reappraisal." In *Agent of Change: Print Culture Studies after Elizabeth L. Eisenstein*, ed. Sabrina Alcorn Baron, Eric N. Lindquist and Eleanor F. Shevlin, 397–408. Amherst: University of Massachusetts Press, 2007.

Chen, Julie, and Clifton Meador. *How Books Work*. Berkeley, CA/Chicago IL: Flying Fish Press/Center for Book and Paper Arts, 2010.

Chow, Kai-wing. "Reinventing Gutenberg: Woodblock and Movable-Type Printing in Europe and China." In *Agent of Change: Print Culture Studies after Elizabeth L. Eisenstein*, ed. Sabrina Baron, Eric Lindquist and Eleanor Shevlin, 169–193. Amherst: University of Massachusetts Press, 2007.

Clark, John Willis. *The Care of Books; an Essay on the Development of Libraries and Their Fittings, from the Earliest Times to the End of the Eighteenth Century*. Cambridge: Cambridge University Press, 1901.

Cormack, Bradin, and Carla Mazzio. *Book Use, Book Theory: 1500–1700*. Chicago: University of Chicago Library, 2005.

Dane, Joseph. *What Is a Book?: The Study of Early Printed Books*. Notre Dame: University of Notre Dame Press, 2012.

Darnton, Robert. *The Case for Books*. New York: Public Affairs, 2009.

Davies, Martin. *Aldus Manutius: Printer and Publisher of Renaissance Venice*. Tempe: Arizona Center for Medieval and Renaissance Studies, 1999.

Drucker, Johanna. "The Virtual Codex: From Page Space to E-space." The Book Arts Web, April 25, 2003. Accessed July 17, 2017. http://www.philobiblon.com/drucker.

Drucker, Johanna. *The Century of Artists' Books*. New York: Granary Books, 1994.

Dworkin, Craig. *No Medium*. Cambridge, MA: MIT Press, 2013.

Edgren, J. S. "The Book beyond the West—China." In *A Companion to the History of the Book*, ed. Simon Eliot and Jonathan Rose, 95–110. Malden, MA: Blackwell Publishing, 2007. Accessed July 17, 2017. doi: 10.1002/9780470690949.ch7.

Edler de Roover, Florence. "The Scriptorium." In *The Medieval Library*, ed. James Westfall Thompson, 594–612. New York: Hafner Publishing, 1939.

Ekdahl, Janis. "Artists' Books and Beyond: The Library of the Museum of Modern Art as a Curatorial and Research Resource." *Inspel* 33, no. 4 (1999): 241–248.

Emerson, Lori. *Reading Writing Interfaces*. Minneapolis: University of Minnesota Press, 2014.

Essick, Robert N., and Joseph Viscomi. "An Inquiry into William Blake's Method of Color Printing." *Blake: An Illustrated Quarterly* 35, no. 3 (Winter 2002): 74–103.

Febvre, Lucien, and Henri-Jean Martin. *The Coming of the Book: The Impact of Printing, 1450–1800*. Trans. D. Gerard. London: Verso, 1976.

Finkelstein, David, and Alistain McCleery. *An Introduction to Book History*. New York: Routledge, 2005.

Ford-Wille, Clare. "Peepshow Box." In *The Oxford Companion to Western Art*, ed. Hugh Brigstocke. Oxford: Oxford University Press, 2001. Oxford Reference. Accessed July 17, 2017. doi: 10.1093/acref/9780198662037.001.0001.

Frost, Gary. *Future of the Book: A Way Forward*. Coralville: Iowa Book Works, 2012.

Fulton, Thomas. "Gilded Monuments: Shakespeare's Sonnets, Donne's Letters, and the Mediated Text." In *Comparative Textual Media: Transforming the Humanities in the Postprint Era*, ed. N. Katherine Hayles and Jessica Pressman, 221–253. Minneapolis: University of Minnesota Press, 2013.

Genette, Gerard. *Paratexts: Thresholds of Interpretation*. Trans. Jane E. Lewin. Cambridge: Cambridge University Press, 1997.

Glassner, Jean-Jacques, Zainab Bahrani, and Marc Van De Mieroop. *The Invention of Cuneiform: Writing in Sumer*. Baltimore: Johns Hopkins University Press, 2003.

Grafton, Anthony. "The Humanist as Reader." Trans. L. G. Cochrane. In *A History of Reading in the West*, ed. Guglielmo Cavallo and Roger Chartier, 179–212. Amherst: University of Massachusetts Press, 1999.

Guo-Qiang, Cai. Statement in *Shu: Reinventing Books in Contemporary Chinese Art*, ed. Wu Hung and Peggy Wang, 26–27. New York: China Institute Gallery, 2006.

Guozhong, Liu. *Introduction to the Tsinghua Bamboo-Strip Manuscripts*. Trans. C. J. Foster and W. N. French. Leiden: Brill, 2016.

Harpold, Terry. *Ex-foliations: Reading Machines and the Upgrade Path*. Minneapolis: University of Minnesota Press, 2009.

Hayles, N. Katherine. *Writing Machines*. Cambridge, MA: MIT Press, 2002.

Higgins, Dick. "A Book." *New Wilderness Letter* 11 (1982): 46–47.

Higgins, Dick. "A Preface." In *Artists' Books: A Critical Anthology and Sourcebook*, ed. Joan Lyons, 11–12. Rochester, NY: Visual Studies Workshop Press, 1985.

Higgins, Dick, and Hannah Higgins. "Intermedia." *Leonardo* 34, no. 1 (2001): 49–54.

Hochuli, Jost, ed. *Jan Tschichold, Typographer and Type Designer, 1902–1974*. Trans. Ruari McLean, W. A. Kelly, and Bernard Wolpe. Edinburgh: National Library of Scotland, 1982.

Houston, Keith. *The Book: A Cover-to-Cover Exploration of the Most Powerful Object of Our Time*. New York: W. W. Norton, 2016.

Hyde, Ralph. *Paper Peepshows: The Jaqueline & Jonathan Gestetner Collection*. Woodbridge, Suffolk, England: Antique Collectors' Club, 2015.

Jabès, Edmond. *The Little Book of Unsuspected Subversion*. Trans. Rosmarie Waldrop. Redwood City, CA: Stanford University Press, 1996.

Jager, Eric. *The Book of the Heart*. Chicago: University of Chicago Press, 2000.

Johns, Adrian. *The Nature of the Book: Print and Knowledge in the Making*. Chicago: University of Chicago Press, 1998.

Johnson, William A. "The Ancient Book." In *The Oxford Handbook of Papyrology*, ed. Roger S. Bagnall, 256–281. New York: Oxford University Press, 2012.

Johnson, William A. "Bookroll as Media." In *Comparative Textual Media: Transforming the Humanities in the Postprint Era*, ed. N. Katherine Hayles and Jessica Pressman, 101–124. Minneapolis: University of Minnesota Press, 2013.

Judge, Elizabeth. "Kidnapped and Counterfeit Characters: Eighteenth-Century Fan Fiction, Copyright Law, and the Custody of Fictional Characters." In *Originality and Intellectual Property in the French and English Enlightenment*, ed. Reginald McGinnis, 22–68. New York: Routledge, 2009.

Kennedy, Amos Paul, Jr. "Social Book Building." In *Talking the Boundless Book*, ed. Charles Alexander, 45–56. Minneapolis: Minnesota Center for Book Arts, 1995.

Kenyon, Frederic G. *Books and Readers in Ancient Greece and Rome*. Oxford: Clarendon Press, 1932.

Kilgour, Frederick. *The Evolution of the Book*. New York: Oxford University Press, 1998.

Kirschenbaum, Matthew. "Bookscapes: Modeling Books in Electronic Space." Paper presented at the Human Computer Interaction Lab 25th Annual Symposium, College Park, MD, May 29, 2008. Accessed July 17, 2017. https://mkirschenbaum.files.wordpress.com/2013/01/bookscapes.pdf.

Knight, Jeffrey Todd. "Furnished for Action." *Book History* 12, no. 1 (2009): 37–73.

Knowles, Alison. *The Big Book*. Leipzig: Passenger Books, 2013.

Knuth, Rebecca. *Libricide: The Regime-Sponsored Destruction of Books and Libraries in the Twentieth Century*. Westport: Praeger, 2003.

Koestler, Frances A. *The Unseen Minority: A Social History of Blindness in the United States*. New York: American Foundation for the Blind, 2004. Accessed July 17, 2017. http://www.afb.org/unseen/book.asp.

Kurlansky, Mark. *Paper: Paging Through History*. New York: W. W. Norton, 2016.

Landow, George P. "Twenty Minutes into the Future: Or, How Are We Moving beyond the Book?" In *The Future of the Book*, ed. Geoffrey P. Nunberg, 209–237. Berkeley: University of California Press, 1996.

Lebert, Marie. *Project Gutenberg (1971–2008)*. E-book, 2008. Accessed July 17, 2017. http://www.gutenberg.org/cache/epub/27045/pg27045-images.html.

Lewis, A. W. *Basic Bookbinding*. New York: Dover, 1957.

Lindberg, David C. *The Beginnings of Western Science*. Chicago: University of Chicago Press, 1992.

Lippard, Lucy. "The Artist's Book Goes Public." In *Artists' Books: A Critical Anthology and Sourcebook*, ed. Joan Lyons, 45–48. Rochester, NY: Visual Studies Workshop, 1985.

Lowry, M. J. C. "The 'New Academy' of Aldus Manutius: A Renaissance Dream." *Bulletin of the John Rylands Library* 58, no. 2 (1976): 378–420.

Lyons, Martyn. *Books: A Living History*. Los Angeles: Getty Publications, 2011.

Mak, Bonnie. *How the Page Matters*. Toronto: University of Toronto Press, 2011.

Mallarmé, Stéphane. "The Book, Spiritual Instrument." Trans. Michael Gibbs. In *The Book, Spiritual Instrument*, ed. Jerome Rothenberg and David Guss. New York: Granary Books, 1996. Granary Books, 2001. Accessed July 17, 2017. http://www.granarybooks.com/books/rothenberg/rothenberg5.html.

Mallarmé, Stéphane. *A Roll of the Dice*. Trans. Jeff Clark and Robert Bononno. Seattle: Wave Books, 2015.

Mallarmé, Stéphane. "The Crisis in Poetry." In *Modernism: An Anthology of Sources and Documents*, ed. Vassiliki Kolocotroni, Jane Goldman, and Olga Taxidou, 123–126. Chicago: University of Chicago Press, 1998.

Man, John. *Gutenberg: How One Man Remade the World with Words*. New York: John Wiley and Sons, 2002.

Manguel, Alberto. *A History of Reading*. New York: Penguin, 1996.

Martin, Henri-Jean. *The History and Power of Writing*. Chicago: University of Chicago Press, 1994.

McKenzie, D. F. *Bibliography and the Sociology of Texts*. Cambridge, UK: Cambridge University Press, 1999.

McMurtrie, Douglas C. *The Book: The Story of Printing and Bookmaking*. New York: Covici-Friede, 1937.

Meador, Betty De Shong. *Inanna, Lady of the Largest Heart: Poems of the Sumerian High Priestess Enheduanna*. Austin: University of Texas Press, 2000.

Mitchell, W. J. T. *Picture Theory: Essays on Verbal and Visual Representation*. Chicago: University of Chicago Press, 1994.

Morley, Simon. *Writing on the Wall: Word and Image in Modern Art*. Los Angeles: University of California Press, 2003.

Murra, John V. "Cloth and Its Functions in the Inca State." *American Anthropologist* 64, no. 4 (1962): 710–728.

Murrell, Mary E. "The Open Book: Digital Form in the Making." PhD diss., UC Berkeley, 2012.

Ong, Walter J. *Orality and Literacy: The Technologizing of the Word*. New York: Routledge, 2002.

Ovenden, Richard. "Bookplate." In *The Oxford Companion to the Book*, ed. Michael F. Suarez and H. R. Woodhuysen. Oxford: Oxford University Press, 2010. Oxford Reference. Accessed July 17, 2017. doi: 10.1093/ac ref/9780198606536.001.0001.

Parkes, M. B. "Reading, Copying and Interpreting a Text in the Early Middle Ages." In *A History of Reading in the West*, ed. Guglielmo Cavallo and Roger Chartier, 90–102. Amherst: University of Massachusetts Press, 1999.

Petroski, Henry. *The Book on the Bookshelf*. New York: Alfred A. Knopf, 1999.

Pflughhaupt, Laurent. *Letter by Letter*. Trans. G. Bruhn. New York: Princeton Architectural Press, 2007.

Piper, Andrew. *Book Was There: Reading in Electronic Times*. Chicago: University of Chicago Press, 2012.

Plato. *Phaedrus*. Section 275c, Perseus Digital Library. Accessed July 17, 2017. http://data.perseus.org/citations/urn:cts:greekLit:tlg0059.tlg012 .perseus-eng1:275c.

Polastron, Lucien X. *Books on Fire: The Destruction of Libraries throughout History*. Trans. J. E. Graham. Rochester: Inner Transitions, 2007.

Pressman, Jessica. "The Aesthetic of Bookishness in Twenty-First Century Literature." *Michigan Quarterly Review* 48, no. 4 (2009): 465–482.

Price, Leah. *How to Do Things with Books in Victorian Britain*. Princeton, NJ: Princeton University Press, 2012.

Queneau, Raymond. *One Hundred Million Million Poems*. Trans. J. Crombie. France: Kickshaws Press, 1983.

Reed, Bruce. "Unpublished review (1967)." In *The Big Book*, Alison Knowles, 37–38. Leipzig: Passenger Books, 2013.

Richards, I. A. *Principles of Literary Criticism*. San Diego: Harcourt Brace Jovanovich, 1985.

Roberts, Colin H., and T. C. Skeat. *The Birth of the Codex*. London: Oxford University Press, 1983.

Rose, Mark. "The Author as Proprietor." *Representations* 23 (Summer 1988): 51–85.

Roth, Dieter. *246 Little Clouds*. New York: Something Else Press, 1968.

Rubery, Matthew. *The Untold Story of the Talking Book*. Cambridge, MA: Harvard University Press, 2016.

Saenger, Paul. *Space between Words: The Origins of Silent Reading*. Stanford: Stanford University Press, 1997.

Saper, Craig. "Introduction." In *The Readies by Bob Brown*, ed. Craig Saper, vii–xxv. Baltimore: Roving Eye Press, 2014.

Saper, Craig. *The Amazing Adventures of Bob Brown: A Real-Life Zelig Who Wrote His Way through the Twentieth Century*. New York: Fordham University Press, 2016.

Schmandt-Besserat, Denise, and Michael Erard. "Writing Systems." In *Encyclopedia of Archaeology*, vol. 3, ed. Deborah M. Pearsall, 2222–2234. Oxford, UK: Academic Press, 2008. Gale Virtual Reference Library. Accessed July 17, 2017. doi: 10.1016/B978-012373962-9.00325-3.

Schraenen, Guy. "A Story to Remember." In *Dear Reader. Don't Read*. Madrid: Museo Nacional Centro de Arte Reina Sofia, 2015.

Sherman, William H. "On the Threshold: Architexture, Paratext, and Early Print Culture." In *Agent of Change: Print Culture Studies after Elizabeth L. Eisenstein*, ed. Sabrina Baron, Eric Lindquist, and Eleanor Shevlin, 67–81. Amherst: University of Massachusetts Press, 2007.

Sherman, William H. *Used Books: Marking Readers in Renaissance England*. Philadelphia: University of Pennsylvania Press, 2008.

Shillingsburg, Peter. "Three- or Triple-Decker." In *The Oxford Companion to the Book*, ed. Michael F. Suarez and H. F. Woudhuysen. Oxford: Oxford University Press, 2010. Oxford Reference. Accessed July 17, 2017. doi: 10.1093/ac ref/9780198606536.001.0001.

Skeat, T. C. *Collected Biblical Writings of T.C. Skeat*. Leiden: Brill Academic Publishers, 2004.

Smith, Andrew F. "Brown, Bob, Cora, and Rose." In *The Oxford Encyclopedia of Food and Drink in America*, vol. 2, ed. Andrew F. Smith, 218–219. New York: Oxford University Press, 2013.

Smith, Keith A. *Non-Adhesive Binding: Books without Paste or Glue*, vol. 1, revised and expanded ed., 5th printing. Rochester, NY: Keith Smith Books, 2007.

Smith, Keith A. "Struggling to See." In *Threads Talk Series*, ed. Steve Clay and Kyle Schlesinger, 116–130. New York: Granary Books; Victoria, TX: Cuneiform Press, 2016.

Smith, Margaret M. *The Title-Page, Its Early Development, 1460–1510*. London: British Library, 2000.

Snow, Michael. *Cover to Cover*. Halifax, Nova Scotia/New York: Nova Scotia College of Art & Design/ New York University Press, 1975.

Spector, Buzz. "On the Fetishism of the Book Object." In *Threads Talk Series*, ed. Steve Clay and Kyle Schlesinger, 56–67. New York: Granary Books; Victoria, TX: Cuneiform Press, 2016.

Stallybrass, Peter. "Books and Scrolls: Navigating the Bible." In *Material Texts: Books and Readers in Early Modern England*, ed. Jennifer Andersen and Elizabeth Sauer, 42–79. Philadelphia: University of Pennsylvania Press, 2001.

Stevens, Wallace. *Collected Poetry and Prose*. New York: Library of America, 1997.

Stewart, Garrett. *Bookwork: Medium to Object to Concept to Art*. Chicago: University of Chicago Press, 2011.

Stoicheff, Peter. "Materials and Meanings." In *The Cambridge Companion to the History of the Book*, ed. Leslie Howsam, 73–89. Cambridge: Cambridge University Press, 2014.

Striphas, Ted. *The Late Age of Print: Everyday Book Culture from Consumerism to Control*. New York: Columbia University Press, 2009.

Suzuki, Sarah, ed. *Wait, Later This Will Be Nothing: Editions By Dieter Roth*. New York: The Museum of Modern Art, 2013.

Symington, Dorit. "Late Bronze Age Writing-Boards and Their Uses: Textual Evidence from Anatolia and Syria." *Anatolian Studies* 41 (1991): 111–123.

Taylor, John H. *Journey through the Afterlife: The Ancient Egyptian Book of the Dead*. Cambridge, MA: Harvard University Press, 2010.

Tschichold, Jan. *The Form of the Book: Essays on the Morality of Good Design*. Trans. Hajo Jadeler. Vancouver, BC: Hartley & Marks, 1991.

Tschichold, Jan. *The New Typography: A Handbook for Modern Designers*. Trans. Ruari McLean. Berkeley: University of California Press, 1995.

Tsien, Tsuen-Hsuin. *Written on Bamboo and Silk: The Beginning of Chinese Books and Inscriptions*. 2nd ed. Chicago: University of Chicago Press, 2004.

Urton, Gary. *Signs of the Inka Khipu*. Austin: University of Texas Press, 2003.

van Vliet, Rietje. "Print and Public in Europe 1600–1800." In *A Companion to the History of the Book*, ed. Simon Eliot and Jonathan Rose, 247–258. Malden, MA: Blackwell Publishing, 2007. doi: 10.1002/9780470690949.ch18.

Vicuña, Cecilia. "Knotations on a Quipu." In *Threads Talk Series*, ed. Steve Clay and Kyle Schlesinger, 76–85. New York: Granary Books; Victoria, TX: Cuneiform Press, 2016.

Vogler, Thomas. "When a Book Is Not a Book." In *A Book of the Book: Some Works and Projections about the Book and Writing*, ed. Jerome Rothenberg and Steven Clay, 448–466. New York: Granary Books, 2000.

Walls, Howard Lamarr. *Motion Pictures, 1894–1912*. Washington, DC: Library of Congress Copyright Office, 1953.

Warde, Beatrice. "The Crystal Goblet, or Printing Should Be Invisible." *The Crystal Goblet: Sixteen Essays on Typography*. Cleveland: World Publishing Company, 1956.

Watkins, Calvert. *American Heritage Dictionary of Indo-European Roots*. 3rd ed. Boston: Houghton Mifflin Harcourt, 2011.

Watson, Rowan. "Some Non-textual Uses of Books." In *A Companion to the History of the Book*, ed. Simon Eliot and Jonathan Rose, 480–492. Malden, MA: Blackwell Publishing, 2007. doi: 10.1002/9780470690949.ch35.

Williams, Emmett. *Sweethearts*. Berlin: Verlag der Buchandlung Walther König, [1967] 2010.

Wilson, Bill. "The Big Book." In *The Big Book*, Alison Knowles, 44–45. Leipzig: Passenger Books, 2013.

Woods, Nicole L. "Object/Poems: Alison Knowles' Feminist Archite(x)ture." *X-TRA: Contemporary Art Quarterly* 15, no. 1 (2012): 6–25.

FURTHER READING AND WRITING

Further Reading

Primary Materials Online

The Atlas of Early Printing: An interactive timeline that visualizes the spread of printing during the incunable period. http://atlas.lib.uiowa.edu/

Artists' Books Online: A University of Virginia project that scans contemporary artists' books. http://www.artistsbooksonline.org/

Cuneiform Digital Library Initiative: A database providing images and transcriptions, where available, of cuneiform tablets from more than thirty national and international collections. http://cdli.ucla.edu/

Digital Scriptorium: A central database for exploring the digitized collections of medieval and Renaissance manuscripts at national and international libraries. http://bancroft.berkeley.edu/digitalscriptorium/

Digitized Medieval Manuscripts Map: Links to scans of manuscripts around the world. http://digitizedmedievalmanuscripts.org/app/

Duke Papyrus Archive: Digital scans of fourteen hundred ancient Egyptian papyri. http://library.duke.edu/rubenstein/scriptorium/papyrus/

Electronic Literature Collections, volumes 1–3: An evolving canon of electronic literature produced by the Electronic Literature Organization. http://collection.eliterature.org

International Dunhuang Project: A multilingual collaboration among eight international institutions providing images and information about manuscripts and other artifacts from the Eastern Silk Road. http://idp.bl.uk/

Internet Archive eBooks and Texts: A site that brings together scanned books from a consortium of international libraries including The Smithsonian, the New York Public Library, the Library of Congress, and many more. https://archive.org/details/texts

Rare Book Room: High-resolution scans of "the world's great books" from the collections of notable American libraries and museums. http://rarebookroom .org/

University of Michigan Artists' Books: A collection of nearly fifteen hundred images and descriptions of works in the library's collection. https://quod.lib .umich.edu/m/mlibrary1ic?page=index

World Digital Library, Library of Congress: A project of the United States Library of Congress and Unesco to provide an online repository of digitized works from libraries and archives around the world. https://www.wdl.org/en/

Secondary Sources

Alexander, Charles, ed. *Talking the Boundless Book: Art, Language, and the Book Arts*. Minneapolis: Minnesota Center for Books Arts, 1995.

Bodman, Sarah, and Tom Sowden. *A Manifesto for the Book*. Bristol: The Center for Fine Print Research, 2010.

Bright, Betty. *No Longer Innocent: Book Art in American, 1960–1980*. New York: Granary Books, 2005.

Bringhurst, Robert. *The Elements of Typographic Style*. Point Roberts, WA: Hartley and Marks, 2002.

Chartier, Roger. *The Order of Books: Readers, Authors, and Libraries in Europe between the 14th and 18th Centuries*. Redwood City: Stanford University Press, 1994.

De Hamel, Christopher. *Meetings with Remarkable Manuscripts*. New York: Penguin, 2016.

Dodd, Robin. *From Gutenberg to Opentype: An Illustrated History of Type from the Earliest Letterforms to the Latest Digital Fonts*. Vancouver: Hartley & Marx, 2006.

Finkelstein, David. *The Book History Reader*. New York: Routledge, 2006.

Gitelman, Lisa. *Paper Knowledge: Toward a Media History of Documents*. Durham, NC: Duke University Press, 2014.

Hayles, N. Katherine. *Electronic Literature: New Horizons for the Literary*. South Bend, IN: University of Notre Dame Press, 2008.

Howsam, Leslie. *Old Books and New Histories: An Orientation to Studies in Book and Print Culture*. Toronto: University of Toronto Press, 2006.

Kirschenbaum, Matthew. *Track Changes: A Literary History of Word Processing*. Cambridge, MA: Belknap Press of Harvard University Press, 2016.

Knight, Jeffrey Todd. *Bound to Read*. Philadelphia: University of Pennsylvania Press, 2013.

Lang, Anouk, ed. *From Codex to Hypertext: Reading at the Turn of the Twenty-First Century*. Amherst: University of Massachusetts Press, 2012.

Levy, Michelle, and Tom Mole, eds. *The Broadview Reader in Book History*. Ontario: Broadview, 2014.

Loizeaux, Elizabeth Bergman, and Neil Fraistat, eds. *Reimagining Textuality: Textual Studies in the Late Age of Print*. Madison: University of Wisconsin Press, 2002.

Ludovico, Alessandro. *Post-Digital Print: The Mutation of Publishing since 1894*. Rotterdam: Onomatopee, 2012.

McLuhan, Marshall, and Quentin Fiore. *The Medium Is the Massage*. New York: Random House, 1967.

Nunberg, Geoffrey, ed. *The Future of the Book*. Oakland: University of California Press, 1996.

Pettegree, Andrew. *The Book in the Renaissance*. New Haven: Yale University Press, 2010.

Phillpot, Clive. *Booktrek: Selected Essays on Artists' Books since 1972*. Zurich: JRP Ringier, 2013.

Rothenberg, Jerome, and Stephen Clay, eds. *A Book of the Book: Some Works and Projections about the Book and Writing*. New York: Granary Books, 2000.

Schnapp, Jeffrey. *The Library beyond the Book*. Cambridge, MA: Harvard University Press, 2014.

Stoicheff, Peter, and Andrew Taylor, eds. *The Future of the Page*. Toronto: University of Toronto Press, 2004.

Suarez, Michael F., and H. R. Woudhuysen, eds. *The Book: A Global History*. New York: Oxford University Press, 2014.

Tribble, Evelyn, and Anne Trubek, eds. *Writing Material: Readings from Plato to the Digital Age*. New York: Longman, 2002.

Museums and Artists' Book Collections

Hamilton Wood Type and Printing Museum (Two Rivers, WI): Hamilton Manufacturing, founded in 1880, was the largest wood type producer in the United States in the nineteenth century. It is now a working museum dedicated to the preservation of wood type that offers studio rental, letterpress, and bookmaking workshops year round. http://woodtype.org/

Historic Rittenhouse Town (Philadelphia, PA): Site of the first paper mill in British North America, this landmark district preserves and maintains an eighteenth-century industrial village for tours and offers workshops in book and paper arts. https://rittenhousetown.org/

Jaffe Center for Book Arts (Boca Raton, FL): A library and gallery of artists' books, broadsides, and Italian futurist publications. http://www.library.fau.edu/depts/spc/jaffe.htm

The Museum of Printing (Haverhill, MA): Dedicated to the preservation of printing technology and craftsmanship, the nonprofit museum boasts "the only collection of phototypesetting machines, fonts, and ephemera in the world." It offers periodic workshops. http://www.museumofprinting.org/

Robert C. Williams Museum of Papermaking (Atlanta, GA): Founded at MIT, and now housed at Georgia Tech, this museum maintains a permanent exhibit on the history and technology of papermaking, along with rotating exhibitions of paper art. Its collection includes a treasure trove of devices and samples related to the historical manufacture of paper. It also offers workshops and papermaking programs. http://paper.gatech.edu/

Sackner Archive of Visual and Concrete Poetry (Miami, FL): Founded in 1979 by Ruth and Marvin Sackner and considered the world's largest collection of text-based art, this collection recently released a portion of its holdings to the Pérez Art Museum in Miami, FL. The website hosts a catalog of holdings. http://ww3.rediscov.com/sacknerarchives/

Further Writing

These resources are limited to the United States, but a quick web search will yield myriad booksellers, galleries, museums, and workshop spaces around the world. For an excellent overview of international resources, I recommend *The Book Arts Newsletter* curated by Sarah Bodman of the Center for Fine Press Research (CFPR) at the University of the West of England, Bristol (http://www .bookarts.uwe.ac.uk/newsletters.html). The Briar Press online community (http://www.briarpress.org/) and Letterpress Commons (https://letterpress commons.com/) can help pinpoint local printers offering classes, apprenticeships, and equipment. A subscription to the Book_Arts-L listserv and the Philobiblion site are also essential references (http://www.philobiblon.com).

Book Arts and Experimental Publishing Programs and Workshops

American Academy of Bookbinding (Telluride, CO): The Academy offers classes at all levels, including credential-based programs in fine binding and integrated studies. http://bookbindingacademy.org/

BookArtsLA (Los Angeles, CA): This nonprofit center offers classes in papermaking, letterpress, and book arts along with youth summer camps. https:// bookartsla.org/

The Center for Book Arts (New York, NY): Founded in 1974, the Center was "the first not-for-profit organization of its kind in the nation." It offers exhibitions, public lectures, workshops, and classes. http://centerforbookarts.org/

Haystack Mountain School of Craft (Deer Isle, ME): The School offers exhibitions, artist residencies, and residential workshops in book arts. http://www .haystack-mtn.org/

Independent Publishing Resource Center (Portland, OR): This nonprofit runs workshops and a certificate program while also providing public access to printing and binding equipment for a nominal per-session fee. http://www .iprc.org/

J. Willard Marriott Library Book Arts Program (Salt Lake City, UT): The studio offers credentialed programs for University of Utah students as well as exhibitions and community programming for those wishing to learn more about printing, engraving, and binding books. http://www.lib.utah.edu/collections/ book-arts/

Mills College (Oakland, CA): Offering an undergraduate book art minor and a two-year MFA in Book Art and Creative Writing, Mills also has its own Center for the Book, which produces publications, exhibitions, events, and workshops. Starting in 2016, the Mills College Summer Institute for Book and Print Technologies offers five-day master classes, professional development seminars, and public presentations for participants with some experience in bookmaking or printing. https://www.mills.edu, https://millsbookartsummer.org/

Minnesota Center for Book Arts (Minneapolis, MN): Committed to the book as an art form, MCBA promotes the artist's book through exhibitions and events, fellowships, and awards. It offers studio rentals, residencies, and youth and adult workshops. http://www.mnbookarts.org/

The North Bennet Street School (Boston, MA): The North End school offers a full-time two-year program in book binding focused on fine bindings and conservation, as well as continuing education courses for both amateurs and professionals. http://www.nbss.edu/

Paper and Book Intensive (Saugatuck, MI): This annual summer residency program at the Ox-Bow artist's retreat near Lake Michigan encompasses intensive workshops and craft talks in all areas of book arts and conservation. Ox-Bow itself offers both space for self-directed work and one- and two-week workshops in a range of fields, including book structures. http://www.paper.bookintensive.org/, http://www.ox-bow.org/

Penland School of Craft (Penland, NC): Founded in 1929, Penland offers artist residencies and year-round workshops in various media, including books and paper. http://www.penland.org/

Pyramid Atlantic Art Center (Hyattsville, MD): Founded in 1981, this 501(c)(3) nonprofit offers residencies, studio and facility rental, and workshops in printing, book, and paper arts. http://www.pyramidatlanticartcenter.org/

San Francisco Center for the Book (San Francisco, CA): Established in 1996, the nonprofit was the first of its kind on the West Coast. It offers workshops at all levels, hosts exhibitions and events, and provides studio rentals. https://sfcb.org/

Triple Canopy Publication Intensive (New York, NY): In this two-week mentorship and education program, participants craft a publication "that hinges on today's networked forms of production and circulation but also mines the history of print culture and artistic practice." https://www.canopycanopycanopy.com/education

Visual Studies Workshop (Rochester, NY): Founded in 1969, this nonprofit artist space offers courses related to books and images through its summer institute and through an MFA program granted by the College at Brockport, SUNY. It also engages the public through exhibitions, programs, and publications of VSW Press. http://www.vsw.org/

Wells College Book Arts Center and Summer Institute (Aurora, NY): The press and bindery offers credentialed classes to Wells students, along with lectures, workshops, and symposia, and week-long summer intensives in letterpress printing and book arts that are open to the community. https://www.wells.edu/academics/book-arts-center

Women's Studio Workshop (Rosendale, NY): This venerated nonprofit, founded in 1974, offers studio rentals, residencies, and summer art workshops to women-identified visual artists, and helps emerging and established artists produce limited-edition books. http://www.wsworkshop.org/

INDEX

AMARANTH BORSUK is a scholar, poet, and book artist working at the intersection of print and digital media. She is the author of *Between Page and Screen*, a digital pop-up book of poetry, and a recipient of an NEA Expanded Artists' Books grant for the collaboration *Abra*, a limited-edition book and free iOS app that recently received the Turn on Literature prize. She has collaborated on installations, art bookmarklets, and interactive works, and is the author of five books of poetry. Borsuk is Assistant Professor in the School of Interdisciplinary Arts and Sciences at the University of Washington Bothell, where she also serves as Associate Director of the MFA in Creative Writing and Poetics.